J. W. (John William) Root

**Tariff and trade**

J. W. (John William) Root
**Tariff and trade**
ISBN/EAN: 9783743395053
Manufactured in Europe, USA, Canada, Australia, Japa
Cover: Foto ©Suzi / pixelio.de

Manufactured and distributed by brebook publishing software (www.brebook.com)

J. W. (John William) Root

**Tariff and trade**

# TARIFF

AND

# TRADE

BY

J. W. ROOT

Subscribers' Edition

*HALF A GUINEA NETT*

LIVERPOOL
ALLOTT, JONES & CO., BIXTETH STREET
1897

# PREFACE.

TRADE economics are constantly assuming greater importance in commercial countries and among industrial communities. Never, perhaps, have theories been so utterly at variance as at present, and never have the respective sides been so determinedly and so fiercely championed. The outcome is very often more dust than anything else, and issues are obscured instead of being made plain. The practical business man abjures economics because they are apparently so contradictory to realised facts, and the economist immediately proceeds to construct new theories to account for the facts.

Though I have been a close student of political economy, I make no claim to be regarded as an expert in the science. Rather do I ask the attention of my readers on the ground that what I have written is based largely on observation during an active business career, and I have endeavoured throughout the following pages to make my meaning plain to those engaged in similar occupations, and not to evolve new and abstruse problems.

There are plenty of these as it is, and in pursuing my work they have crossed my path at every turn. I have never burked them, but sought always to provide some sort of solution, though I must expect that a few of them at anyrate will be challenged. One consequence has been that this volume has assumed larger dimensions than I originally intended, and I can only trust that what it has gained in size, will not be lost in any interest it may evoke.

An author dealing with such a subject is beset by innumerable difficulties. The free use of statistics is absolutely necessary, and there are few weapons more dangerous, or more likely to be turned against those who handle them. Reference to page 364, or to the second footnote on page 283, will show how utterly unreliable they may be. Anyone who has to analyse large masses of figures emanating from different sources, is liable to be completely bewildered, and so frequently are they contradictory, that they may be made to prove almost anything. I wish it to be distinctly understood therefore, that in no single instance have I used statistics favourable to my case, well knowing them to have been produced by exceptional circumstances. I have always availed myself of the latest obtainable, provided they came from reliable sources, and whenever I have departed from this, I have given definite reasons for so doing. Moreover, I have rarely based my arguments on statistics, rather have I used the statistics to illustrate the arguments. Differences of ten or twenty per cent. in the former, will merely intensify or diminish the force of the latter, but will not destroy them. In more than one instance where a legitimate choice has been presented to me, and where my contentions have been overwhelmingly borne out, I have deliberately selected the least favourable. So far therefore from dreading criticism of the figures I have given, I confidently invite my readers to compare them with those of succeeding or preceding years, provided always the conditions of such comparison are fair.

I have not troubled readers with footnotes giving the authorities for statistical and other information. I will simply say here that my sources have been principally official, and, in addition to the various abstracts published by the English Board of Trade, I have had frequent recourse to the official publications of other countries, while occasionally I have been favoured with the inspection of private documents. Now and again I have availed myself of unofficial material, but never when its publication has been for purely controversial purposes.

I take this opportunity of expressing my indebtedness and heartfelt thanks to all who have in any way rendered me assistance, by placing documentary and other matter so freely and unreservedly at my disposal, without which it would have been impossible to produce this work. In one or two instances, probably the worst return I could make for their kindness, would be to refer to them by name, and I abstain therefore from mentioning any individually. I shall take care however that this public acknowledgment is brought to their notice.

J. W. R.

*1st September* 1897.

# CONTENTS.

## CHAPTER I.

### THE PURPOSES OF TARIFF.

PAGE

Beginnings of English Tariff :—Insidious Operation—Indifference of Taxpayers. REVENUE :—Influence on Value—Indirect Taxation a Necessity—Principles which should regulate it—Temptations to depart from them—Stimulus to Home Production—The Taxation of Great Communities. MORALITY :—Checks on Over-indulgence—Limits to which they can be imposed—Public Opinion—Duties and Licences. PROTECTION :—Primary Basis—Uncertainty of Revenue Returns—Conflict between National and Private Interests—Demands for Frequent Revision—Resulting Disturbance to Trade—Restriction of Benefits—Logical Issues—Revenue and Protection an Impossible Combination, . . . 1-25

## CHAPTER II.

### INFANT INDUSTRIES.

The Growth of Primitive Manufactures—The Conditions Necessary—Coal and Iron — Textiles — Impatience of Settlers — Natural Advantages of the United States—Wages—Their Gradual Equalisation on the Two Continents—Rapidity of American Expansion—Europe unable to cope with it—Industrial Development in Germany—Former Conditions in Great Britain—Protection really confined to Agriculture—Expansion following Repeal of the Corn Laws—Natural and Artificial Stimulus, . . . 26-42

## CHAPTER III.

### TAXING THE FOREIGNER.

Antipathy to Taxation—Value of Natural Monopolies for Revenue Purposes. EXPORT DUTIES :—Nitrate of Soda—Sugar—Mint Seigniorage on Mexican Dollars—United States Wheat—Cotton -

British Salt and Coal—Textile Machinery. IMPORT DUTIES:—
French Wheat—Analogy to United Kingdom—The Steel Rail
Pool in America—Trusts—Antagonism of Free Trade to Trusts—
Influence of Protection on Price—Incidence of Revenue Duties—
Price *versus* Market Value, . . . . . . . 43-64

## CHAPTER IV.

### THE BRITISH TARIFF.

Customs and Excise Revenue—Antiquated Nature of Existing Tariff
—Spirit Duties—The Beer Duty—Wine—Tobacco—Cigars—A
Neglected British Industry—The Breakfast-Table Duties—Non-
Dutiable Imports—Breadstuffs and Food—Raw Materials—
Labour—Sugar—Effect of Foreign Bounties—How to meet
them—Sources of Tea and Sugar Supplies—Manufactured
Articles—Cotton and Woollen Textiles—Leather—Glass—Iron
and Steel—Paper—Watches and Clocks—Gloves—Silks and
Ribbons—Linen Fabrics—Sundries—Summary of Suggested
Reforms, . . . . . . . . . . . 65-99

## CHAPTER V.

### THE UNITED STATES TARIFF.

Frequency of Changes—Avowed and Real Purposes—Extent and
Detail of the Tariff—Summary of Schedules—Principles of their
Construction. CHEMICALS:—Drugs—Chemical Manufactures—
Vegetable Products — Exemptions. EARTHENWARE:—Building
Materials—Domestic Utensils—Glass and Glassware. METALS:
—Tin—Iron and Steel—Cotton Ties—Tinplates—Cutlery and
Tools—Copper and Lead. TIMBER:—Conflicts between Succeed-
ing Administrations. SUGAR:—The Domination of the Sugar
Trust—Resulting Scandals. TOBACCO AND CIGARS. WINES AND
SPIRITS. AGRICULTURAL PRODUCTS:—Breadstuffs—Dairy Pro-
ducts—Fruit and Vegetables—Meat and Provisions—General
Result of Protection on the Industry. TEXTILES:—Raw Materials.
COTTON :—Yarns — Tissues — Complicated nature of Duties—
Extent of Import Trade. WOOL:—Yarns—Fabrics—Severity of
M'Kinley Tariff—Illustrations—Effect of Duty on Raw Wool—
Extent of Trade. SILK. FLAX, HEMP, AND JUTE:—Linen
Tissues and Embroideries. PAPER AND BOOKS. MISCELLANEOUS:
—Coal—Leather and Gloves. THE FREE LIST:—Agricultural
Implements—Tourists' Wearing Apparel—What Protection has
done and is doing for the United States, . . . . 100-152

## CHAPTER VI.

### THE TARIFFS OF FRANCE AND GERMANY.

FRANCE :—Prevailing Economic Conditions of the Country—Tariff as a Source of Revenue—The Nature of French Protection—Analysis of Foreign Trade—Export Statistics—Absence of Competition in French Products—National Character and Economic Policy—Tariff Rates—Textiles—Iron and Steel—Chemicals—Exemption of Raw Materials—Agricultural Products—Surtax on Indirect Imports—Colonial Tariff Policy—Reciprocity.

GERMANY :—Moderation of Tariff—Simplicity of Arrangement—Revenue Duties — Protective Duties — Chemicals — Iron and Steel—Textiles—Leather—Earthenware—Agricultural Products —Advantages enjoyed by Home Manufacturers—Retaliation and Reciprocity—Tariff Wars with Russia and Spain—Strained Commercial Relations with United States—The Denunciation of the British Treaty—Causes of Industrial Expansion in Germany, . . . . . . . . . . 153–192

## CHAPTER VII.

### BOUNTIES.

SUGAR :—Nature of Drawbacks—Tendency to Develop into Bounties —Efforts to Stimulate the Beet Industry—Continental Bounty Wars—Germany Antagonistic to the System—Cost to Consumers —Hidden Bounties—Surtax on Foreign Sugar in France—Futility of the System—Possibilities of Increased Consumption—Decline of the British and Colonial Industry—Fairplay but no Protection.

SHIPPING :—British Subsidies—Carriage of Mails—German Subsidies —French Construction Bounties—Navigation and Mail Subsidies —Other European Bounties — United States Shipbuilding—American Coasting Service—Mail Payments—The Canadian Subsidy.

RAILWAYS :—The German System — Cost compared with Great Britain—Watered Stock—Results of German State Control—French Subventions—Division and Remuneration of Capital—Total Cost to the Treasury—American Railroads.

MISCELLANEOUS :—France — Canada — Australia — Sale of Surplus Products—General Influence on Trade, . . . . 193–236

## CHAPTER VIII.

### TARIFF AND TAXATION.

Sources of Indirect Taxation—Proportion to Direct—Distribution of Taxation in Great Britain—Taxation in United States—Revenue Derived compared with Actual Burdens—Cost of Collection—Effect of Protection on National Finances—Taxation in France—Sources of Revenue compared with United Kingdom—National Expenditure—Cost of Debt—Why France is able to prosper under it—Taxation in Germany—Imperial and State Systems—Moderation of Debt and Taxes—State Contributions—Prussian Budget—Immense Advantages enjoyed by Germany over her Industrial Competitors, . . . . . . . 237-279

## CHAPTER IX.

### IMPERIAL CUSTOMS UNION.

Discovery of America — Spanish Colonies — Portugal and her Possessions—Germany in Africa and Oceana—French Colonies—Extent of Trade — Algeria and Tunis — Madagascar — The Egyptian Question — Relationship between France and her Colonies. GREAT BRITAIN :—Crown Colonies—Colonial Tariffs—Colonial Trade—The Basis of Union—Schemes Propounded—Proportion of Colonial to Foreign Food Supplies—The Canadian Preferential Tariff—Distribution of Canadian Trade—Origin of Dutiable Imports—Analysis of Canadian Exports—Possibilities of Canadian Expansion—The Belgian and German Treaties—What their Denunciation may mean—Constitutional Aspect of the Question—Australasian Trade—Australian Federation—Free Trade in Agricultural Products—Australasian Loans and the British Trustee Act—The True Basis of Imperial Federation—Phœnicia and Greece, . . . . . . . . 280-335

## CHAPTER X.

### THE BALANCE OF TRADE.

Mistaken Notions concerning it—The United Kingdom Balance of Trade—How it is made up—Influences affecting it—Its Fluctuations—The Meaning of them—Remedies when unfavourable—The United States Balance of Trade—Wild Fluctuations—Their Principal Cause—The French Balance of Trade—Its Dependence on the Wheat Crop—The German Balance of Trade—Influences

# CONTENTS

affecting it same as in United Kingdom—Trade Fluctuations in the Argentine Republic—Trade Movements in Japan—Unreliability of some Trade Statistics—How Balances are settled—Gold Movements—The Balance of Trade in South Africa—Why Great Britain imports so largely from France—The Importance of the Question, . . . . . . . . . . 336-375

## CHAPTER XI.

### HOME AND FOREIGN TRADE.

Relative Importance—Effects of Protection—Arbitrary Divisions of Territory—Wasteful Labour—Incidence of Taxation on different Industries—The Agricultural Rating Act—Light Dues—Railway Preferential Rates—Reckless Foreign Trading—Education—Internal Competition—Independent Traders—Capitalist Influences—The Directions in which they are exerted—The True Aims of Home Traders—The West African Trade—General Possibilities of Foreign Development, . . . . . . . 376-407

## CHAPTER XII.

### FREE TRADE OR PROTECTION?

Slow Growth of Free Trade Principles—National and Individual Interests—General Growth of National Indebtedness—Decrease of the British Debt—Military and Naval Expenditure—The Commercial and Industrial Classes—Re-export Trade—Protection in its Relationship to Commercial Morality — The Causes of Over-production—The Working Classes—Spread of Protectionist Sentiment in Great Britain—Increasing Competition in Wholesale Trade—Great Prosperity of Retail Trade—Bullion Movements—What Free Trade and Protection do for the various Classes of the Community, . . . . 408-432

## APPENDIX.

THE NEW AMERICAN TARIFF, 433-448

INDEX, 449

# TARIFF AND TRADE.

## CHAPTER I.

### THE PURPOSES OF TARIFF.

Beginnings of English Tariff:—Insidious Operation—Indifference of Taxpayers. REVENUE:—Influence on Value—Indirect Taxation a Necessity—Principles which should regulate it—Temptations to depart from them—Stimulus to Home Production—The Taxation of Great Communities. MORALITY:—Checks on Over-Indulgence—Limits to which they can be imposed—Public Opinion—Duties and Licences. PROTECTION:—Primary Basis—Uncertainty of Revenue Returns—Conflict between National and Private Interests—Demands for Frequent Revision—Resulting Disturbance to Trade—Restriction of Benefits—Logical Issues—Revenue and Protection an Impossible Combination.

TARIFF is inextricably bound up with the still larger question of taxation. For whatever ultimate object it is levied, the first result is always to affect the national revenue, and either to intensify or diminish the strain upon the more direct or internal taxes. From its earliest inception this method of raising money has lent itself peculiarly to abuse, inasmuch as, though its incidence in the long run, if not actually universal, falls upon the great majority of any community subjected to it, direct interference with the liberty of the individual is confined within narrow compass. From the days of King Edward I.—who systematised and legalised the exactions of his father Henry III. upon the woolfells exported from the kingdom, which, owing to the absence of any native weaving industry, practically included all that was grown—down to the present day of taxation on imports of the same commodity wherever it may be in vogue, the amount of the levy has been nominally paid by a very small number of merchants or factors engaged in the foreign commerce of the country, but has actually come out of the pocket of the humble peasant who reared a few sheep, or the industrious and often poorly paid artisan whom the laws of decency, to say nothing of health or the desire of comfort, compel to be clad. But it would rarely occur to either the peasant or the artisan that in the very pursuit of his ordinary avocation, or in compliance with the most elementary of demands, he was casting his mite into the national treasury, while, assuming the form of a poll tax, it might have dawned on him that it was altogether out of proportion to his means, and led him to protest, if not actually to rebel against it. However legitimate a tariff may otherwise be, it is always possible for it to fall with crushing weight on those least able to stand it, without them being aware of the fact, while those who should bear the burden escape almost scot-free.

Yet it rarely happens that ultimate incidence is taken into account in the imposition or rearrangement of tariff. The unfortunate consumer is about the last person to be considered in the negotiation of a commercial treaty; he is quite as likely as not to be sacrificed to the interests of some specially favoured class in the foreign country which the Government of his own seeks to conciliate, and if he venture to complain, an attempt is made to silence him by appealing to his loyalty and to the general welfare, represented, it may be, by some branch of trade with which he is not in the remotest degree concerned. A prominent English statesman complained not very long ago that his country had thrown away the keys which might unlock the door of foreign markets to English manufacturers; in other words he regarded it as a misfortune that the general consumer was not called upon to pay an annual premium to insure markets at some indefinitely future period to a limited number of producers. So far from this opinion being isolated, it represents a very important basis, on which many tariffs are constructed.

To the student of human nature it must be a matter of surprise that under these circumstances the consumer remains so docile, and only on very rare occasions seeks to throw off the yoke. It may be well padded to make it sit easy, but it galls all the same after being worn long in one position, and though we do see constant signs of discontent it has nowhere yet broken into open rebellion. The reason of this is not far to seek. National expenditure everywhere is increasing by leaps and bounds, and funds must be provided to meet it. Nothing is so annoying to the individual taxpayer as personal application. He will resist to the uttermost the payment of half a crown while he is awake, but if someone puts a hand in his pocket and extracts five shillings when he is asleep, he feels that it cannot be helped and is not worth worrying about. By this apparent indifference he becomes the object of attention from three distinct quarters, and eventually succumbs to the attack of their combined forces. The Government desires to replenish its exchequer, the social reformer aims at diminishing the temptations to vice by enhancing their cost, and the wily producer avails himself of the opportunity of adding to his profits by shutting out foreign competition. Thus tariff is made to answer the purposes of revenue, of morality, and of protection.

## I.—REVENUE.

A commercial age like the one in which we live, lends itself eminently to the easy raising of revenue by indirect means. The enormous burden of taxation now resting on the shoulders of every civilised as well as most semi-civilised peoples, would often be well nigh intolerable were it realised. Were it possible for instance, to make every

Englishman who drank a glass of spirits or smoked an ounce of tobacco, every German or Frenchman who used a pound of sugar, and every American who purchased a suit made from imported cloth, pay for them in two separate amounts, the one the actual cost of the article, the other the sum reserved for the Government, he would be amazed at the disproportion between them, and the extent to which he was contributing to the support of the national exchequer. To ignorance in this respect is largely owing the ability to raise and maintain those bloated armaments which are a constant menace to the peace of the world, though declared so often to be necessary for the protection of commerce, which would however be still more flourishing without them, if for no other reason than that the vast sums expended would be diverted to industrial channels, where they would be likely to yield a more or less profitable return.

The dependence of Government on this source of revenue naturally varies in accordance with its situation. In a country sparsely inhabited over a widely scattered area, the collection of direct taxation is a practical impossibility, and it becomes a necessity to levy it upon some particular and generally used fixture—such as land, or upon commodities which have to pass through a limited number of defined places for distribution, whether as imports or exports. No community in these days is so self-contained as to be independent of its neighbours, both near and distant, and even if it strive to supply most of its own wants, it is at least anxious to raise and dispose of surplus products in order to exchange them for luxuries, or some tangible and permanent form of wealth which it may hoard.

So far then from the Government of a newly settled territory ever being likely to experience difficulty in procuring funds for its due maintenance, it has invariably a wide choice for operation, increased rather than diminished in proportion as the territory over which it exercises sway is undeveloped, because in a primitive state the demand for foreign material of all sorts must be considerable. It is just here however that a wise discretion is absolutely necessary if success is to reward the efforts to attain prosperity. There will always be a strong inclination to tax such articles as are imported in the greatest abundance, or are declared of the highest value, because by limiting the scope of the impost, trouble and expense may be saved. It may nevertheless be unsound policy, because upon the cheapness at which these articles can be obtained may depend the rapidity of the progress made. Take for instance a country opened out to agricultural settlers. Among their earliest requirements will be implements for preparing the land for cultivation, to be followed quickly by machinery for the economic ingathering of the fruits of the earth, and possibly subsequent treatment to render them marketable. Or suppose again a rush to a mining district where there has been a discovery of the precious metals, or the more sober appropriation of territory where the baser ones are known to exist in rich abundance. Mining machinery of complicated and costly character will be required before a large, or even a payable yield can be obtained. In any of these cases therefore, implements and machinery are likely to figure as an important item in trade returns, a tariff on which would produce a substantial income towards the expenditure on administration, and that protection of life and property which is one of the first essentials in every newly constituted community.

Such material, however conveniently it may offer, should be kept off the tariff list until every other source of revenue has been exhausted. Following in the same line, we shall arrive at the principle on which a tariff ought to be constructed. Implements and machinery are not the only materials requisite for agricultural and mining development, and whether it be in this direction or in some other, everything required for production should be rendered as cheap as possible. There is no form of production into which the simplest articles of food and clothing do not enter, and they likewise demand immunity from every charge which is not imperative. In fact, exclusion from taxation of every article and commodity largely entering into the production of another, is the only sound basis of economic progress and prosperity.

We are at once shut off from a very wide field in which the tax-gatherer has long revelled, but it leaves a still wider one untouched. The days are long past since any considerable aggregate of individuals confined expenditure to bare necessaries, and we are now in an era when in most countries a very large part is for the provision, first of comforts and then of absolute luxuries. The strict line between these is difficult to draw, and no despotic distinction is possible, but there is in the mind of every thinking person some sort of classification which grades the one into the other. The justice of taxing pure luxuries is rarely denied, even by those who most largely indulge in them, and who offer a stout resistance whenever an effort is made to put theory into practice. The advisability of including everything which legitimately falls under this designation is, however, another matter. They are sometimes capable of being confined in so small a space, that detection is difficult, and contraband trading rendered so easy as to place the honest and legitimate dealer at a serious disadvantage, and the gain to national revenue is more than offset by injury to national morals. Moreover, luxuries in their narrower and more exclusive sense are nowhere sufficiently distributed to make them an important source of revenue; how much less then in a new country, whose inhabitants have still to win their way to wealth.

Yet in all climes and under most conditions, there is a considerable, often a wide margin for personal expenditure, which is not strictly applicable either to production or the maintenance of life and health, and it is here that the legitimate imposition of indirect taxation becomes alike possible and profitable. The individual is then called upon to contribute out of his abundance, and is neither penalised for his poverty nor handicapped in his industry. Articles of ornament and of general but not necessary utility, the higher and better grades of food and clothing, are sure to be wanted in sufficient quantities to provide a moderate revenue on a reasonable tariff, without seriously inconveniencing those who pay, and afterwards profit by the security they enjoy as well as by the public works which tend to enhance the value of their labour by reducing cost of transport, or in a hundred other ways. Only when a Government has failed to meet its expenditure or finds it impossible to economise, is it justified in extending its system of indirect taxation beyond these limits.

At the same time care must be taken in imposing a revenue tariff that it does not defeat its own object. By framing it on too high a scale, an unhealthy impetus may be afforded to the manufacture or preparation of commodities for which the country is in no way suited, and tariff, instead of being a necessary adjunct to Government, will become the battlefield of contending factions.

There remains of course the safeguard of an excise duty, but that would mean the creation of another department with its staff of officials, whose salaries and expenses might not be defrayed by the revenue they collected, especially if the manufacturing industry were spread over a wide area, and not concentrated in a few settled districts. On the other hand, it would be absurd to exclude an article from a tariff list, merely on the ground that its inclusion might encourage native production. Provided the tax is in every way legitimate, it is a matter of indifference to the consumer whether the product he purchases is of foreign or home manufacture. Perhaps patriotism may lead him to prefer the latter if he has not to pay more for it. When the duty becomes prohibitive, or so materially reduces the import as adversely to affect the revenue, it will be time enough either to lower it to an attractive basis, or to see that those who are profiting by the exclusion make good the deficiency. It is quite possible for a revenue tariff to encourage and assist local industry without becoming extravagantly or unwisely protective; but it must not be overlooked that the moment indirect taxation threatens to grow oppressive, or a direct impost becomes more lucrative and economical, as well as fairer in its incidence, that moment does the protected industry become a drag on the progress of the country. That it would be unfair to leave it suddenly in the lurch is the strongest reason for the exercise of caution in stimulating it.

The policy of raising revenue by indirect taxation is not however, by any means confined to new and sparsely peopled, or even densely populated but poverty-stricken countries, where the percentage of the well-to-do and wealthy is infinitesimal, and the scope for the tax collector correspondingly limited. Great Britain, which is pedantically Free Trade in its economic creed, still imposes a large annual contribution on various commodities entering its ports, though in no instance could the most delicate olfactory nerve detect the scent of protection. No other great country is so scrupulously careful, rather do they seek to combine national income with what they are pleased to regard as national prosperity, fostered by harassing foreign competition. But we have for the moment only to consider the principles which ought to guide them from a purely revenue standpoint.

These do not widely differ from what has been already laid down. The same care is necessary to avoid hampering production, or to increase its cost by the taxation of the materials or labour that may be required in any indigenous branches of industry.

A country whose import runs up to tens and hundreds of millions of pounds sterling, and whose population can only be expressed in eight figures, enjoys a very wide selection, because in no such instance are the climatic conditions within its borders so diverse, that it is not compelled to draw many of its requirements from other sources, though, like the United States it may be capable of producing every absolute necessary. There is consequently less excuse for such a country imposing burdens likely to prove grievous to any class of its hybrid population, and still less to favour one at the expense of another. In every case there will be commodities of almost universal consumption which readily lend themselves to taxation, and thus extract a moderate contribution from the pockets of those who are too poor to make a large or direct one. For it must be remembered, that in every well-ordered country the poor like the rich benefit from at least some part of the national expenditure, and while they may fairly look to Government to place no impediment in the way to maintain existence, they are under obligations when that is provided for, to apportion some small amount of the surplus towards the protection they are afforded in the enjoyment of whatever civil rights they are entitled to.

That indeed must always be a strong argument against the entire abolition of indirect taxation. Still, even when limited in extent, it is capable of inflicting great injustice, which there is invariably less disposition to redress than if the scope were wider. Channels of trade as well as habits of life are continually changing, and what may be wise to-day may become oppressive ten years hence. Not even a tariff imposed purely for revenue should become hidebound, but must be regarded as open to revision and transition whenever altered circumstances render such a course expedient. Too rigid an adherence to what has become an antiquated system, may bring contempt on the policy underlying it, which in itself may be as sound as on the day it was adopted.

It is evident then that a tariff for revenue requires more scientific construction than for any other object. The number of commodities upon which it may be economically imposed is limited, because most of those which are theoretically best fitted are likely to be of too trivial a character to make them sufficiently productive to the exchequer for the time and labour devoted to them. Whatever is selected should not enter largely into the fabric of native industry, while it should be distributed among as many of the well-to-do sections of the community as possible. Absolute equality of incidence in this or any other form of taxation is impossible, but in most, if not all the trading countries of the present day, it is quite practicable to impose the burden in such a way that its inconvenience shall be reduced to a minimum.

II.—MORALITY.

We now enter a field where the question of revenue becomes of secondary importance to the well-being of the people. Human nature as it is exhibited to us in the history of the past, as it presents itself to-day, and as it will most certainly be found in the centuries ahead, is prone to indulge in some form of narcotic, which, when taken in excess, leads to demoralisation of the mental, and collapse of the physical faculties. Usually it is a distillation of strong waters, occasionally a powerful drug like opium. Nature supplies the raw material with so profuse a hand, that when manufactured into a fit state for consumption, few of them are costly, and persons of moderate means would ordinarily be able to obtain them in dangerously large quantities with but little sacrifice. Social reformers have hit upon a method of enhancing the cost to such an extent, that only those in affluent circumstances are able to partake copiously or even freely, without depriving themselves of the more innocent comforts, and possibly of the very necessaries of life, while governments, not always too eager to assist in the promotion of morality, find that in this instance at least the pecuniary reward is worth the effort. Thus many of the liquors can only be retailed at several times the price at which they are actually produced.

So strong however does the craving sometimes become, that no price would place these stimulants beyond the reach of the most needy individual while they had it in their possession. Entire prohibition has proved fruitless in checking those who are sufficiently determined, and only adds to the evil, the further one of law-breaking. The most that can be done is to impose a wholesome restraint, and many an individual is undoubtedly deterred from excess, either from absolute want of means, or from the more laudable desire to avoid financial embarrassment. These duties therefore, while not totally destroying the mischief, do modify it to a very material extent.

This modification ought to become more favourable in proportion as cost is increased. In practice however it is always found that there is a point beyond which this ceases to have any effect, if brought about by artificial and removable causes. There are few things men will not do in desperation, and the distillation of spirits is not one of them. In every country where the duty is at all heavy, not the least important part of the work of Government officials connected with the department controlling it, is to prevent evasion of the law, whether directly, or by the thousand and one subterfuges which ingenuity is always ready to invent; and just as stringency approaches the border line of prohibition, so will the law be set at defiance.

Besides, all countries do not regard the matter in quite the same light, and while most impose restrictions on the traffic, they are very unequal. Carefully as coasts are guarded, there are scores of quiet coves and inlets to be found on the most unpromising, where a contraband trade can, and under exasperating conditions will, be conducted. Just as a metallic currency tends to flow to those places where it can be most profitably employed without undue risk, so will commodities, not always quite so legitimately, pass to lucrative markets even with considerable attendant risk.

Nor can public opinion be ignored; indeed this is one of the most important matters on which public opinion is constantly asserting itself. Upon many countries the curse of intemperance rests so lightly, that it is not an evil demanding legislative interference and repression, and a temperance reformer would be laughed to scorn. Even where excess is prevalent, the numbers who partake moderately are so large, that they are able to make their wishes respected. That there is a growing perception among this class of the necessity of adopting stringent measures to check abuse, is evidenced by the increasing readiness with which restrictions are tolerated, and even advocated on legitimate use, and among English-speaking people at any rate there is no longer any fear of a successful movement in favour of stimulating consumption. When agitation is not making practical progress in the opposite direction, the worst that happens is stagnation.

Unlike a revenue tariff, that imposed for purposes of morality is more costly and cumbersome as area and population are disproportionate. The trade is an internal rather than an external one, for though foreign imports are everywhere to be found, the national beverage is invariably of home manufacture. In thickly-peopled districts it is easy to control, because each factory is generally of some importance, and able to bear the expense of one or more revenue officers. Where towns and villages are small and far apart, the business is often conducted on a corresponding scale, and could not bear the cost of regular, much less of permanent inspection, and thus a system of licences takes the place of fixed tariff. It is not unknown indeed where tariff is high, but generally occupies a subsidiary position, and is sometimes little more than a registration for ensuring more efficient oversight, as well as a guarantee for good behaviour. It is, however, at any time possible to convert it into a principal instrument, and as such is to be found in operation in rising but sparsely-peopled districts, where the direct duty might easily be evaded.

A somewhat novel but very efficacious expedient has been adopted to check the undue multiplication of drinksellers. It may not be altogether creditable, but it is nevertheless true, that this is one of the first wants of a new community, and is rarely long in being supplied. Inasmuch as the first arrival is welcomed, he is dealt with tenderly, and the tax imposed is light. But as each successive competitor puts in an appearance, the cost of the licence is raised all round, and even the original holder, when the period of his grant lapses, must fall into line with the others. It becomes a question of the survival of the fittest, because a point will sooner or later be reached when the licence becomes too onerous to maintain, and some must be allowed to lapse, or else there must be an entire cessation of new ones. Thus, as the community grows, the local exchequer swells, while a guarantee is afforded that it will not be flooded and demoralised by an incubus of licensed houses.

The main point to be borne in mind in connection with tariff under this heading, is that Government is rarely the supreme arbiter in its imposition. Liquor laws have played havoc with more than one political party on both sides of the Atlantic, and they would have been everywhere in a more satisfactory condition to-day had there been less zeal and more discretion displayed in framing them or seeking their alteration. The custodian of national finances must be content to receive whatever the public will give him; if he endeavour to secure more, he will be ejected, and very likely his friends with him. The day has gone when occupants of that office will volunteer to accept less, and considerable pressure will have to be used to compel them to do so. It is eminently desirable therefore that opinion upon the question should be healthy and guided by moderation, not only that the exchequer may be protected against unwelcome and unexpected revolutions, but that the standard of national morality may be raised to a higher level.

### III. PROTECTION.

No more thankless task can well be undertaken by any Government, than the construction of a protectionist tariff. The articles which common sense denote as specially suitable for taxation have to be excluded, because it is nobody's interest to have them on the list, while room must be left for others, which, when included, cannot fail to be productive of hardship. For plumbing the depth of human selfishness, nothing more effective has ever yet been invented than what is called a protective tariff. While those who clamour for it are preaching the virtue of patriotism, and extolling the merit of sacrifice for the encouragement of home industry, the moment their schemes come within the range of practical politics, they resemble nothing so much as a victorious army turned out to loot a captured city. The grower of raw material wants protection against what he chooses to designate the pauper labour or superior advantages of a keen competitor; the manufacturer of that raw material wants it cheap, and expresses surprise that the grower should desire to enhance the cost of the finished article. So many interests must eventually be disappointed, either by getting nothing at all, or much less than they consider their due, that the claims of the party which can survive the shock must be great indeed, for political gratitude is ever the anticipation of favours to come, never of benefits conferred.

National finance dependent upon a protective tariff must always be in a nebulous and unsatisfactory condition. First to tax the commodity, and then to be compelled to tax the individual because the commodity remains at a respectful distance, is adding insult to injury, but unless it is done the exchequer must go bankrupt. The foreign manufacturer or shipper who was to provide ways and means, pay the salaries of officials and find the pensions of veterans, diverts his energies to another sphere; and to conceal the chagrin which his want of thought, or still worse, his revengeful disposition has roused, a substantial addition is made to the national debt, and the cautious investor is added to the number of beneficiaries under the system. He wants interest of course, but perhaps by the time it is payable the foreigner will have lost some of his shyness, and be prepared to part with a portion of his treasure.

A nation generally regards an expanding revenue as a sure sign of prosperity, and sound finance will always aim at exceeding rather than falling short of estimates. But every increase of revenue from tariff, must be gall and wormwood to the citizen whose products are being displaced, while he openly rejoices at the falling off which can only finally result in embarrassment. The public need is in fact his opportunity, and he measures his success and prosperity by the adversity of the national exchequer. So long as his profits remain untouched, it is of small consequence to him how the adverse balance is redressed; should it become necessary to lower the tariff in order again to attract revenue, he will fight hard against the selection of his particular commodity, and offer innumerable reasons why another should be chosen. Nothing in short raises such keen enemies to the exchequer as protection. Those who live under it and upon it, are constantly exercising their minds to waylay the contributions, which, in the ordinary course would find their way thither, and to pocket them instead. Defrauding the revenue as a rule sits lightly on the conscience, but openly to war against it creates animosities, compared with which the satisfaction of having done something improper but rather smart, becomes a positive virtue.

Nor is there any finality or continuity in financial arrangements. A revenue tariff or direct taxation may be steadily continued year after year. Not only is its yield calculable to within a very small percentage, but those who have to contribute to it may sink their capital in investments or enterprises with little fear of a disturbing hand being laid upon them. A manufacturer will know that in the extension of his premises or plant, he will be free from any demand until a profit has been made which he can either save or spend. On the other hand, such an extension may be commenced in anticipation of advantages which are never conferred, or if granted, may be snatched away before they can be availed of. There is either an element of speculation in all private enterprise, or if the policy of protection be persistently followed for a course of years, it has to be made continually more stringent, and the speculation and uncertainty are transferred to the national finances.

However wide a protective tariff may be, there are always large numbers of persons who cannot possibly benefit by it. In every country there are many, indeed the majority of industries, in which foreign competition is impossible. Ready-built houses cannot be imported from abroad and laid down on the sites selected for them. Clothing made to measure cannot be tried on and fitted a thousand miles away. The daily and weekly newspaper would be rather stale if made in Germany, and its contents might also be regarded with suspicion. There are agricultural products so perishable, that forty-eight or even twenty-four hours' delay in consumption renders them unfit for food. What equivalent can be given to these? The producers are compelled to pay an artificial price for many of their requirements, and yet get nothing in return. A paternal Government might grant them a bounty, but bounties are rarely given except to those who undertake to dispose of their commodities abroad. They must struggle on as best they can, and if they create a supply in excess of demand, must take the best price obtainable, instead of selling in the home markets on their own terms, and dumping the surplus on a foreign one at anything it will fetch. No wonder that discontent enters the mind and permeates the soul, until the wildest socialistic theories gain possession of the whole system.

Nor does the trouble end here, for degrees of protection cause even more heartburning than none at all. One set of producers secures a tariff which results in absolute prohibition, and their industry consequently contributes nothing whatever to the national revenue. Another set has still to wage a fierce struggle against foreign competition, and demands consideration on the not unjust ground that their particular trade is paying a large amount of taxation. There is no logical half-way house in a protective policy. If a country be capable of producing all it wants of any particular commodity, every inhabitant should be forbidden, under severe penalty and punishment, to obtain it elsewhere, because a Government which accepts a duty is entering into a conspiracy with the foreign plunderer to rob the innocent manufacturer, and is an accessory before as well as after the offence. Surely when Æsop wrote his fable about the man and his son and his donkey, he had obtained a glance into futurity, and witnessed the high priest of protection labouring to propitiate the worshippers assembled round its altars!

All this is no mere theorising. Ample illustration will be given in succeeding chapters of the actual existence of the evils which sound reasoning on the subject would be likely to deduce. The world has had experience of freedom as well as restriction, but wide as it is, most of its inhabitants still find it difficult to divest themselves of their immediate surroundings, and, travelling round a circle, arrive at the point from which they started. Man does reach that stage where he honestly conceives that what suits him personally must be good for everybody else, and setting a goal before him at which he may or may not eventually arrive, bids others follow, however impossible it may be of general attainment. Because protection does open a road to wealth, there is an eager rush to enter it, utterly oblivious of the fact that it is so narrow that a crowd will be trampled under foot. But the victims below are lost sight of in gazing at the victors above.

A combination of two of the three purposes for which tariff is levied is generally possible, but the first and the last will no more mix than oil and water. By a coincidence one may lapse into the other, but when revenue ceases to flow freely, protection occupies the field, unless indeed there is no longer any demand for the particular commodity.

Contrariwise, when revenue becomes elastic, protection is no longer afforded, unless it be for a brief period when demand has, without warning, outrun supply, and cannot be immediately filled. But a tariff for revenue and protection combined is an anomaly, and where it is supposed to exist it will be found on analysis to consist of two distinct parts, the first operating in one direction, the second in the other. Where this is the work of a democracy and a freely-elected legislature, the hindrance to political progress is incalculable, for so much time is spent in wrangling over disputed points of finance and trade, that the more important questions of social progress and individual liberty and well-being are thrust into the background. Monarchs divert the attention of their subjects from domestic grievances by plunging into foreign complications. Those responsible for the management of democracies maintain control by raising all sorts of intricate economic problems, which would puzzle the brain of a Solon to solve. Government must be carried on and revenue raised, but the one will work more smoothly if the other can be depended on. Either fix an amount, which under ordinary circumstances will be forthcoming from the indirect sources selected, or abolish them altogether and make trade free or entirely prohibit it, in each case resorting to the pockets of those who are most likely to profit.

# CHAPTER II.

## INFANT INDUSTRIES.

The Growth of Primitive Manufactures—The Conditions Necessary—Coal and Iron—Textiles—Impatience of Settlers—Natural Advantages of the United States—Wages—Their Gradual Equalisation on the Two Continents—Rapidity of American Expansion—Europe unable to cope with it—Industrial Development in Germany—Former Conditions in Great Britain—Protection really confined to Agriculture—Expansion following Repeal of the Corn Laws—Natural and Artificial Stimulus.

No more specious doctrine has ever been preached than the economy of building up new industries by means of protective duties. We might be disposed to admit the wisdom of it, if the infant grew to man's estate and gave evidence of self-reliance. It is true such industries do grow under the forcing process, sometimes at a rapid rate, but as they shoot upwards and outwards they lose rather than gain in strength, so that while a sapling was sufficient to support them in their youth, by the time old age is upon them the strongest oak of the forest is scarce stout enough to prevent their collapse. Industries are much like human beings, so long as they are kept by extraneous help they rarely exhibit any haste to emerge from the stage of infancy.

Just as it is natural food that stimulates the development of the child into youth, and youth into the strong man or the healthy woman, so a new country or community must feed upon its own resources if it desire to attain a real measure of prosperity. People do not go into the bush of Australia, or adventure into the wilds of Central Africa, to build locomotives and establish silk manufacturing. There must be something already there to attract them. Either gold casts its magic spell, or the colonist, full of energy, burns to wield the axe and clear a space where the fruits of the earth may have free play to yield their increase, and in due course provide sustenance for man and beast. He requires tools, from the axe and spade to the complicated reaper or crushing machinery, and he wants them as cheaply as they are to be had. Very likely he takes his first supply of the simplest with him, and whether he wants more complex ones or not, those he has soon wear out. But not only has he to pay the price at the town depôt or the country store, but the cost of conveyance to a remote station possibly doubles it. Axe heads and spade irons he must continue to buy, but the handles he can make himself from the timber he has felled, and thus without knowing it he introduces the first primitive manufacture into the settlement. In due course he is surrounded by neighbours. A mechanic arriving in their midst discovers he can obtain constant employment in making handles for axes and spades, and a host of miscellaneous odds and ends which the settler would not have troubled about getting had they not been brought to his very door. So the first manufacturer establishes a factory, and manufacturing industry begins to grow up side by side with agricultural pioneering.

But to the protectionist, or the man who desires to see his country go ahead, anything so primitive is regarded with scorn. That is not manufacturing they say. We want to see the building with the tall chimney-stack by its side; to hear the thud of the steam hammer as it falls on the molten metal; to listen to the deafening buzz of the spindle, or drink in the music of the loom as it meanders to and fro, gathering up the weft and the warp. Wait a little, and all that will follow.

To begin with however, a few questions must be asked and answered. Are coal and iron to be found in close proximity to one another, and in such a situation that they or their products can be easily transported to other fields of industry? If so, then in due course iron manufacturing will become not only a possibility, but a paying occupation for capital and labour alike. But first, steel rails, waggons, and locomotives will be wanted to tap the source and freely disperse its stream in all directions, and these will be obtainable best and cheapest in some old country where the industries have been long established, and are economically worked.

Then may the forge with all its accessories be erected, not necessarily to duplicate the rails and the waggons and the steam engines, but to make the more modest articles which in turn help to make civilisation.

Or are large quantities of sheep and cattle raised? Then why should their wool and hides be sent thousands of miles away to be returned as clothing and leather, or even boots and shoes? Perhaps the community is too small to make the carding, spinning, weaving, and tanning industries possible on a sufficiently important scale to render them remunerative. Then it is waste of energy as well as money to carry them on. Very likely the conditions and wages of labour are such, that competition with countries where these are more favourable is out of the question. Then that must mean that the demand for labour in the existing industries, whatever they may be, is large enough to absorb the supply on very much its own terms, and it were folly to attract it where at the same rate it would be unremunerative.

Once more, does the cotton plant flourish? Then the same problem presents itself as in the case of wool and hides. If not, are the conditions favourable for converting it into calico, should the raw material be imported? Are there places where water is abundant, either as motive power in driving the machinery, or for the purposes necessary in the process of manufacture? Is the atmosphere sufficiently humid to ensure cohesion of the threads? If so, is the spot where all these advantages are found sufficiently near a port of shipment or discharge to reduce cost of transport to a minimum? All this granted, then cotton spinning may fearlessly advance.

Unfortunately, neither communities nor individuals are willing to allow this to take place in proper sequence. Agriculture may be said to be the basis of all settlement, for though gold or some other form of adventure be the original attraction, the discarded and rejected earth will sooner or later bury disappointed hopes in her fruitful womb, and cherish them into new life. Virgin soil, and the keen air and free life of the prairie combined, afford a stimulus which causes everything for a time to be viewed through rose-tinted spectacles. What matters it if clothing and other necessaries do cost half as much again as they ought to? Is not the recompense ample when the farmer, visiting the rapidly growing city on the occasion of his annual holiday, views the smoke belching forth from the factories and darkening the atmosphere, and prides himself on being the unit of a nation which is well on the way to independence of all others. Thus the very people who are eventually to feel the first pinch of adversity, animate and encourage those who, by dipping freely into the national funds, see their way to the easy accumulation of handsome fortunes.

Let us apply these tests in a practical manner. No country ever discovered, and there remain but few still beneath the veil, has been so abundantly blessed by nature as the vast territory enclosed within the boundaries of the United States of America. An immense coast-line fronting two oceans, and magnificent harbours. Every conceivable variety of climate, from the soft airs and perpetual summer of Southern California, to the icy blizzard of the north. Lakes which are inland seas, and mighty rivers which for hundreds of miles are highways of commerce. costing nothing to construct or keep in repair, the levees or embankments, upon which so much money has been spent, being designed for the protection of the adjoining lands, among the richest in the world and requiring no artificial stimulus whatever for the regular production of abundant and exhausting crops. Mountains teeming with mineral wealth, and rolling prairies providing sustenance for millions of four-footed beasts. Gold and silver, coal and iron, light and heat, poured forth from the bowels of the earth, and last, but by no means least, the most intelligent and enterprising beings in God's image who ever trod God's earth. And yet forsooth, these last appeal to the State for protection! What would public opinion say of the giant, splendidly proportioned and gorgeously equipped, crying out for help against the pigmy who scarce reached to his knees, and whose every advantage had been gained by long toil and patient plodding?

Is it possible to believe that Pennsylvania and Alabama could never have flourished as coal and iron-producing centres, unless propped up by protective duties against the industries of far-distant nations, whose output in years gone by was severely taxed by the cost of transport from the inland foundry to the port of shipment, and then across the Atlantic? The latter, it is true, has diminished, sometimes well-nigh to vanishing point, but the former, as far at anyrate as Great Britain is concerned, remains solid and unimpressionable. Or can it be that Fall River would never have been utilised, or the scores of spinning mills in the very midst of the cotton plantations never erected, unless a heavy tariff had been imposed on foreign goods made from cotton entering the country, and that it would still have been necessary to send the raw material from Georgia to Manchester or München Gladbach, in order that the Georgian negro might have a coloured shirt to his back? If these things are possible, then is the inventive genius and untiring energy of the native-born American a sham and a delusion, and he himself the most overrated man, whether in his own or other people's estimation, that ever breathed.

Wages of course is the reason assigned for inability to compete. The American labourer scorned the miserable pittance afforded by the manufacturers of Europe, and rightly so, as long as he could do better by cultivating the soil elsewhere.

So great and so genuine were the inducements offered, that a broad stream of immigration flowed from across the Atlantic, and the population of the United States advanced by enormous strides. But that at once began to equalise matters, slowly and imperceptibly at first, rapidly and visibly as time progressed. The more abundant supply of labour told on the wages of the American agricultural labourer, and helped to depress them. The relief from over-pressure on the European labour market, assisted no doubt by combination, which only however became possible under the altered circumstances, brought about a rise in wages which thus drew gradually closer together on the two continents. The process was deferred by the introduction of protected industries, which for a time at least tend to maintain the reward of the artisan, but it has not prevented in some cases, and will not eventually prevent in the rest, the final and natural consummation. Already we see immigration, at one time so enthusiastically welcomed and earnestly encouraged, scotched if not killed by legislative enactments. It was the labour first that had to be protected, now it is the labourer, though before the United States will have attained the present density of population of the United Kingdom, their inhabitants must multiply fifteen fold.

Had this process of equalisation been left alone, manufacturing industries in the United States would have sprung up without assistance at a period very little later than they were actually forced upon the country. Agricultural wages would have fallen more rapidly, or else those in Europe would have taken less time in attaining the level they have since reached. Manufacturing wages in America would have started on a lower basis, and sooner reached the rates they now stand at. Again the protectionist says, see what a long innings of prosperity the workman had while wages were high. Quite so, but the cost of living was also high, and for a fair comparison between the continents it would be necessary to consider, not what was paid, but what could be saved after the same comforts had been provided. That the balance would long have been in favour of America is undoubted, because the capabilities of expansion were so enormous, and an intelligent man had so many more chances of exercising his ingenuity than in an old and already well-populated country like Great Britain. But that would have occurred with an entire absence of protection to manufacture, just as it did to agriculture, and Pittsburg and Fall River would still have competed successfully with Staffordshire and Oldham, though paying a higher rate of wage.

It is quite possible that another and perfectly legitimate influence would have been at work on a small scale. I have previously maintained, that provided a Government has to support itself by indirect taxation, it need not necessarily avoid a commodity which may some day be produced at home, so long as the double condition is fulfilled, of obtaining a revenue and imposing no restraint on the domestic industries actually in existence. That in itself would foster enterprise. But the question is naturally asked, what is the difference between this and protection pure and simple? It is admittedly difficult to define, but the same intangible border line often exists between revenue and protection, as we have already noticed between comfort and luxury. Moreover, the individual who avails himself of the opportunity thus offered steps warily. He asks himself what the consequences would be if the protection were withdrawn, because the tax ceased to be productive. Could he so arrange his affairs as to be able to stand alone in the course of a few years? He may rightly ask that no change shall be sprung upon him unawares, but he will have no reason to complain if due warning be given that artificial support is to be withdrawn. In such a case an industry may come into existence earlier than it otherwise would, but it is attended by greater risks than one which patiently waits for maturer conditions.

The sudden expansion of the United States, moreover, was such that Great Britain would not under any circumstances have found it possible to keep pace with. The great trunk lines of railroad were commenced, and for a time continued, not because of the existence of coal and iron in the country, but because the products of the soil had to be carried to the consumer. True, railroads were constructed later because furnaces and mills had been erected to manufacture iron and steel, but those roads went into the receiver's hands and bankruptcy; and had they never been built, or their construction deferred, we should have heard less of railroad scandals, and the occupation of the railroad wrecker would have been a sinecure. Had America been content to take a little more of the material from Europe, and a little less eager to supply it all herself, millionaires might have been less plentiful, but stock would not have been watered to such an extent, that in the struggle to earn a dividend on a portion of it, presidents and directors alike have earned the animosity of nearly every independent trader in the Republic. When the enormous cost of land to English railway companies is contrasted with the free gift of millions of acres to the American ones, we may well ask what has happened to make freights approach anything like as close as they do.

A larger demand upon European supplies of material, particularly if distributed over a wide area and for a prolonged period, would have tended to raise European wages rather than to lower American ones. Activity in the iron trade does not necessarily imply prosperity in cotton or wool-spinning, though there is a thread of sympathy running through all the great industries of any country, and were trade universally free it would encircle the world. But even should special causes arise to depress one while another is progressive, that can only continue for a very limited period. So rapidly do masters and workmen fall out of the ranks, that unless they are replaced the staff of an industry is quickly depleted, and where one is more prosperous than another, recruits naturally seek it. Whether iron had preceded cotton or cotton iron, both would long since have established a firm footing in America without the smallest assistance, and ought to-day to be able to compete with any similar industries in the world. But America chose rather to play the part of the prodigal son, with the difference between it and the typical one, that it spent its substance in riotous living at home instead of in a far land. Signs are not altogether wanting that it desires to return to steadier habits, but it must be remembered that repentance precedes the fatted calf.

What is true of the United States is equally so of every other country. Conditions may be less favourable and progress slower, but the race is not always to the swift. The industrial expansion of Germany is scarcely less marvellous than that of the great American Republic, and protection is again singled out as the chief cause of it. The same thing may be said of Westphalia as of Pennsylvania, only with this in favour of the former, that the scale of wages began at the bottom and has gradually ascended, instead of the reverse.

The same results are discernible in both the countries named, a deplorable decline in agricultural prosperity, and that notwithstanding the fact that in Germany it is the best protected industry. The phlegmatic character of the people was bound to win it success the moment it got fair play and was relieved from the constant strain of political anxiety which weighed it down until a quarter of a century ago. Its progress has been artificially stimulated, but at what will some day inevitably prove to have been too great a cost.

It were useless to follow each country where protection reigns supreme, and where the same arguments are urged in its support. It would only mean ringing the changes on a higher or lower keynote. One country, and one only, has not yet been engulfed in the vortex, though one at least of its self-governing dependencies has emerged from it. It is sometimes contended however, that Great Britain could not have attained her commercial and manufacturing supremacy had she not started under the powerful patronage of protection, and that at least is worth inquiring into.

The conditions prevailing fifty years ago and those in existence to-day are so totally distinct, that comparison is difficult, if not impossible. But protection in England never aimed at the encouragement of infant industries, it sought rather to maintain the oldest of all—agriculture. The most perfervid protectionist of modern times is willing to admit that English manufacturers were well able to take care of themselves. The immunity of the soil from invasion while all Europe was a battlefield, the employment of the people in the arts of peace, while those of other nationalities wielded the sword, though they were largely subventioned at English expense, constituted in themselves a premium which rendered competition prohibitive. True, there was a tariff on all imported manufactures, but it was a hindrance rather than otherwise, and imposed on the chance of mulcting anything that strayed into the kingdom, for the benefit of the treasury, which, reeling under a load of debt, found the greatest difficulty in making ends meet. As the wealth of the nation increased and direct taxation became possible as well as profitable, the worn-out and rusty shackles were struck off trade, which became more and more free without attracting the manufactured goods of the foreigner, who indeed rather increased his custom to his English rival. To protect manufacturing industry therefore, was about as productive an employment as gilding refined gold.

Far otherwise was it with agriculture, and the wonderfully constructed sliding scales invented by our forefathers almost lead us to the conclusion, even in this scientific age, that the science of pure mathematics has been either lost or stolen. In any case it was labour wasted, because nearly every other nation on the face of the earth found it rather more than it could manage to feed itself, and only the inducement of very high prices persuaded people to starve themselves a little more for the sake of the offered reward. Then the sliding scale became so like free trade that only an expert could detect the difference.

This is not the place to discuss the motives which animated Richard Cobden and those who acted with him in the great Corn Law League. That many of the men concerned were actuated by pure love of their species, and on the highest grounds of a noble and unselfish philanthropy is absolutely beyond dispute, that others thought only of the cheaper cost of living, the possibility of reducing the wages of their workpeople, and the probable stimulus to their trade, is equally certain. What is more apparent than anything else, is that any man who values his future reputation should never adopt the profession of prophet, for many on both sides have thus far been hopelessly wrecked. The greatest prosperity ever enjoyed by British agriculture was under Free Trade, and though it now languishes, it can hardly be said to be worse off than in countries where protection is still rife, and where the farmer and landowner are objects of tender solicitude. At anyrate we may dismiss it for the time being, the clamour for protection is not to inaugurate a new, but to resuscitate an old industry, and therefore rests on totally different grounds, though ruled by exactly the same principles as we have been discussing.

What might have happened had Great Britain started on even terms with her manufacturing rivals of the present day, I do not care to surmise after penning the preceding paragraph. Financial and economic heresies might have taken as deep root there as elsewhere, and then the great tariff battle would have been still further embittered. Most Englishmen and all Scotchmen, however, are fervent advocates of Free Trade, because it suits their pockets; and as there is hardly likely to be any change in this respect, the dulcet tones of the protectionist charmer only fall on deaf ears. For exactly the same reason the American manufacturer stands by protection, and not because he desires to see his workpeople earn high wages; he would reduce them below the European standard if he could, though there are honourable exceptions of course. There can be no hope therefore of convincing him, the appeal must rather be made to that wider circle which includes within its circumference the victims of the system.

Nobody would ever dream of erecting a cotton factory on the summit of Ben Nevis, or constructing blast furnaces on the roof of the Alleghanys, even though subsidised. At least the man who attempted it would more likely than not be escorted by his fellows to the nearest lunatic asylum. Yet experiments almost as foolish are constantly attempted throughout the world. For what can be more ridiculous than to endeavour to establish an industry where the true economic conditions are entirely absent. Either the raw material, of little value, has to be transported an immense distance at considerable cost, or labour has to be attracted by higher wages from some established and profitable trade. And yet Governments will deliberately compel their subjects to pay 50 and 100— yes, and 200 per cent. more than the real value of particular commodities, in order that some prentice hand may prove his ability to make them. The same Government, as likely as not, will refuse to permit the establishment of another industry or branch of it, because the cost of production is so small. Hard working but poverty-stricken foreigners, with a trade at their finger ends, are forbidden to enter the country and pursue it, while complaints are loud of the competition they create at home. Surely the true policy is to encourage every trade and industry which, beginning on a cheap basis, can work its way to a higher level and carry its labourers with it, rather than to stimulate those inaugurated at immense cost, which, were the props removed, would collapse like a house of cards, and bury all connected with them beneath the ruins.

## CHAPTER III.

### TAXING THE FOREIGNER.

Antipathy to Taxation—Value of Natural Monopolies for Revenue Purposes. EXPORT DUTIES:—Nitrate of Soda—Sugar—Mint Seigniorage on Mexican Dollars—United States Wheat—Cotton—British Salt and Coal—Textile Machinery. IMPORT DUTIES:—French Wheat—Analogy to United Kingdom—The Steel Rail Pool in America—Trusts—Antagonism of Free Trade to Trusts—Influence of Protection on Price—Incidence of Revenue Duties—Price *versus* Market Value.

MANKIND is so constituted as to be ever seeking to diminish, or altogether avoid its obligations to the State. Men, and women too, will spend money recklessly on the most foolish objects which benefit neither themselves nor anyone else; but was there ever one who did not grumble at paying a tax? Whenever it is proposed therefore to make the foreigner provide the national revenue, there is always a delighted crowd ready to applaud the method suggested, without knowing exactly how it is going to work. The worst of it is that no national patent is possible for so clever an invention; every country in turn will adopt it when once discovered, and people are not always economical when spending their neighbour's money. Perhaps therefore it is better on the whole that each nation should raise its own revenue and control its expenditure, than that it should hand it over to another to do what it likes with.

That there are methods of exacting tribute from other nations without appealing to the fortune of war is certain. They are few however, and becoming gradually fewer, because while people can establish and permit monopolies in their own midst, they can rarely enforce them on others. A country which is fortunate enough to possess a commodity which does not exist elsewhere, and others must have, is thus able to tax the foreigner by the imposition of an export duty. Salt, for instance, is a necessity in India as in all other lands, and yet is only found there in the most meagre quantities, and for that reason is made an important source of revenue. But suppose Great Britain desired to exploit her great dependency and make it a source of revenue, as colonies have been made in the past: by prohibiting the importation of salt from other countries, she could secure the monopoly to herself, and impose an export duty which the Indian native would be compelled to pay, together with the import duty on his own side.

A few instances still survive where something of the sort is done, independent of relationship between colonies and mother countries. The nitrate industry of South America is subjected to such an impost for the benefit of the Chilian Government, which raises nearly half its revenue in this way, and hitherto it has been a tax on foreigners, because nitrate of soda is not produced elsewhere, and is a favourite manure on the continent of Europe, where its properties are found suitable for certain lands and special crops. Whether chemical research, now so busy, will eventually find a cheaper substitute in an artificial manure, it is of course impossible to say, but should this happen, then if Chili desires to retain the trade, the duty will have to be abolished.

Other export duties are to be found which are not so successful, and are indeed continued with the full knowledge that they press on the home producer. Since the abolition of slavery in the West Indies, it has been impossible to secure a sufficient quantity of negro free labour for the cultivation of the plantations, and recourse has been had to the East Indies, whence coolies are imported under indentures. As far as the islands and territories under British control are concerned, every care is taken to attend to their welfare, and a fund accumulated to send them home again when their terms have expired, and this is raised by a small export tax on sugar. It should of course be regarded as a slight increase in the cost of labour rather than a tax.

Another instance is to be found in Mexico. The Philippine Islands were once dependent upon the viceroyalty of that country when it was a Spanish colony, and all trade between them and Europe passed through Mexico. Every year a large quantity of silver coin or bullion was despatched from Acapulco to Manila in payment of merchandise sent from Manila to Acapulco, and was afterwards disseminated throughout the whole of the East Indies by means of local trade. Thus the Mexican dollar became, and remains to-day, the most accepted currency in many countries in the East, and Mexican silver is minted before being exported. The Government imposes a seigniorage which somewhat more than covers the actual cost of minting, and thus a duty is imposed on one of the principal articles of Mexican export, which is only paid for by the foreigner however, at the value of the silver contained, and the tax consequently falls on the silver mine owner.

Morocco is another instance where a small duty is levied on almost every article of export, and needless to say this does not contribute to an extension of its trade. Some of the smaller colonies are likewise compelled to make up their revenue by this method, otherwise import duties would be excessive, while the object, in French and German colonies especially, is to encourage the import of manufactured goods rather than the export of native produce, the dependence of one upon the other being apt to be lost sight of.

Occasionally an export duty is imposed which is meant to be and actually proves prohibitive, as for example in South Africa, where an ostrich can only be exported on payment of a fine of £100, and the eggs of the bird, £5 each.

The question naturally arises, whether any of the great commercial countries could possibly subsidise their revenues by similar duties. What is there, say in the United States upon which they could be levied? That country exported in 1895-96 60,000,000 bushels of wheat, and had a duty of 5 cents a bushel (equal to about 1s. 8d. per English quarter) been charged on it, it would have realised $3,000,000. For the second half of 1896 the export of wheat was unusually heavy, and it is not at all unlikely that the duty would have been paid by the foreigner, as the Indian famine and the Australian drought, with the consequent failure of the wheat crops in both countries, gave the United States the control of the market, and enabled them to some extent at any rate to fix the price, which there might have been little difficulty in raising another 5 cents a bushel. Still, even had that really happened, it would have been difficult to persuade the farmer that he would not have received those 5 cents had there been no duty. Besides, how often now do the United States control the wheat market? Year after year for many years, there has been a surplus in the world's production, and the consuming, not the growing countries have established the price. Under such circumstances they certainly would not pay an export duty, which must consequently fall upon the farmers. To tax the export of wheat therefore is an impossibility on economic grounds, putting altogether on one side the morality of taxing food at all.

The most important crop grown in the United States for export, is cotton. An export duty of half a cent. a pound on the crop of 1894-95 (a large one) would have realised $17,500,000, on that of 1895-96 (a small one) $12,000,000. Surely here if anywhere is an opportunity for taxing the foreigner! Moreover, the American staple has never yet been cultivated economically elsewhere, and is so far a practical monopoly. The rich alluvial lands of the Mississippi and its numerous tributaries, or the virgin and well-watered soils of Texas, seem to defy competition. India and China, it is true, grow much cotton, but for the purposes for which American is utilised, all but the very choicest of it is valueless. The production of Egypt has rapidly increased, but the Valley of the Nile is so much more fruitful than even the Mississippi, that its yield is as superior as that of the Indies is inferior. There is still another advantage. America retains from one-fourth to one-third of the crop for consumption in its own mills, and an export duty on the raw material would afford the domestic spinner an equivalent bounty on the manufactured article, and enable him to compete with his foreign rival, even in foreign markets.

Again however, it is the foreign consumer who more often than not rules the price of cotton, and to enable American planters to do so they would need to enter into a combination to limit the output. That in its turn would be extremely difficult, as, independent of jealousies, the weather affects the yield of the seed put in the ground to fully 25 per cent., and no ring or trust has yet been able to control that. A crop planted to produce a normal consumption might consequently fall short of, or exceed it by more that 10 per cent. When there was a shortage, the European consumer would pay the duty; when a surplus, the American planter; that is, when the price was high owing to scarcity, it would be forced still higher, and when low in consequence of abundance, the result to the planter would be more disastrous than ever. An export duty on cotton therefore is as much out of the question as on corn.

There is no occasion to go through the entire list of commodities, in which scarcely one is to be found to which objection would not be taken, and to tax the foreigner by this means would necessitate the annual readjustment of the tariff. American traders find a quadrennial one quite frequent enough as it is.

Turning now to the exports of Great Britain, the bulk of them are at once out of court. They consist of manufactured articles. British manufacturers find it hard enough to meet foreign competition, and the most trivial additional burden would destroy their trade altogether. There are one or two natural products however, which, like wheat and cotton in America, it is at least advisable to pass under review. Salt and coal form more or less important items in the trade returns. Anyone acquainted with the history of the Salt Union will hardly require to be told the consequences that follow an artificial rise in the price of that particular commodity ; those who have not the knowledge may find it profitable to acquire it. But coal is on a somewhat different basis. It is a raw material entering more or less into the production of every other. The output of the mines in Great Britain is colossal, and in 1896 reached 195,000,000 tons. Such figures are bewildering, and to a non-scientific mind it must appear incredible that this can go on year after year without the surface of the earth collapsing. Certain it is however that, though there is no sign of it yet, exhaustion must be somewhere in the not very remote future.

Of the quantity named, about 150,000,000 tons was retained for home consumption, some 10,000,000 used for steamer coal, and the remaining 35,000,000 tons exported for use abroad, to some extent also for the supply of steamers at foreign ports. It is contended that a duty should be imposed on this export, in order if possible to put a stop to it, as it would most effectually, because coal is an article of world wide production, and can be raised in other countries quite as cheaply as in Great Britain. Germany in particular is stimulating its foreign trade in coal, and of an output in 1896 of upwards of 80,000,000 tons, exported 13,500,000, or about 17 per cent. of the total against the British 23 per cent.; but then it must be remembered that both the merchant and naval fleets of the two countries are altogether disproportionate to their size and trade. Should our industries and our hearths ever be threatened with natural scarcity, restriction may become a necessity, but under existing conditions it need not be anticipated. Electrical science is making such rapid progress, that in another generation it may provide most of the motive power as well as light and heat, and then the demand for coal will become extremely limited. British coal owners are therefore acting wisely in disposing as rapidly as possible, provided it is on profitable terms, of what in the future may be a drug. It will be time to cry halt when the danger really looms in sight.

Besides, to prohibit, or even to check the export of coal, would inflict enormous loss on British shipowners, whose principal outward cargo it is. Indeed in the same year, 1896, though the total tonnage cleared from the various ports of the United Kingdom reached a figure exceeding 52,000,000 tons, that of general merchandise was under 8,000,000, and the rest was coal. No more serious blow therefore could well be aimed at British commerce.

Among British exports of manufactured goods, textile machinery was accountable in 1896 for £6,750,000. We are told that we are making a whip for our own backs, and that the countries which take our machinery eventually take our trade with it. In the manufacture of textile machinery however, which during the last few years has been very largely for foreign account, as most British manufacturers have supplied themselves with the latest and best, some 30,000 hands are constantly employed, and after all it matters very little whether they are earning a living in machine shops, or in cotton and woollen mills. Indeed, in the former they not only receive a higher rate of wage, but the material used is produced almost entirely by British labour, and employs many thousands more, while cotton and wool are brought from the ends of the earth. And if England refused to supply the machinery, it would be made elsewhere; a foolish restriction of this sort is said to have led to the establishment of the greatest ironworks in Belgium, which now compete so keenly and so successfully with the British trade.

The hope of taxing the foreigner for the benefit of the British exchequer by placing a duty on exports, is consequently a delusive one, and few if any Englishmen are foolish enough to indulge it. Either they must go on paying, or find some other way out of the difficulty.

It is in the realm of imports where the protectionist feels himself on firm ground. He points confidently to the rates and taxes paid by the native manufacturer which add to the cost of his goods, while free imports escape. Not altogether though, for the shipowner who carries them, the railway company, the distributor, and the retailer, all have to bear their share like the manufacturer. All the same it does on the surface look unfair, until we come to consider that these foreign commodities have already been more or less enhanced in price in their own country by similar rates and taxes, though perhaps not levied in the same way. The state, county, and municipal taxation in the United States, for instance, levied on real and personal property, averages eight dollars per head of the population, one-third of which is devoted to purposes of national education. The only exception is when bounties are granted, with which we shall have occasion to deal hereafter.

It is bad policy to spoil a good case by claiming for it more than is really due. As a Free Trader therefore, I frankly and unreservedly admit that protective duties are not always paid in full by the consumer, but they are still less often paid by the foreigner. No such sweeping assertion can be made on either side, and to arrive at the truth we must analyse each individual case. That of course is utterly impossible here, but one or two illustrations will serve to draw out a few of the principles which have invariably to be considered.

In highly protected France, foreign wheat must pay a duty of 7 francs per 100 kilogrammes, or double hundredweight as it is called in England, before it can pass to the consumer. This is equal to about 12s. 6d. a quarter, or 38 cents. a bushel. It rarely happens however that French wheat sells in the home markets at this excess over the prices quoted say in London, Liverpool, or New York, therefore the consumer is not mulcted in the entire 7 francs. But the reason of this is that France, as a rule, imports little foreign wheat, and grows what she wants at home, and as supply and demand are fairly balanced, competition makes the market price. But two things may, and one of them at least sometimes does happen. France grows more wheat than she requires for home consumption, and wants to sell the surplus abroad. This she can only do by taking the price ruling in foreign markets, and as cost of production has been enhanced by the general system of protection, that results in a severe loss. France therefore cannot grow wheat for export like Hungary or Russia, and it is only when nature has been more than usually bountiful that this can ever occur. She merely tries to meet her own requirements. Now it is most improbable that this is the real economic capacity of French land. Either it ought to be able to produce more and become exporting, or part of it could be more advantageously applied to another purpose, and some of the wheat purchased abroad.

Occasionally however the French wheat crop fails, and for the people to be fed, large foreign supplies are necessary. This happened in the year 1891, and as the Russian crop failed at the same time, the outlook was somewhat serious. It was recognised by the Government that the price of wheat in France would be the price ruling in foreign markets, with the cost of freight added, plus the duty, every centime of which in this case would have to be paid by the consumer, not only on the wheat imported, but on that grown at home as well. Even a protectionist French Government dare not face an angry populace clamouring against dear bread, and the duty was temporarily reduced to 3 francs, in spite of the protests of the agricultural community, who wanted high prices to compensate for short crops. This was all the more significant from the fact that it occurred while the French Parliament was engaged in framing a new tariff, under which most duties were considerably augmented; yet the utmost concession made to the protectionists, who were in a large majority, was that the reduction should not become operative until August the first, and should cease on June the first following.

Surely no franker admission was ever made of the utter helplessness of protection to meet an unlooked-for emergency.

As a rule France needs a small foreign supply, and as the market for wheat is a very fluctuating one, a favourable moment has to be seized for securing it. Purchases may be made during a time of depression when holders are anxious to realise, and a cheap sale is concluded to move an important parcel. In such a case the seller may really be paying a portion of the duty, but this can only happen on rare occasions on a scale far too insignificant to establish a principle or base an argument upon.

English protectionists may perhaps claim that the moral of all this is, that protection enables France to feed herself with wheat, and that if imposed in England it would do the same. Had English land actually gone out of cultivation through the operation of Free Trade, its continuance would have been a matter for serious consideration, if not an impossibility, because after all, agriculture is still and must remain the greatest British industry. But what has really taken place has been a gradual displacement of wheat in favour of other crops, and the land is more widely and intensely, as well as more diversely cultivated than ever. Much loss and suffering have doubtless accompanied the process, as they always must when a body so conservative as farmers can no longer trudge along the time-worn ruts. Some land has become derelict, but only on account of the excessive and inalienable charges upon it. There is no other country in the world where the land could bear such burdens of rent and tithe combined, and in many instances of tithe alone, and remain profitable to the cultivator.

Moreover, it is quite certain that unless an excessive import duty were imposed, it would be many years before England again harvested enough wheat to meet her own requirements, if indeed that ever occurred; and, meanwhile, the whole duty would be paid by the consumer just as it was in France in 1891, because the price of foreign wheat, plus the duty, would rule the English markets with very occasional exceptions. The risk of scarcity of food in case of war is no doubt unpleasant to contemplate, but there are others still greater, and it would be madness for England to cast away her commercial and industrial supremacy in order to make preparations for an eventuality that may never arise.

With France it is different, and the abandonment of protection to agriculture there is for the present impossible. It would be manifestly unfair to the French farmer to tax him heavily for bounties and to make him pay dearly for protected commodities, and then leave him in the lurch. Fiscal reform in France must begin at the other end. Besides, she is exposed to greater risks than England in case of war, and cannot rely upon foreign sources for her food supply. Protection therefore is the curse of militarism, and the penalty imposed for a Europe armed to the teeth, and not by any means a sound and wise economic policy.

Let us now for change of scene travel across the Atlantic. The United States is the land of railroads, and as might be expected, the plant set up for equipping them is gigantic. Everything however is protected, from the locomotive to the sleeper, and protected so highly, that it amounts to prohibition.

In the autumn of 1896, an announcement was made that the manufacturers of steel rails, amalgamated into a pool, would thenceforth charge at least $28 a ton, and might shortly raise the price. American railroads have discovered too often that there is a hook under that sort of worm, and they did not bite. English mills could have rolled and laid down rails in the United States at much below $28, but the duty prevented them.

In February 1897, the pool suddenly collapsed, and in three days sales of about 700,000 tons, sufficient to lay a single track more than 6000 miles in length, that is, to build a new double track railway right across the American continent, were made at prices varying from $15 to $18 a ton, probably below actual cost. Many railroads supplied their requirements for a long time ahead, and orders are said to have been booked for further large quantities on very little better terms. Such are the facts; what do they signify?

Secure in their own market and able to make big profits, the American steel rail makers were too greedy, and turned out more than were wanted. Instead of competing against each other and bringing down the price, they agreed to pool their stocks, charge $28 a ton to all buyers, and divide the proceeds on some principle agreed to among themselves. But nobody would buy, and some of the makers who needed money could no longer wait. Could we penetrate the secrets of the ring, we should probably discover that diligent enquiries were made as to what chance there was of disposing of a large quantity of rails abroad. It would have paid to sell half a million tons to foreign consumers at $12.50 a ton, and make a loss of $4 or $5, if by so doing they could have ensured the sale to their own railroads of another half million at $25, and netted a profit of $7 or $8. Either for so large a quantity no demand existed, or the weight of the rails was unsuitable, so the American railroads got them at cost price instead.

Now here is protection, yet so far from the consumer paying the duty, he gets his commodity at less than the price at which it could be imported free. But that was never the intention of the steel rail makers, and only indirectly their fault. If indeed rails can be produced in the United States at $15 to $18 a ton, then the argument set forth in the preceding chapter is incontrovertible. Pennsylvania does not require protection, and every cent imposed, so far from going to assist an infant industry, is a flagrant robbery of the consumer for the benefit of the producer. The latter wanted the duty, not to keep him alive, but to make $12 a ton profit. The protectionist says to-day his system is necessary to encourage native industries against foreign competition, to-morrow he gloats over the fact that these same industries are selling their commodities at lower prices than the foreigner, and that protection makes things cheaper, not dearer. There is some inconsistency here, and the only explanation of it is, that when thieves fall out, honest men come by their own.

What befell the steel rail pool is of course liable to happen to any other protected industry, and if such a thing became at all general, the consumer would indeed have occasion to rejoice. But protected industries, in America especially, have learned how to protect themselves against this calamity. They no longer form pools liable to sudden dissolution, but Trusts under despotic management, and impervious to every attack from within or without. Having first combined a sufficient number of the concerns interested, they either force the rest to join, or proceed to ruin them, and then, not only dictate the price of the commodity they deal in from New York to San Francisco, and from Maine to Southern Texas, but defy competition, domestic or foreign. The former is easy, the latter only a matter of calculation. They know what the foreign article will cost after the duty has been paid, and sell their own at 1 or 2 per cent. less. The profit may be 5 per cent., or it may be 150, but they allow nobody else to share it with them.

President M'Kinley during his electoral campaign propounded one of the most extraordinary fallacies ever uttered, when he maintained that Trusts were the offspring and outcome of Free Trade. Under it they could not exist, because foreign traders with large capital could not be crushed like the smaller ones at home. They might be invited to enter the ring, but the swarm would be so great that the profit eventually pertaining to each member would not be worth taking. President M'Kinley and Free Trade are as far asunder as the poles and the equator, yet the offspring of the latter poured out their money like water, and worked day and night to secure the return of the candidate of Protection. Surely here is another inconsistency!

Two broad principles may be laid down as the result of a protective tariff. When it is prohibitive of course nobody pays any duty. The foreigner loses his trade and, if he cannot transfer it elsewhere, his profit, but contributes nothing to the revenue of the protected country. The consumer however, on every purchase he makes of a protected commodity, pays to the producer, not to the Government, a tax equivalent in amount to the difference between his actual outlay and the cost he would have incurred had the market been open to free foreign competition.

When the duty is not prohibitive, and the Government derives a revenue, in three cases out of four, if not nine out of ten, the consumer and not the foreign producer contributes it. The latter may, when a tariff is raised, consent for a time to cut his prices and work at a loss, in the attempt to retain his market, but after a very short experience he invariably relinquishes it to his more favoured rival. Only in such instances, or where surplus stock is shipped to a protected market for the purpose of being got rid of, does the foreigner pay, and he never does that while there is a free market open elsewhere.

No pretence is ever made that a revenue tariff is a tax on the foreigner, and in that respect it is perfectly honest. The British duties on spirits and tobacco, on tea and coffee, are paid by the consumer, and are meant to be. They are as much an internal tax as the house duty, or the income tax, or a licence to use armorial bearings. Their incidence may be unfair, but they claim to be just what they are. Still, it does not follow that no portion of them is ever paid by the foreign producer. Stocks may have accumulated to such an extent that, to force them off, concessions in price must be made. The public will increase their consumption if they can get them cheap enough, and care nothing about the duty. Did it not exist at all they might be willing to pay just as much, and consequently the producer or merchant loses it. But that is an accident of the system, not its design.

Arguments as to who pays the duty based on prices are altogether misleading, as so many elements enter into the making of them. It is no uncommon practice in countries where protection is rampant, to endeavour to prove that it cannot hurt the consumer, because prices of protected commodities have fallen so heavily during the last five or ten years. But all commodities have been affected alike, and protection has more than once been invoked in the effort to maintain them. Comparisons must not be made with last year, or even with last month, but with the same commodities in a free market. If the protected market is relatively no higher, then the consumer is fortunate, but the difference is the measure of his loss, rarely, if ever, of his gain.

Two instances will suffice in conclusion. In 1874 the remaining duty on sugar in the United Kingdom was abolished. The price at that time was 30s. per cwt., now it is under 10s., yet nobody would contend that the abolition of the 3s. tax has been the cause of the decline. The consumer did almost at once obtain the benefit, but a long series of events which would make a history by themselves, have gone to reduce sugar to its present price. Similarly in the negotiations for a treaty of commerce with Greece in 1890 the British Government agreed to reduce the duty on currants from 7s. per cwt. to 2s. The price on the English market then was 26s., now it is 18s. It has been many shillings lower, and probably would be so now but for the political misfortunes of Greece, and the attendant risks to the crop, but even the smaller difference is much greater than the rebate of 5s. Greek currant growers hoped to retain some of the advantage; as a matter of fact the British consumer promptly secured it all. Other circumstances have tended to lower the price still further, notably over-production, the refusal of the French government to allow distillation to be continued except on onerous terms, and last, but by no means least, the disordered state of Greek finances, and the depreciation of the currency. A tariff may relatively alter prices, it cannot control market value.

The inventor who can saddle his own and his nation's taxes on the back of the foreigner, has yet to be born.

# CHAPTER IV.

## The British Tariff.

Customs and Excise Revenue—Antiquated Nature of Existing Tariff —Spirit Duties—The Beer Duty—Wine—Tobacco—Cigars—A Neglected British Industry—The Breakfast-Table Duties—Non-Dutiable Imports—Breadstuffs and Food—Raw Materials— Labour—Sugar—Effect of Foreign Bounties—How to meet them — Sources of Tea and Sugar Supplies — Manufactured Articles—Cotton and Woollen Textiles—Leather—Glass—Iron and Steel—Paper—Watches and Clocks—Gloves—Silks and Ribbons—Linen Fabrics—Sundries—Summary of Suggested Reforms.

The tariff imposed in the United Kingdom is unique in the small number of items it contains, and is one of the very few possessed by any civilised and trading country, which can be printed in good type on two ordinary octavo pages and leave a wide margin. It is nevertheless, an eminently productive one, the receipts from customs duties aggregating for the financial year ending 31st March 1896[1] no less a sum than £21,040,000, while excise duties levied on beer and spirits made at home were responsible for £27,530,000 more. The total revenue of the kingdom was £109,527,831,

[1] Since the above was written the figures for the year ending 31st March 1897 have been given by the Chancellor of the Exchequer in his budget speech. As they have not yet been issued in detail, I prefer to deal with those of 1896.

but this included a considerable sum derived from the post office, telegraphs, and other productive sources, for which the public receive full value in return. The amount collected from taxation was approximately £92,500,000, and out of this customs and excise contributed some £49,000,000, or over fifty per cent.—not a bad proportion for a country which long ago discarded protection. Between seven and eight millions of this total was diverted to the relief of local taxation, and the balance applied to Imperial purposes.

There is not however in any single item, the faintest tinge of a protective tendency, and in this respect the tariff is thoroughly sound. Nevertheless, it is full of anomalies, and like most institutions verging on to a venerable age, demands radical reforms. Nothing of any consequence has been added, and nothing excluded, since the abolition of the sugar duties in 1874, and it is impossible for a period of a quarter of a century to elapse without many changes in the channels of trade and the economic conditions of the people. The specific rate on nearly every article has been altered to suit the exigencies of the revenue, but while on the one hand no Chancellor of the Exchequer has ever been bold enough to eliminate an item, and deprive himself and his successors of a source of income which can always be made elastic, none on the other has dared to suggest an addition in face of the prevailing sentiment of the country. Yet it is quite possible that a tariff might now be framed, differing in many essential points from the one in operation, which, without departing a hair's-breadth from the principle underlying it, might be more in consonance with modern requirements. Unfortunately, free traders sometimes bring discredit on their cause by upholding an antiquated system as it is, because it cannot be abolished either in whole or in part, while periodic consideration and readjustment would destroy many of the objections urged against it.

Let us first of all then, consider the tariff as it stands. The most important part of it constitutes a combination of revenue and morality, inasmuch as the duties on intoxicating liquors are aimed at, and do most materially check consumption. For the financial year 1895-96, nearly eight and a quarter million gallons of imported spirits paid £4,420,000, while 32 million gallons distilled at home contributed £16,860,000,[1] the former at the rate of 10s. 10d., the latter 10s. 6d. a gallon. As in most cases this exceeds the original cost, the price of the liquor to the consumer is more than doubled. The purchaser of a pint of whisky or brandy, for instance, not only pays for the raw materials, the cost of distillation, and the profits of the distiller and any intermediate hands through which it may pass, but one-eighth of the 10s. 6d.

[1] A drawback on spirits and beer exported somewhat reduces the net revenue.

duty, say 1s. 4d., plus the profit which the seller demands on the outlay of that sum, so that the consumer in reality pays about 15s., and not 10s. 6d. a gallon, as a consequence of the customs and excise duty.

Without entering into the question of the advisability of increasing or diminishing the rate, we can, from the moral point of view for which it is partially imposed, see the possibility of very material improvement in the manner in which the duty is levied. The temperance reformer has been very busy since the principle of the spirit duties was established. The chemist and the medical man have also taken their share in the work, and their researches have brought to light many important facts. We need not side with the extremists who declare alcohol in every form to be rank poison, nor with those who declare that except in very excessive quantities it is harmless. It is probably largely a matter of the physical constitution of the individual consumer. But there is ground common to both. The defamer of alcohol admits that some kinds are worse than others, that, for instance, newly-distilled spirit is maddening in its effects, while the matured article may be temporarily soothing. The advocate proclaims the latter to be positively beneficial, and admits that the former does possess some drawbacks. One thing is beyond dispute, that the man whose regular beverage is well-matured whisky does not often drink to excess, and rarely becomes a confirmed drunkard, because when that inclination takes hold of him, he craves for something stronger. Of course it may, and often does happen, that the one leads to the other. Yet no distinction whatever is made between the two in the matter of duty.

Now it stands to reason that new spirit must be cheaper than old. In the first place, the materials used in the distillation of the article made for immediate or early consumption, are invariably cheaper than those entering into the composition of one meant to stand the test of time. Nor can the latter be kept for nothing. There is loss of interest on the capital sunk, besides warehouse rent, fire insurance, and a certain amount of leakage. A universal and indiscriminate duty of 10s. 6d. a gallon therefore is a direct encouragement to the consumption of new, cheap, and deleterious spirit.

The remedy is a simple one. Raise the standard of duty to 12s. 6d. a gallon, and allow a rebate of 1s. for every year the spirit is kept in bond up to a period of say five years, which will probably cover the cost of keeping it. These figures are not absolute, and to maintain the national income from this source, elaborate calculations would have to be made before an exact basis could be arrived at. But the principle can be adopted, the revenue will not suffer, good old spirit will be as cheap as the bad new, public morality will gain, and the temperance reformer will for once have scored a point without incurring the hostility of any but the more unprincipled members of "the trade" who aim at profiting by the misery and crime they create.

The beer duty for the year with which we are dealing was paid on 33,825,000 barrels, at the rate of 6s. 9d. for the specific gravity of 1055, and amounted to £11,305,000. As a barrel contains 36 gallons, the cost to the consumer of a pint, inclusive of the profit on outlay, is not more than a halfpenny, and he may be considered therefore to escape very cheaply. Indeed, there are several reasons why the duty should be materially increased. Beer drinking may not be responsible for a proportionate amount of crime to spirits, its results tend rather to debauchery. In proportion to the alcohol it contains however, it pays nothing like its equivalent. A gallon of beer of 1055 specific gravity contains one-tenth part of a gallon of proof spirits, which pays 10s. 6d. duty. The corresponding beer duty would be 1s. per gallon, or 36s. per barrel, instead of the 6s. 9d. now charged. Finally, the report of the Royal Commission on the Finances of Ireland has demonstrated that country to be considerably over-taxed, due largely to the fact that whisky is the national beverage, and not beer. Part of the injustice at anyrate can be remedied by increasing the beer duty, and reducing taxation in some way from which Ireland will benefit, without interfering at all with the spirit duties.

Similar questions enter into the brewing of beer as into the distillation of spirits, and there is a Pure Beer League in existence which advocates differential duties. Experts are not altogether agreed about the facts, and I lay no claim to be one, and therefore make no pretence to settle the dispute. The great bulk of the liquor brewed is pure and wholesome, and therefore the question is of minor interest compared with spirits.

Of the wine duties little need be said. It has been the policy of successive Governments to encourage the consumption of the lighter kinds in the hope of displacing spirits. Nearly 11 million gallons of this description contributed £540,000, while less than half the quantity of the more highly alcoholised produced £565,000, the respective rates being 1s. and 2s. 6d. a gallon. Sparkling wines, to whichever class they belonged, paid 2s. a gallon more, amounting to £150,000. As wine is, with rare exceptions, an undoubted luxury, and one indulged in principally by the wealthy, the duties do not err on the side of being excessive. But here the graduated principle has already been introduced, and it commends itself as both just and wise.

After alcoholic liquors, the item of by far the greatest importance is unmanufactured tobacco. 64,500,000 pounds yielded a gross revenue of

£10,200,000, at the rate of 3s. 2d. per pound. The duty on tobacco cannot in any sense be said to be a moral tax, and if such a thing as an Anti-Smoking League does exist, it counts discretion the better part of valour.[1] Tobacco is a comfort rather than a luxury, and is the solace of poor and rich alike. The use of it is rarely demoralising, its abuse, like that of everything else, carries its own punishment, which does not necessarily involve other people. Its consumption is moreover limited by natural bounds. A man may empty his pockets of a considerable sum on beer or spirits in a very short time; he may smoke like a furnace, and find it difficult to get through an ounce of tobacco costing threepence or fourpence in several hours. He may be none the better after the performance, but few people attempt it, and there is probably no pleasure in life enjoyed on the whole with such moderation as tobacco.

Yet this is the commodity singled out for an altogether exorbitant tax. Were it originally an expensive one, something might be said in favour of the impost as being not out of proportion to its value. But for the year ending 31st December 1896, the import of unmanufactured tobacco into the United Kingdom was 83,558,757 lbs., valued at £2,410,949, or an average price of sevenpence

---

[1] Since writing the above, my attention has been drawn to the "English Anti-Smoking Society and Anti-Narcotic League" (not Limited in name, though I should judge so in membership).

per pound, yet a duty of 3s. 2d. is imposed, more than five times its original cost. It may be maintained that threepence to fivepence an ounce is not an excessive price to pay for the limited quantity each individual consumes, but that is not the question if the principle be wrong. A lower price would not greatly stimulate consumption; it would rather provide millions of wage-earners throughout the kingdom with a few pence per week to spend on other things. A steady and persistent reduction should be made in this charge, until it is brought down to no more than half the present rate. The Exchequer certainly cannot afford to lose the £5,000,000 per annum involved, but compensation must be sought in other directions. Were the beer duty, for instance, raised one shilling per barrel for three successive years, bringing it up to 9s. 9d. or 10s., and the corresponding rebate made on tobacco, the latter would, at the end of the term, be reduced to 1s. 6d. per pound, and still be largely in excess of say Germany and the United States. Moreover, as Ireland is a large consumer of tobacco, she would directly benefit, and gain relief from some portion at least of her excessive taxation.

Of manufactured and partly manufactured tobacco, embracing negrohead and cavendish, the import was trivial, 875,000 lbs., and at rates varying from 4s. to 4s. 6d. per lb. contributed £175,000 to the revenue. Any concession to the unmanufactured article must be extended to this as well.

When we come to cigars we are on different ground. The quantity cleared from bond during the period under review was 2,180,000 pounds, and paid duty at the rate of 5s. per pound, amounting to £545,000. Cigars are very often expensive luxuries, and the 5s., instead of being many times their value, may be only 5 or 10 per cent. of it. The tax therefore is not an unjust one. But the price of cigars varies enormously, and what is a severe impost on one costing twopence or threepence, is light on another worth a shilling. A great quantity of the cheaper kind are manufactured in the United Kingdom, and here at last we have an opportunity of benefiting a home industry without any infringement of free trade principles. Were the duty on foreign cigars retained as it is, and no question asked as to what became of unmanufactured tobacco after the duty on it was once paid, a great stimulus would be afforded to British cigar-making, and employment found for many hands. It is doubtful even whether the foreign import would be curtailed, as the penny or twopenny cigar of fair quality would largely displace the pipe or cigarette. It is nothing uncommon to see the German mechanic returning from his work, or the drayman driving his horses through the streets, with a cigar rather than a pipe between his teeth, while the consumption in the United States equals about sixty per annum of the entire population, against four in the United Kingdom.

We pass now to articles of general consumption other than alcoholic liquors and tobacco, which find a place in the tariff. We are at once in the realm of taxation falling largely on the poorer classes, but still legitimate enough if levied in moderation, because it avoids what may be termed strict necessaries, and places no restraint on production. Tea, coffee, and cocoa, currants and raisins, are provided after bread and meat and clothing, or at any rate should be, and those who can afford to buy them can also afford to contribute their mite to the treasury, and indeed this is frequently the only taxation they pay. Most of the articles named however are too insignificant to be economically taxed, and during the financial year under review, coffee, cocoa, and chicory, contributed between them £350,000, and dried fruits £400,000, or a total of only three-quarters of a million. In a budget exceeding one hundred millions sterling, these might easily be replaced, but as they do not inflict any special hardship, and no agitation exists against them, they are permitted to remain. Some day, a Chancellor of the Exchequer hard pressed to balance his accounts may exact another one or two millions from them, so that each one in turn avoids disturbing so promising a milch cow. We might almost invent a fourth purpose of tariff in addition to the three dealt with in the first chapter, and call it "opportunist." Under this heading these duties would undoubtedly fall.

Tea however is another matter. The consumption for the same period exceeded 225,000,000 lbs., and at fourpence per lb. increased the national income by £3,750,000. It responds to its purpose therefore far more readily and efficiently than the others. We will have something more to say about it presently.

Having exhausted what is on the list, we must now turn to what is not there, in order to determine whether, among the multitude of articles imported into the United Kingdom, there are not some which might be made dutiable. Exports have already been dealt with in the previous chapter, and need not therefore be brought under review again. I am aware that many free traders consider it rank financial heresy to suggest the addition of anything to the tariff, but even at the risk of being disowned and finding myself homeless—for I cannot expect any protectionist to pity me and afford me shelter—I must subject free imports to a rigid analysis.

First and foremost we meet with articles of food. So far as they are necessaries of life, they are beyond the pale of argument. Living animals and dead meat, wheat and all kinds of bread stuffs, bacon and hams, butter and cheese, eggs and poultry, perishable fruits and vegetables, must be held sacred as the sustenance of the common people, whereby life is rendered tolerable, and they

are enabled to pursue their daily avocations.
Immense as the import of these articles is, the home
production of many of them is still greater, and
keen as is the competition, farmers thrive and landlords draw big rents. Changes in cultivation must
continually go on, and the old-fashioned rotation of
crops go by the board, but the very diversity of what
the land now produces has done much to improve the
health and stamina of the nation by constant change
of diet. For agriculture there is no protection
other than just laws wisely administered.

The next great class of commodities consists of
raw materials. Where they cannot be produced
at home, even protectionists concede that their
import should be free. Possibly however that
very circumstance may rouse the suspicions of the
free trader, but the protectionist, this once at any
rate, is right. To increase the cost of the materials
of manufacture would mean to handicap the export
trade of the country. If protectionists would only
see that labour is the most important of all raw
materials, they perhaps would not be so anxious to
tax that by increasing the cost of living, and
necessitating the payment of high and sometimes
extravagant wages. The labourer is entitled to get
all he can, but the living wage, if the minimum he
demands, is also not very far removed from the
maximum he can at present hope to obtain. In
one sense the protectionist does recognise labour
as a commodity, because in some countries he

is endeavouring to prohibit its importation altogether.

As far as the United Kingdom is concerned, the most important raw materials are cotton and wool, jute and hemp, hides and tallow, timber and metallic ores—whether of iron, lead, copper, or tin. In a minor category, but in their way of no less consequence, are chemicals and dye stuffs, paper materials and ivory, oils and indiarubber, if indeed the post office does not deliberately destroy the last-named trade by its red-tapism, for by refusing to forward the samples of English merchants on the ground that they emit an unpleasant odour, it is driving the business into continental hands. So rigidly indeed has it attempted to enforce its rules, that blocks of wood, carefully wrapped up and bearing the stamp of rubber merchants on the covers, have been refused transmission, and returned to the senders with the postage stamps defaced.[1] There are others too numerous to mention, but they are either trivial or too essential to meddle with.

There is still another large class from which the tariff list is really recruited, articles of consumption not strictly necessaries. Wines, spirits, and tobacco are heavily taxed as it is,—tea, coffee,

---

[1] The Post Office authorities have lately begun to evince a greater sense of their responsibilities towards the trade and commerce of the country in general.

cocoa, and dried fruits less so, but yet sufficiently. Spices are a semi-luxury and might be included, were it not advisable to abolish all the smaller duties. Sugar is a large item in this class, and is free.

Under ordinary circumstances, sugar should undoubtedly remain where it is. It has however been the subject of the most extraordinary financial legislation of modern times. When the sugar duties were abolished in 1874, this commodity was imported in the raw state principally from the British West Indies, Cuba, and the East Indies, and refined either in England or Scotland. But by the stimulus of bounties, beet cultivation has been engaged in to an enormous extent on the continent of Europe, and bounty-fed manufactured beet sugar has largely driven out its cane rival, and closed refinery after refinery engaged in its manipulation. The process has provided the United Kingdom with cheap sugar, which is an unqualified blessing, but it has almost destroyed an important industry, which is an equally unqualified misfortune.

Had this occurred by fair means, it would have been a matter for regret, but like many another unfortunate industry, it would have been impossible to render it national assistance. The pity of it is however that it has been deliberately brought about by methods which cast every principle of political economy to the winds. It is not necessary to maintain, as some people do, that the object of France, Germany, and Austria is first to ruin the British refiner, then destroy the cultivation of cane sugar, and finally, when the monopoly is safe for their own beet, charge whatever price they think proper. Under such conditions no monopoly would last very long. These countries have thought simply of themselves and altogether ignored the foreigner, and where they have compelled their own consumers to pay extravagant prices, while selling abroad at nominal ones, it has been solely with the view of helping agriculture, and encouraging an infant industry, which, as we have but recently experienced, is only another instance of becoming weaker as it grows older.

Can this state of things be remedied without injury to the British consumer? Is it possible so to tax sugar as to relieve those who pay the impost of an equivalent sum in another direction? It is practicable by substituting sugar for tea.

Moreover, a graduated scale of duties can be introduced. It would not be possible to tax Continental beet and leave West Indian cane free, because that would be contrary to commercial treaties to which Great Britain is a party. But it is possible to establish a classification without infringing them. Let raw cane sugar pay a stipulated duty, raw beet the same amount, plus the continental bounty, and manufactured beet plus the additional bounty again. Let the rate be fixed to bring in to the revenue the amount now received from tea, and abolish the duty on that commodity entirely.

But before we can settle so large a question in so offhand a manner, we must consider the results, not only financially and economically, but from a utilitarian point of view as well. Would the health or comfort of any considerable body of people suffer? Sugar is much more largely consumed than tea, of the former about ninety pounds per annum for every man, woman, and child in the kingdom, and of the latter only six pounds. If the one were restricted and the other encouraged, might not some injury accrue?

In the first place, 90 pounds is not the real individual consumption. Brewers have used upwards of 100,000 tons per annum for many years past, the latest return crediting them with 114,000 tons. Jam and marmalade manufacturers, bakers, confectioners, and biscuit makers, use enormous quantities, which however it is utterly impossible to get at, and only a rough estimate can be made. Probably fully one-third, and possibly nearly one-half the total consumption of sugar in the United Kingdom is accounted for in this way; many single firms use 1000 tons per annum. Domestic requirements therefore do not at the outside exceed 60 pounds per head of the population. Now should an extra charge of say a halfpenny a pound be imposed, this would hardly be likely to affect the use of the article: it has certainly not been noticed that a rise of 5s. per cwt. in the price interferes with consumption. Besides, it would not be an extra payment in reality, because the same households use tea, and would have the money refunded to them on that. As a pound of fruit and a pound of sugar go to make jam, the manufacturer would recoup himself by charging an additional farthing a pound on his production. Brewers, bakers, and others use such small quantities in proportion to their outturn, that they could not well charge the impost to their customers, and it would serve to reduce slightly their own profits.

Let us see then, how the amount of £3,750,000 now received from tea would be levied, and how subsequently distributed.

For the year ending 31st December 1896, the import of sugar into the United Kingdom was 385,000 tons cane, 400,000 tons raw beet, and 740,000 tons refined beet. The actual consumption was about 100,000 tons less, but that does not greatly affect the calculation. The average bounty paid by exporting countries on their beet is now supposed to be 1s. 3d. per cwt. on raw, and 1s. 9d. per cwt. on refined. The sum works out something like as follows :—

## SUGAR BOUNTIES

```
385,000 tons cane at 1s. 6d. per cwt.,      . .  £577,500
400,000   „   raw beet at 1s. 6d. + 1s. 3d. = 2s. 9d.
              per cwt.,     .   .   .   .   . 1,100,000
740,000   „   refined beet at 1s. 6d. + 1s. 9d. =
              3s. 3d. per cwt., .           . 2,405,000
                                              ──────────
                                              £4,082,500
```

The average duty would thus be 2s. 7½d. per cwt., but to be on the safe side we must calculate that the consumer would have to pay the maximum, though that is hardly likely, and even with the addition for profit on outlay the tax would not reach a halfpenny a pound but any small difference would probably be rectified in the better quality supplied. As a matter of fact the duty might be levied at threepence less, but the Chancellor of the Exchequer would naturally want to be on the right side in case of any falling off in the consumption, or displacement of the various proportions.

Though the nominal rates of bounty are well known, their incidence and distribution are matters of considerable doubt, as the calculations are made, not always on the quantity actually exported, but on the sugar supposed to be contained in the beets, and it is acknowledged that manufacturers by this means secure much more than the official figures would point to. It has been stated indeed that the French bounty amounts to 4s. 6d. per cwt. Into that question I do not propose to enter here, and have contented myself with the supposition that the published rates are the real ones. Strict inquiry would, of course, have to be made before the details of such a scheme were finally settled, and the result might be a reduction on raw, and a further increase on refined.

Nor is such discrimination any novelty, as the duties prior to repeal in 1874 were divided into four classes on raw sugars, varying from 2s. to 2s. 10d. per cwt. according to quality, while refined was charged at 3s. The variation is of course greater in this instance, but there is good reason for it.

Just as there would be a profit charged on the outlay of the sugar duty, so would there be a saving on that of tea, and the consumer would receive, not the fourpence per pound only, but fourpence plus another penny, say fivepence in all. Then he would pay—

½d. per pound on 60 pounds sugar, . 2s. 6d., and receive
5d. per pound on 6 pounds tea, . 2s. 6d.
the one just compensating for the other.

He might also have to pay an additional farthing a pound on any jam purchased. But the financial portion of the scheme is practically equalised.

The advantages of the substitution are not yet exhausted. An excessive consumption of sugar is perhaps less injurious than of tea. The mischief done by the latter is generally in the mode of its preparation, and caused by people drinking the liquor after it has stewed for hours, or by adding fresh boiling water to old leaves. Were the retail price of a fairly good tea reduced from 1s. 2d. or 1s. 3d. a pound to 9d. or 10d., there might be no great increase in the consumption of the liquor, but there would be of the leaf, a fresh spoonful of which might often be emptied into the pot after it had been relieved of its exhausted contents. By this means health might actually be conserved.

Again, the average consumption of sugar in a wealthy household is greater than in a poor one, and the reverse is the case with tea. Sugar is used for so many things where money is plentiful, and a lavish or even abundant table provided. On the other hand, the rich have a multiplicity of drinks and divide their favours. Among the poor, where alcohol is excluded or moderately partaken of, tea is the principal, often the only other beverage, and the tea bill quite an important item in the weekly household expenditure. Thus the incidence of a tax on sugar would be more largely against the rich, and in favour of the poor, than on tea.

But the most obvious advantage of all is the justice of the change advocated. Protests have been made in vain against the unfair operation of the bounties, and it is now time to adopt more practical measures. If British refiners can hold their own with fair play, they are entitled to it, and if the industry of British colonies can be saved, common sense demands it. If continental nations like to continue the bounties, by all means let them do so, but let the money go into the British exchequer. That would afford an object lesson in protection which they would not forget in a hurry, and instead of taxing the foreigner, they would be able each year, by calculating the difference between the duty actually paid on beet sugar, and the amount chargeable at the minimum rate, to realise what relief they were themselves affording to the British taxpayer.

Some day continental Governments will grow tired of the system and abolish the bounties. When they do so, and not till then, they will be entitled to claim and receive equal treatment with cane sugar. The loss of revenue which this would entail might be made good by increasing the minimum duty, or by transferring the loss intact to some other tax, and thus affording relief to the consumer. And eventually a British Chancellor of the Exchequer, gladdened by a handsome budget surplus, may again abolish the sugar duty, and, by a round-about method, the taxation of tea will be got rid of. Meanwhile, there is nothing to fear from retaliation. The Governments concerned would be the first to recognise, if they did not openly admit, the wisdom of the proceeding, and would be too anxious to retain the British markets for their producers to hanker after revenging so obvious an act of justice.

Had the existing state of affairs prevailed when the budget surplus of 1874 was disposed of, it may reasonably be presumed that tea rather than sugar would have been the favoured commodity. Sugar was then largely the product of British colonies, tea principally of a foreign country, and a man does not usually slap his friend in the face and confer his favours on a perfect stranger. How different the circumstances are now will be seen at a glance from the following figures :—

IMPORTS OF SUGAR.

|  | 1874. | 1896. |
|---|---|---|
| Cane from British possessions, | 245,000 tons. | 155,000 tons. |
| „ Foreign countries, | 335,000 „ | 230,000 „ |
| Beet, raw, from Foreign countries, | 125,000 „ | 400,000 „ |
| „ refined „ „ | 126,500 „ | 740,000 „ |
|  | 831,500 tons. | 1,525,000 tons. |

There was also imported in 1874 about 10,000 tons refined cane from foreign countries.

IMPORTS OF TEA.

|  | 1874. | 1896. |
|---|---|---|
| From China, | 133,452,693 lbs. | 35,299,730 lbs. |
| „ India, | 17,608,598 „ | 127,721,885 „ |
| „ Ceylon, | 484,135 „ | 94,859,965 „ |
| „ Other countries, | 11,237,384 „ | 7,512,542 „ |
|  | 162,782,810 lbs. | 265,394,122 lbs. |

All things being equal, British possessions are certainly entitled to receive generous treatment in preference to foreign and rival countries.

There still remains an interesting class of British imports to be dealt with, namely, manufactured articles, which figured in the trade returns of 1896 for £81,250,000. To lump these together and suggest a duty of twenty or twenty-five per cent. on the lot is a manifest absurdity, and again separate analysis is the only way of arriving at sound conclusions.

There are many insignificant items amounting in value to a few hundred thousand pounds each at the outside, some of which might perhaps reasonably lend themselves to taxation. Where trade is conducted on so gigantic a scale however, they are not worth consideration, and may be summarily dismissed.

Of the first importance are cotton and woollen textiles, because Great Britain depends largely for prosperity on these very industries. Cotton goods figure for £3,525,000, but we soon realise how small this is, when we find British exports of yarns and textile fabrics made from cotton during the same period were valued at £61,250,000, or nearly eighteen times as much. Besides, some portion of the 3½ millions consists of goods sent merely to some continental country for a finishing process, perhaps only to be returned as French prints, for which there is always a demand, and £500,000 was re-exported. At anyrate cotton manufacturers have not yet been heard to complain of foreign competition on English soil, and they almost entirely monopolise the home market.

With woollen fabrics it is somewhat different. Their value amounted to £10,770,000, or allowing for re-exports, to a little over ten millions net, while woollen yarn was responsible for a further £2,050,000. These figures compare with British exports of the same goods of £18,270,000 and £7,225,000 respectively, and are therefore much less favourable than the case of cotton. The export of wearing apparel, the bulk of which would be of woollen material, though no doubt largely mixed with cotton, was valued at a further £5,230,000. Yarn, for the industry in which it is used, is a raw, or at the most a partly manufactured material, and may be allowed to escape on that plea if on no better. The fabrics do compete severely with British manufactures, but they owe their advantage largely to their foreign name and production, as French dress materials are frequently insisted on. If that were all there would be no harm done in making the purchasers pay a little more for them, but there is a principle at stake. Among the imports are large quantities of cheaper goods, and clothing is as necessary as food. Once begin to tax it, and it is impossible to draw distinctions or to say where it may end, and it is better to forego a little satisfaction and revenue combined than run the risk of committing a wide-reaching injustice. Cotton and woollen fabrics alike therefore may retire from court.

Leather and dressed hides amounted in value to £7,600,000, straw plaiting to £910,000. As these are partly manufactured materials for covering the feet and the head respectively, they claim immunity. In view of the enormous quantity of hides available in the United States, it is but natural that the tanning industry should flourish there, particularly as the weight of a wet hide is so much greater before than after conversion into leather. While Great Britain tans her own, she may fairly concede the same right to America, and purchase whatever additional quantity of leather she wants in the cheapest market. Boots and shoes, principally French and Belgian, amounted to £520,000, again an item for which fashion is largely responsible. Our own export of them amounted to £1,800,000, so there is not yet any danger of foreigners ousting British manufacturers from their own markets.

Glass of all kinds, including window glass and bottles, was imported to the extent of £2,740,000. Here, for some reason or other, continental manufacturers fairly beat the British on their own ground. There is no pretence that foreign glass is sold in England at a loss, and yet the English works cannot successfully compete. There is something wrong somewhere, and what it is can best be explained by the glass manufacturers themselves. To impose a duty would be naked protection. Besides, glass is a necessity, and used much more by the poor than by the rich in most of its varied forms. Taxation would fall directly on the consumer, who would gain no corresponding benefit, and it is therefore out of the question. An export valued at £900,000, demonstrates that the British industry is not yet played out.

Manufactured iron and steel, including sewing machines worth £300,000, finding its way into the country, was valued at £6,000,000, but as £900,000 was again exported and consisted evidently of transit goods, the net result was only some five millions. Again this is insignificant when compared with the British exports, valued at £23,800,000, together with machinery for a further sum of £17,000,000, implements, tools, and railway carriages and waggons for £3,000,000, cycles for nearly £2,000,000, hardware and cutlery £2,120,000. The British iron trade has recently shown an amount of vitality which has surprised its warmest friends, and is well able to take care of itself without Government intervention. Some portion of the import was no doubt legitimate enough, but how the remainder came over will be a matter for consideration later on.

Paper is responsible for the very respectable total of £3,140,000. British paper manufacturers must bestir themselves. They possess one of the oldest and most respectable industries in the kingdom, and have largely gone to sleep over it. They are able to turn out work which cannot be touched in quality, and should be equally able to produce material that cannot be beaten in price. They have adhered far too long to old methods, and failed to keep pace with modern invention and modern requirements, relying upon their reputation and the monopoly they formerly enjoyed. The consequence has been that they have looked on while foreign rivals have captured their business. It were greater kindness to stir a few of them up with a long pole, than to afford the entire industry protection. There are plenty of firms fully alive to the necessities of the hour, and these not only manage to do a large and profitable trade at home, but to export £1,630,000 worth into the bargain.

Watches and clocks and the different parts thereof were valued at £1,550,000. These may be either comparative luxuries or necessaries, but in this instance they fall under the latter rather than the former description. Imported watches and clocks are mostly of a cheap, but by no means inferior description, and find their way largely to the pockets and chimney-pieces of the working classes. As it is as necessary for a working man to turn up punctually at his appointed task as to leave it or take his meals, he must not be deprived of the means that enable him to do so. English watch and clock makers are skilled mechanics who earn good wages, and whose lot will remain a satisfactory one while they prevent the trade from becoming overcrowded,—not a difficult matter, as a long apprenticeship must be served.

The list is becoming exhausted, and thus far we have arrived at nothing practical. Two items now appear however, which call for closer scrutiny. Gloves were imported to the value of £2,340,000, and silks and ribbons and materials made from them, to the large sum of £16,700,000. Now these are luxuries pure and simple, for the gloves are of the kind which are not necessaries, and include few of the woollen ones so useful in winter to protect the hands from the inclemencies of the weather. The poorer classes no doubt buy gloves and silks, and especially ribbons, but they only do so with surplus earnings, or if otherwise they deserve no sympathy. No principle of free trade will be infringed by taxing them, and as there is a more or less important home manufacture, it is quite possible that the foreigner may have to cut his profit to compete, and so contribute part of the revenue. An import duty of 10, 15, or even 20 per cent. would realise a considerable sum, and if it enabled Macclesfield and Spitalfields to hold up their heads once more, no Englishman need cry over it. If the French Government, to retain the market for its own manufacturers, granted them a further bounty, that too would go into the British exchequer, and leave the British wearer of French silks and gloves no worse off than before, though the British industry might not revive.

Nor is there in this instance any important export trade to jeopardise. Silks in 1896 were shipped of the declared value of £1,420,000, and there was a re-export of foreign goods amounting to £725,000, upon which of course, in case of duty being levied, a drawback would be allowed. It is also just possible that some portion of the larger item was wrongly described, and consisted really of foreign manufactured silks which may or may not have gone through an additional process in Great Britain. In the case of being subjected to duty, scrupulous care would naturally be taken to preserve the identity of the imported goods, in order that the drawback might be claimed. The export of haberdashery and millinery, worth a further £1,520,000, would scarcely be affected, as the value of such goods is generally much more in the workmanship than the material. Nearly the whole of it moreover is to British colonies and would be retained. Of gloves the re-export was under £200,000, again almost entirely to the colonies.

And if by some strange chance the entire industry were to be transferred from foreign to British hands, the revenue would not suffer total loss of duty, because it would be necessary to import either the raw material or the partly manufactured yarn, upon which a charge would likewise be imposed, though not necessarily on so high a scale as on the finished fabrics.

The monthly Board of Trade returns lump a number of items together as "other articles," and only publish details in the annual digest, but some of them at least are of sufficient importance to deserve mention.

Rubber manufactures figure for £630,000, cork £640,000, cordage and twine, £690,000, matches £360,000, and are all too insignificant, even were there no other objections. China, porcelain, and earthenware, a good deal of it of an ornamental rather than a general character, was valued at £850,000, but on the other hand the export amounted to £2,170,000. Diamonds for £4,600,000, not included in the official Board of Trade returns at all, would be a fair object of taxation, were concealment less easy. Musical instruments, for £1,170,000, afford an undoubted incentive to the cultivation of musical taste, and the cheaper descriptions of German pianos at anyrate are an immense improvement on similar priced goods of English make. Toys also figure for £1,050,000, but afford infinitely more than that amount of pleasure to those into whose hands they fall, and the cause of the children must be held sacred.

Linen yarns and manufactures were worth £1,180,000, but only £400,000 consisted of tissues, the rest being yarn—mostly from Belgium—and consequently a semi-raw material. On the other hand, exports of linen fabrics amounted to upwards of £5,000,000, and of yarn to a little over £1,000,000. The linen trade has suffered much more from Lancashire than from foreign competition, by the gradually extending use of cotton goods for domestic purposes; and of late years a new enemy in the shape of jute has put in an appearance.

What is wanted is the demonstration of the superiority of flax over both cotton and jute to those who can afford it, or else greater economy in the cost of production, and it is to these that the north of Ireland must pay most attention. Climatic conditions are unequalled in the production of these fabrics, and with proper enterprise Belfast should experience no difficulty in retaining its position as the centre of the world's linen industry.[1]

Laces were valued at £1,100,000, and embroideries at £840,000, together £1,940,000, and here once more we are on less solid ground. Still, they are necessary to make our wives, our sweethearts, and our homes becoming, and enter so largely into the adornments of everyday life that it were cruel to enhance their cost, particularly when their use is helping to elevate the tastes of the people. Expensive laces and embroideries are luxuries no doubt, but their inclusion with a large class of cheap goods makes discrimination difficult. Besides, some of them are made from silk, the laces alone of that material being valued at £225,000, and would be included in the schedule. Then £400,000 worth are re-exported, so that the final total is by no means as formidable as it looks.

Ornamental feathers for £1,140,000, and artificial flowers for £560,000, are in every respect

[1] A report from the British Consul-General in Germany, issued since the above was in type, states that linen tissues manufactured in that country are actually sent to Belfast to be bleached, because nowhere else in the world can the same purity of colour be obtained.

more suitable objects of taxation. But here we are met by a fresh difficulty, inasmuch as half the former item is imported from British possessions, South Africa contributing most of it in the shape of ostrich feathers. In theory that ought not to stand in the way, but it would hardly be politic to single out an article in which a colony is so largely interested. Besides, nearly half are re-exported, and against the £413,000 received from France there is a set off of £120,000. Germany took £125,000 and the United States £210,000, against an import from both these countries of only £13,000. The same objection does not apply to artificial flowers, but by themselves they are hardly worth attention.

Prepared skins of the sheep, goat, rabbit, and seal represent a value of £2,700,000, but again British possessions are responsible for over £1,700,000, Australia and South Africa being specially prominent. For this reason then, if for no other they must be passed. Furs, however, were valued at £1,060,000, and fur manufactures at £780,000 respectively, and the same objections would hardly apply here, for though Canada is interested in the trade, she supplied less than 15 per cent. of the total. They are, too, distinct luxuries, and fall into the same category as silks and gloves. But the re-export of the one was valued at £1,020,000, and of the other at £210,000. The number of skins imported was upwards of 9,600,000, and of those exported only 7,250,000, so that the British trade appear to have secured some 2,350,000 for the small sum of £40,000. On this basis it must be extremely profitable, and it would be a pity to disturb it by any custom-house regulations, particularly as the value upon which the duty would ultimately have to be paid would only be some £600,000.

The list is now exhausted, and resolves itself into two articles, namely:—

|  |  |
|---|---|
| Silks and Ribbons. . . | £16,700,000 |
| Gloves, . . . | 2,340,000 |
|  | £19,040,000 |

which at an *ad valorem* duty of 20 per cent. would yield a revenue of nearly £4,000,000, and would be contributed in a manner which offends against no principle either of justice or political economy.

It is evident that the British tariff, satisfactory though the basis upon which it is constructed may be, is very far from perfect, and may be radically reformed without much ultimate change in the revenue derived from indirect taxation, to very great advantage. The plan upon which this can be carried out may be briefly summarised as follows:—

(1) A readjustment of the spirit duties without altering their amount.

(2) The substitution of a duty on sugar equivalent to that on tea.

(3) The increase of the beer duty to a more adequate level with that on spirits, the revenue derived to be applied to a reduction on tobacco.

(4) The inclusion in the tariff of certain specified manufactured goods.

(5) The abolition out of the proceeds of these new duties of those on the minor articles of consumption.

(6) The application of the balance of the new and increased duties to a remission of other taxation, preferably the income tax.

This need not by any means be a final readjustment, but once adopted, wise consideration should be given to the tariff at not too frequent intervals, but within such reasonable periods as important changes in the habits of the people and the variations of trade may demand.

# CHAPTER V.

## THE UNITED STATES TARIFF.

Frequency of Changes—Avowed and Real Purposes—Extent and Detail of the Tariff—Summary of Schedules—Principles of their Construction. CHEMICALS :—Drugs—Chemical Manufactures—Vegetable Products — Exemptions. EARTHENWARE :— Building Materials—Domestic Utensils—Glass and Glassware. METALS :—Tin—Iron and Steel—Cotton Ties—Tinplates—Cutlery and Tools—Copper and Lead. TIMBER :—Conflicts between Succeeding Administrations. SUGAR :—The Domination of the Sugar Trust—Resulting Scandals. TOBACCO AND CIGARS. WINES AND SPIRITS. AGRICULTURAL PRODUCTS :—Breadstuffs— Dairy Products—Fruit and Vegetables—Meat and Provisions— General Result of Protection on the Industry. TEXTILES :—Raw Materials. COTTON :—Yarns—Tissues—Complicated nature of Duties—Extent of Import Trade. WOOL :—Yarns—Fabrics— Severity of M'Kinley Tariff—Illustrations—Effect of Duty on Raw Wool—Extent of Trade. SILK. FLAX, HEMP, AND JUTE : —Linen Tissues and Embroideries. PAPER AND BOOKS. MISCELLANEOUS :—Coal—Leather and Gloves. THE FREE LIST :— Agricultural Implements—Tourists' Wearing Apparel—What Protection has done and is doing for the United States.

WHICH ? As during the years 1890-94 the country was under three distinct ones, and at the beginning of 1897 a fourth is well within sight,[1] there is an abundant selection, and amid such superfluity one finds difficulty in making a choice. There is common ground in all of them however, and it is well fenced round with pro-

[1] The new tariff has become law just as this is going to press, and will be dealt with in an Appendix at the end of the volume.

tection. That is never the avowed object. The tariff which came into operation on the 6th October 1890, and which has always been associated with the name of President M'Kinley, is officially described as "An Act *to reduce the revenue*,[1] and equalise duties on imports, and for other purposes," and so rapidly and effectively did it accomplish the first purpose, and bring the national treasury to the verge of bankruptcy, that the object of the Act of the 1st August 1894, usually known as the Wilson Tariff, was declared to be "to reduce taxation, *to provide revenue for the Government*, and for other purposes." The "other purposes" in each instance are delightfully vague, and may mean anything and include everything.

The strongest condemnation of the M'Kinley Tariff is to be found in President M'Kinley's own words. Referring to the anticipated re-enactment of that measure in all its main features, he is reported to have said in his inaugural address delivered on the 4th March 1897 :—" I earnestly hope and expect that Congress will, at the earliest practicable moment, enact a *revenue* legislation—fair, reasonable, conservative, and just—which, *while supplying sufficient revenue for public purposes*, will be also generally helpful to every section and every enterprise. . . . *The paramount duty of Congress is to stop deficiencies by restoring protective legislation, which is always*

[1] The italics are the author's.

*the firmest prop of the Treasury."* Is it the facts or only the opinions which have undergone so radical a transformation since 1890?

Needless to say, the simplicity we noticed as so marked a feature of the British tariff, is entirely absent in those of the United States, and they present more the appearance of substantial text-books for the use of advanced students, though hardly in the science of political economy. The M'Kinley Act, with the accompanying instructions as to its operation and enforcement, covered seventy-two large and closely printed pages in the edition issued by the International Customs Tariff Bureau. The clauses of dutiable articles numbered 472, the index alone covering nearly four pages in double columns, and enumerating 370 commodities or groups of commodities. As in such a catalogue, doubt would often arise as to whether a particular article were included or not, a free list had to be appended, which specified 289 more, and if at any time an unexpected seven-hundred and sixty-second commodity put in an appearance at a United States port, it was graciously stipulated that it should be admitted on payment of a 10 per cent. *ad valorem* duty if unmanufactured, and 20 per cent. if otherwise.

The Wilson Tariff is a slight improvement on this. Printed in precisely the same form, it is compressed into forty-one pages, though most of the instructions, being unchanged, are not repeated. The dutiable clauses number 362, the free list is responsible for 328 more, and the index occupies only 3 pages, and confines itself to 334 commodities or groups. The more important transfers from one list to the other we shall have occasion to notice as we go on.

To attempt to analyse so stupendous a mass of detail, would in itself demand a volume much larger than this, an expenditure of time, most of which might be devoted to better purposes, and an amount of technical knowledge such as no one individual ever yet possessed. We must content ourselves therefore with an examination of general principles, and an occasional application to specific industries. Moreover, as anything earlier than the year 1890 in United States tariffs has long since been regarded as ancient history, it will answer no present purpose to stray beyond the two bearing the names of M'Kinley and Wilson.

There is a further advantage in confining ourselves within these limits, as both proceed on much the same lines, the one in fact is an amendment of the other. So many disputes are constantly arising regarding the classification of specific articles, that after a decision is once arrived at, the customs authorities are naturally anxious that changes in the tariff should be in the rates of duty, not in the groupings of commodities.

The schedules then in each instance are lettered A to N. and are as follows :—

- A   Chemicals, Oils, and Paints.
- B   Earths, Earthenware, and Glassware.
- C   Metals, and Manufactures of.
- D   Wood, and Manufactures of.
- E   Sugar.
- F   Tobacco, and Manufactures of.
- G   Agricultural Products and Provisions.
- H   Spirits, Wines, and other Beverages.
- I   Cotton Manufactures.
- J   Flax, Hemp, and Jute, and Manufactures of.
- K   Wool, and Manufactures of.
- L   Silk and Silk Goods.
- M   Pulp, Paper, and Books.
- N   Sundries.

The conundrum propounded to any one after reading this list, omitting even Schedule N, "What has been omitted?" would be a poser, yet possibly a more than usually intelligent guesser of riddles and solver of mysteries, particularly if he were an Englishman acquainted with the tariff of his own country, might reply tea, coffee, and cocoa, and truly they have to be sought for on the free list. Not that I would advocate their displacement for a moment, but the very mention of these commodities provides us with a key to the underlying principle, which is to tax nothing that cannot be produced at home, and everything that can.

Bearing this in mind, a flood of light will be

let in upon many of the schedules and clauses, which might otherwise remain enshrouded in darkness. Where details of imports or exports are given by way of illustration, it will be understood that they are, unless otherwise stated, for the fiscal year ending 30th June 1896, which represented a full working year under the Wilson Act. As it only actually came into operation on the 28th August 1894, two of the twelve months of the previous year were under the M'Kinley Act ; indeed, the figures for both 1893-94 and 1894-95 were influenced by tariff changes, prospective and actual, and must be scrutinised in consequence with more than usual care.

Schedule A, embracing chemicals, oils, and paints, is further subdivided into acids, ammonia, coal tar productions, oils, paints, colours and varnishes, lead products, potash, medicinal and chemical preparations, soap and soda. In the M'Kinley Act it is represented by ninety-two distinct clauses, and in the Wilson by seventy-nine. It is indeed fitting that so far-reaching and inclusive a tariff should commence with a class of articles which in some form or other enter into the daily life of every man, woman, and child. The humble blacking, which nevertheless adds so much to the personal appearance, is rated in the one at 25 per cent. and in the other at 20 per cent., and still the value of the import was $137,611. Most of this was from France, but the United States exported blacking to the value of $533,000, of which upwards of $300,000 was to the United Kingdom. To move to the other extremity, hair washes, pomades, dentifrices, and such like are taxed 40 per cent., reduced from 50 per cent.

There is some crisis in the life of nearly every individual, and often more than one, when drugs more or less expensive are necessary to preserve existence, and here we might expect that a Government would at least abstain from doing anything to increase their cost. Yet an all-round duty of 10 per cent. is imposed if in anything but their raw state, meaning considerably more to the needy patient. Even such simple preservatives of health as magnesia and Epsom salts are taxed respectively 3 cents, and ½ cent per pound, about 30 per cent. of their value, and were nearly half as much again. Such an impost is as unwise as it is exasperating. Castor oil is eminently a poor man's remedy, and was taxed at 80 cents a gallon, mercifully reduced however to 35 cents, while cod liver oil, the great preservative of weak chests, likewise pays 20 per cent. on its value. Many of these are not American productions at all, but their enhanced cost enable cheap United States concoctions of doubtful value, both pecuniarily and remedially, to be palmed off instead of the simple provisions of beneficent nature. The United States is eminently the land of patent medicines, and the annual export alone is valued at upwards of two million dollars, of which unfortunately the United Kingdom gets about half. How many millions worth more United States citizens themselves swallow is wisely excluded from the purview of Government statistics.

Paris green and London purple look innocent enough, and most people would no doubt ask what they were for. When the fatal cotton worm attacks the cotton plant, an immediate application of one or other of these substances is absolutely necessary to save the crop. So effectively have they been used in past years, that the pest, if not exterminated, is now but a rare visitor, so Paris green and London purple are enhanced in value by an import tax of $12\frac{1}{2}$ per cent., plus any additional profit the seller likes to put on.

Important as are the domestic items in this schedule, they sink into insignificance when placed alongside those which enter into the great manufacturing industries. Chemical research has done more to cheapen commodities than any other single agent, and the chemical industry is but the handmaiden to nearly every other of importance it is possible to name. In the promotion of American manufacturing enterprise, cheap chemicals are an absolute necessity of progress, yet even they must as far as possible be produced in the United States, and not purchased in the most favourable markets. Caustic soda, soda crystals, and soda ash, are all commodities of wide use, yet are rated at $\frac{1}{2}$ cent, $\frac{1}{4}$ cent, and $\frac{1}{4}$ cent per pound respectively, half of what they formerly were. This looks very moderate until expressed as $11.20, $2.80, and $5.60 a ton[1] respectively, and contrasted with the actual value, when they are found to be equal to something like 30 per cent. *ad valorem*. As some 27,500 tons of caustic soda, of the value of upwards of $1,000,000, and over 110,000 tons soda ash, were imported and paid the duty, the increased cost was in this instance at anyrate paid by the consumers, as English chemical works do not ship their products to the United States at a loss. One of the principal firms in the trade indeed pays its proprietors from 30 to 50 per cent. per annum on a very large capital. Other chemicals, coal tar products, colours, etc., paying duty, were imported to the value of $10,000,000 additional, and increased in price to the consumer by at least 30 to 50 per cent. Little wonder that every other schedule of the tariff becomes a necessity, for Schedule A handicaps them all.

Cotton seed oil was rated under the M'Kinley Act at 10 cents a gallon, but freed under its successor. Few items are quite so utterly absurd as this, as the United States is pre-eminently the home of the seed-crushing industry, where the material is actually on the spot. Salad olive oil pays 35 cents a gallon, but despite this, 942,598 gallons were imported. Well refined cotton oil is an excellent substitute, and was at one time

[1] The ton is taken at 2240 pounds. Throughout the North American Continent the hundredweight is literally 100 pounds, and the ton consequently 2000 pounds.

largely shipped to Spain and Italy, where a change of casks was supposed to transform its nature, as it did its name, and the duty was no doubt imposed, yet unsuccessfully, to encourage the domestic use of the native product. The latest returns show France to have taken nearly five million gallons, partly no doubt for similar purposes.

The most justifiable article on the list is opium, and, though a drug, there is a strong tendency to use it as a narcotic, which should be checked. The duty of $12 per pound has been reduced to $6, and the import was valued at $900,000, a decided increase on previous years under the higher tariff. In the realm of paints, not even artists' oil and water colours are exempt, and anyone artistically inclined, desirous of making use of the preparations of some of the famous makers in Europe, is compelled to pay an additional 25 per cent. on their value.

There are of course important exemptions, particularly of natural products not indigenous to the United States. The import of logwood in its rough state was valued at over $1,500.000, and of indigo at slightly under $1.750,000. Gums amounted to $7,000,000, and vegetable and essential oils to upwards of $4,000,000. 127,000 tons of so valuable a fertiliser as nitrate of soda were admitted free, though the United States pay great attention to the manufacture of manures, principally however of phosphates, in which some parts of the country are naturally rich, and of which four or five million dollars worth are annually exported. Bleaching powder is also welcomed, and together with free chemicals, such as potashes and brimstone, and others of more or less indefinite nomenclature, represented something like $20,000.000. Whether so important a group will escape the next readjustment it is impossible to predict. One effect a high tariff on chemicals most certainly has. While it does not prevent a total import valued at $50,000,000, it destroys all chance of a considerable export trade, the total, exclusive of patent medicines, being only some $6,500,000 of an extremely miscellaneous character.

Such are a few of the leading features of the first schedule, and the entire tariff will be found to maintain its reputation, good or evil, from whichever point it is looked at. It contains scarcely an item that does not offend on economical or humanitarian grounds, and has apparently been framed to give impartially as much annoyance as possible to a nation of seventy millions of people.

Schedule B devoted to earths, earthenware, and glasswares, is also subdivided into brick and tile, cement, lime, and plaster, clays or earths, earthenware and china, glass and glassware, marble and stone and manufactures of, stone and slate. Here the domestic threshold is crossed, and the privacy of the dwelling invaded, for both in the construction of the home and the furnishing of it with the most necessary utensils, the hand of the tax-gatherer lies heavily.

There is absolutely nothing in this class admitted duty free beyond glasses suitable for optical instruments, imported to the value of $93,600. Bricks and tiles are rated at 25 per cent. upwards, according as they are plain, or glazed and decorated, but this class of material surely needs no protection. Clay is so universal a commodity, that ordinary building brick will rarely stand addition to its cost beyond cartage or drayage for a short distance, and railroad, much less ocean freight and charges is out of the question. Fancy brick and tile made from special clays may occasionally be an exception, but their use is limited. It is hardly surprising that the import recorded is exceedingly small, the wonder would be if it were greater, even without the check of any duty at all.

Not all building materials however are so favourably situated. Roman and Portland cement is required from abroad in immense quantities, 535,000 tons being valued at upwards of $3,800,000. This is a trade which Germany has specially laid itself out to capture, and England is being gradually elbowed out, the former now supplying about twice the quantity of the latter country. The duty at 8 cents per 100 pounds, equal to about $1¾ per ton, thus realises about $1,000,000, too small an amount if regarded as revenue, too large to add to a commodity so necessary to ensure stability and strength to public and private works alike. In rough marble we meet for the first time a method of levying duty which we shall henceforth come across in varying forms, the rate being 50 cents per cubic foot, reduced from 65 cents, while manufactures of the stone pay 45 per cent. *ad valorem*, against a former 50 per cent. ; granite, freestone, sandstone, and limestone, pay now 7 cents per cubic foot, and formerly 11 cents ; slate tables, chimney pieces, etc., 20 per cent. ; and roofing slates also 20 per cent., which effectively shuts out the superior qualities found in such abundance in Welsh quarries.

It is inside rather than outside the dwelling where the pressure of this schedule is most severely felt. Everything alike, from the commonest brown or yellow earthenware mug, to the choicest china teacup, falls within its scope, and everything costs fully half as much again as it ought to, while under the M'Kinley tariff most things cost double. On common earthenware the charge is 20 per cent., against a former 25 per cent., but in the other descriptions the fall has been from 60 per cent. to 35 per cent., while the cost to the consumer includes of course the profit on the outlay of these heavy duties. Nor is this an instance where the home manufacturer is able to shut the foreigner out, as the import amounted to $10,500,000, and English potteries are known to earn fair profits, so that this is eminently one of the instances where a remission of the three or four million dollars duty would benefit the users of china and earthenware to the extent of several millions more. Needless to say there is no export trade in American earthenware worth speaking of, its total value falling short of $150,000.

Glass bottles or utensils of any sort pay from ¾ to 1½ cent per pound, according to capacity, nor do they escape the vigilant eye of the customs collector when entering the United States filled with some liquid, for they must pay the duty just the same, lest as empties they should compete with home bottle makers. Cut and decorated glass pays 40 per cent., and the interests of scientific research were carefully guarded by the imposition of 45 per cent. on laboratory glass. It is window, crown, and plate glass however which appeals most to patriotic sentiment for support against the foreigner, and the care taken to exclude him from dipping too deeply into the American pocket will be best illustrated by quoting intact clause 91 of the Wilson Act, and placing in brackets the corresponding duties charged under the M'Kinley Act :—

"Unpolished cylinder, crown and common window glass, not exceeding 10 × 15 inches square, 1 cent per pound (1⅜ c.); above that and not exceeding 16 × 24 inches square, 1¼ cents (1⅞ c.); above that and not exceeding 24 × 30 inches square, 1¾ cents (2⅜ c.); above that and not exceeding 24 × 36 inches square, 2 cents (2⅞ c.); all above that 2¼ cents (3¼ c.): *Provided*, That unpolished cylinder, crown and common window glass, imported in boxes, shall be packed fifty square feet per box, as nearly as sizes will

8

permit, and the duty shall be computed thereon, according to the actual weight of glass."

These duties vary from about 15 to 70 per cent. *ad valorem*.

Such a clause may work more smoothly than it reads, it certainly converts the Government into trade inquisitor, and dictates to the foreign manufacturer how he is to conduct his business and pack his goods, if he wishes the inestimable privilege of trading with the United States of America. The four succeeding clauses, dealing with crown, plate, and silvered glass of various descriptions, are framed in the same manner, only the duties are chargeable on the still more intricate scale of measurement per square foot, instead of weight per pound. Not only the tax, but the method of levying it, is well calculated to frighten the most enterprising manufacturer or merchant. It is indeed fairly successful in accomplishing this, as the value of cylinder, window, and bottle glass imported, was but little over $1,500,000. Silvered glass was valued at $1,200,000, plate glass at $800,000, and other glass not specified in detail, at nearly $4,000,000.

The remarks made in the previous chapter regarding the English glass trade are amply illustrated here. Belgium, France, and Germany supplied the United States to the extent of $5,750,000, Great Britain following far in the rear with less than $500,000.

Schedule C, metals and metal manufactures, embraces, as may well be imagined, almost every conceivable article extracted from mineral ores—iron and steel, copper, lead and zinc,—but tin is conspicuously absent, as so far every effort to discover this metal in payable quantities in the United States has been unsuccessful, and there exists a strong inclination to reprimand Providence for want of foresight.

The M'Kinley tariff did indeed tempt Providence to amend its ways, and imposed a duty of 4 cents per pound, or $90 per ton, to stimulate prospecting and production. Unless however the latter reached 5000 tons in any year up to 1st July 1895, the duty was to be abolished and tin to resume its place on the free list. The condition was not fulfilled, only the Wilson Act hastened the transfer by nearly a year. Tin remains a foreign commodity, and 22,500 tons, of the value of $6,750,000, had to be imported during the year.

All iron and steel manufactures as a matter of course are included; bars and rods, hoops and bands, beams and girders, sheets and plates, are indiscriminately intermingled. Steel ingots and billets, rails and railroad iron of every description, and wire of all sizes follow. Hammers and anvils, nails and screws, bolts and bars, locks and keys, are not omitted; indeed here we have the typical country store, supposed to supply everything from an anchor to a needle; only Government wants $1\frac{3}{10}$ cents per pound on the weight of the one, and 25 per cent. on the value of most kinds of the other—if the American manufacturer cannot waylay it.

The duty of $4 a ton on pig and scrap iron is quite as effective in keeping it out, as the M'Kinley tax of $6.75; indeed, unless it were conveyed free as ballast from a foreign country, it is difficult to see how a product costing no more than $8 to $12 a ton could enter, as it could not naturally pay freight and charges to a country so prolific in iron ore as the United States, where an export trade of considerable magnitude is now in process of development. The year 1895 was one of enormous activity in the American iron industry, and the domestic output of pig was close upon nine and a half million tons. 1896 experienced a sharp falling off, but the import was 88,000 tons, a mere fraction compared with the total; the United Kingdom being responsible for 58,000 tons[1] and Germany for 23,000 tons. Judging from the average value of nearly $25 per ton, it must have been special brands of high quality.

Despite the heavy charge of $12 to $25 per ton on bar, hoop, and sheet iron, and steel ingots, 60,000 tons entered United States ports of the value of $3,300,000, showing that the country is not yet quite independent of foreign makes of special qualities. This quantity is of course infinitesimal in

[1] This must have been principally during the last six months of 1895, as the British returns record an export of pig iron to the United States for the whole of 1896 of only 30,000 tons.

comparison with the total American output and consumption, and affords the best proof that the duties, if needed at all for protective purposes, are absurdly high. Steel rails and railroad iron for instance, are rated at $\frac{7}{20}$ cent a pound, or $7.84 a ton, against $\frac{6}{10}$ cent under the M'Kinley Act. Yet immense quantities have been sold at prices varying from $15 to $18 a ton. The price then ruling at tide water in Great Britain was about $22 or $23, inclusive of overland carriage and makers' profit. Adding freight and duty they could not be laid down in the United States at less than $30, and American makers were free from foreign competition at anything below that figure. They too could have sold at $22 or $23 and made a good profit, yet availing themselves of protection, they endeavoured to exact $28, and only failed for reasons already alluded to.

Hoop iron was rated under the M'Kinley tariff at 1 to $1\frac{3}{10}$ cents a pound, equal to $22 to $29 a ton, under the Wilson Act 30 per cent. *ad valorem*, which is generally speaking a considerable reduction. The M'Kinley Act however specially singled out cotton ties for baling purposes, and imposed $\frac{2}{10}$ cent a pound, or nearly $5 a ton extra, raising the duty on them to about $30 a ton. The avowed object of this was to compel cotton planters to buy American instead of English ties, as they had long been accustomed to. There was a particular hardship in this exaction. They were already compelled to pay a high price for the jute bagging to wrap round the bales, which was heavily protected, and under section J of the M'Kinley Act still appeared at $1\frac{9}{10}$ to $1\frac{7}{10}$ cent per square yard, equal to about 50 per cent. of its value. Some years earlier a bagging trust had been formed on very similar lines to the larger ones which have since gained such notoriety, and its members demanded an extreme price for their manufacture, limiting it only to the cost at which it could be imported from Europe. Planters and all interested in the trade revolted, and a determined effort was made to substitute a material made from low grade cotton for the jute. It failed, principally for reasons concerning weight into which there is no need to enter, and the cotton interest remained at the mercy of the jute-bagging manufacturers.

The redeeming feature was that the iron bands or ties could be purchased on reasonable terms. But while before they had been chastised with whips, the M'Kinley Act proceeded to chastise them with scorpions, by increasing the cost of the ties likewise by $30 a ton, equivalent to a tax of 10 to 12 cents a bale. Cotton planters and merchants sent Democrats to represent them in Congress, bagging and tie manufacturers, well knowing on which side their bread was buttered, consistently supported the Republican party. The Wilson Bill recognising the crying injustice inflicted by this special legislation, placed both bagging and ties on the free list, and the import of the latter, which had almost disappeared for several years, rose again in the autumn of 1895 to 3500 tons, equal to the binding of one million out of a total crop of over seven million bales. They were valued at an average price of $30 per ton, just the figure the M'Kinley tariff sought to impose on them. The new tariff, it is said, will resuscitate the duties on both bagging and ties.

Perhaps the most striking feature of the M'Kinley Act was its determined attempt to establish, at all costs, a domestic manufacture of the tin plates so extensively used in the canning and other industries of the United States, and previously obtained almost exclusively from South Wales. The duty imposed was $2\frac{2}{10}$ cents per pound, practically $50 per ton, which meant the doubling of the price of an article so essential to the great agricultural and fishery interests. Even so exorbitant an impost as this entirely failed to destroy foreign competition, while it naturally exasperated those who had to pay it. The later Act just halved the duty.

No tariff legislation for many years so utterly disorganised a trade as this attempt to force an industry on an unwilling people before the time for it was ripe. The duty was not to become operative until the first of July 1891, nine months later that is than the general enactment, ostensibly to give the American manufacturers time to conclude their arrangements. This period of grace was made use of for another purpose, and the import of Welsh plates was enormous. The British export to the United States for 1891, nearly the whole of it in the first six months, reached 325,000 tons, and it might have been supposed that that would have been the end of it. Not so however, for the American market became so over-stocked and demoralised, that the home manufacturers were completely at the mercy of importers, and made little or no attempt to compete. The demand consequently continued to fall on the Welsh material, and the export during 1892 and 1893 was still upwards of 250,000 tons, despite the excessive duty, which meant that American consumers were going on paying something like double the actual value.

But the years 1895 and 1896 witnessed an immense growth in the American industry, and high tariff enthusiasts will need all their wits to explain how this could happen under a $25 rate when a $50 one failed to accomplish it. The British export in 1896 fell to below 120,000 tons, and the capacity of the American works is said to have risen to some 300,000 tons per annum. The real facts of the case are that the industry has now become possible owing to the immense fall in the price of sheet iron, coupled with more economical methods of manufacture; and were the duty entirely abolished, it is extremely doubtful if South Wales could win back the trade without the assistance of some huge trust to raise the price of the sheets to an abnormal figure. Meanwhile, it is affirmed that Welsh tin plates have actually been manufactured from American iron imported for the purpose, because it is cheaper than English.

The more highly finished and expensive articles are treated in quite proportionate terms to the commoner and heavier descriptions of iron and steel. Wire pays from $1\frac{1}{4}$ to 2 cents a pound, say $28 to $45 per ton. Cutlery 25 per cent. to 50 per cent. of its value, files 3 to 8 cents a piece, according to size and value. Common nails pay $22\frac{1}{2}$ per cent., wire nails 25 per cent., and horseshoe nails 30 per cent., all about half the rates ruling under the M'Kinley Act, yet quite high enough to amount to prohibition. Pens pay 8 cents per gross, and pins 25 per cent. of their value. Even quicksilver, so necessary to the mining industry, is charged 7 cents per pound, and the flasks additional.

The total value of all iron and steel imported was $25,000,000, nearly the whole of it from Great Britain, Germany having supplied less than $3,000,000. English protectionists who call out against foreign competition, would do well to contrast this with the £5,000,000 imported into their own country during the same period under absolutely free trade conditions. The British export amounted, as I mentioned in the last chapter, to £31,000,000, and of machinery to £17,000,000 more. The corresponding figures for the United States were £5,250,000 and £3,000,000 respectively. The year 1896-97 will probably show a considerable increase in United States exports, owing to trade depression, the collapse of the ring, and great cheapening in the cost of production, in other words, to the triumph of natural causes over protection.

Copper and lead are mined in great quantities in the United States, and in the former there is an export trade which amounted in the year under review to 87,000 tons. Under such circumstances foreign competition is hardly likely or even possible, yet to make assurance doubly sure a duty of $28 per ton was imposed by the M'Kinley Act. It is now on the free list, and the import, never more than trifling, has actually fallen off.

On the other hand, the production of lead is insufficient to meet domestic requirements, and the 85,000 tons of pig lead and lead ore required to make good the deficiency must pay one cent and three-quarter cent per pound respectively, and formerly had to pay just double, a present exaction in round figures of one and a half to two million dollars per annum.

One of the features of the Wilson Act was the transfer of timber from the dutiable to the free list, and schedule D consequently contains but four clauses, one of which provides for a duty of 35 per cent. on tooth-picks. The preceding tariff had exempted many of the fancy and expensive furniture and cabinet woods, grown chiefly in Central and South America, but had rigorously maintained an impost of $1 to $2 per thousand feet on the commoner kinds in every-day use, thus reversing the natural order of things. The primeval forests of the United States have long since fallen beneath the woodman's axe, and though there is still abundance of timber throughout the country, it is no longer so prolific as to be valueless. The duty consequently can only have been aimed at Canada, where the lumber industry is still an important one, and was an attempt to make Canadian timber at least dear, if it could not be entirely excluded. There was something particularly spiteful about such a tax, as rough timber is not an article which can bear heavy transport charges, and as a consequence Canada could only supply the wants of a few of the boundary States, or where lengthier transport is possible by water. The trade is of considerable value, amounting to about $20,000,000, of which only $3,500,000 of manufactured wood came under the operation of the tariff law. The state of affairs under the M'Kinley Act teaches an instructive lesson. The value of imports under this schedule in 1891-92 was $20,000,000, in 1892-93 $23,000,000, both years of protection. No sooner was free trade instituted than the figures fell off. The effort to destroy the Canadian lumber trade resulted in fact in ignominious failure, the only outcome having been to impose a heavy tax on northern builders and users generally. There is an export trade in timber worth about $30,000,000 per annum, but chiefly from southern ports.

Schedule E, consisting of but three clauses in the Wilson Act, though reduced from eleven in the preceding one, created more discussion, and resulted in greater scandal than all the rest of the Bill put together. It deals with sugar, and there is no more powerful monopoly in the United States than the Sugar Trust, which has given ample proof of its ability to destroy all dangerous competition wherever and whenever it arises. It always wants to buy raw sugar cheap and sell the refined product dear, and a prolonged and bitter contest took place over the fixing of the tests and the settlement of the duty.

As Louisiana is an important sugar-growing State, the planters located there naturally wanted protection against the product of Cuba and the Philippines, and this was accorded them under the M'Kinley Act in the form of a bounty of 2 cents per pound, for Europe is not the only continent where this vicious system has thriven. The Sugar Trust triumphed by methods which will not bear investigation, and a committee of the United States Senate deputed to make one has been openly defied.

A prominent broker, who rightly enough refused to divulge the names of his clients, engaged in gigantic speculations, was committed to gaol, while his principals, who were really the guilty parties and well known, escaped on technical subterfuges, and allowed their agent to bear the punishment, though only at the expense of greater ignominy to themselves.

The Wilson Act, true to its avowed object of providing revenue, abolished the bounty which had proved so severe a drain upon the Treasury, and substituted a duty on imported raw sugar of 40 per cent. *ad valorem*, affording protection to the home grower to that extent. A differential duty of $\frac{1}{5}$ cent per pound additional on refined sugar gave the Trust that much advantage, increased by a further tenth of a cent on sugar imported from bounty-paying countries. The Trust moreover had been actively preparing for the event. The import for the year ending 30th June 1894 was valued at \$127,000,000, for the one ending 30th June 1895 at \$76,500,000 only, and of that \$30,000,000 was rushed in before the duty became operative. The history at best is a sordid one, and the motives which made it purely personal, and to the selfishness of protection must in this instance be added the tyranny which can be and is sometimes exercised by mammoth capitalists.

To Schedules F and H, dealing with tobacco, wines, spirits, and other beverages, there can be little objection.

Tobacco is a natural product of the United States, a country capable not only of supplying its own requirements, but raising a large additional quantity for export. Nevertheless there is only one place in the world able to supply the wants of the connoisseur, and America, like every other country, must import its choice leaf from Cuba. The duty of 35 cents per pound on unstemmed and of 50 cents on stemmed, though many times the excise rate imposed on the leaf of native growth, which has to be paid in addition, must be regarded as a tax on luxury rather than rank protection. On wrapper tobacco the duty is exceedingly high, $1.50 per pound on unstemmed, and $2.25 on stemmed. Cigars, cigarettes, and cheroots pay a specific duty of $4 per pound, and a further 25 per cent. *ad valorem*, and these rates are much the same in every tariff.

Alcoholic beverages are also largely of home production, and the duties imposed on those of foreign countries can hardly be regarded as protective, though Californian wine growers desire to make them so. In beverages of this sort however it is usually more a matter of taste than of price, and the duties on still wines of 30 cents per gallon if under 14 per cent. of alcoholic strength, and of 50 cents if over, and on sparkling wines at the rate of $4 per dozen pints, will certainly not tend to the consumption of native liquors by those who do not appreciate them. Neither will French brandy at $1.80 per gallon be displaced by rye whisky and similar distillations rated much lower.

Schedule G is in many respects the most extraordinary in the whole tariff. It deals exclusively with agricultural products and provisions, and here at least we might suppose that protection was absolutely useless. A country which annually exports hundreds of millions of dollars worth of breadstuffs, meats, vegetables, and animal products of almost every description, must be a cheap producer to make headway against so many competitors throughout the world. We naturally wonder therefore what can be contained in the 57 clauses of the Wilson Act, not to mention the 82 of its predecessor.

It will be news to most people that the wheat growers of the Western, or indeed of any of the States of the Union, are being ruined in their own country by foreign competition, whatever may be taking place elsewhere. Yet in the later tariff, wheat is scheduled at 20 per cent. *ad valorem*, and in the previous one at 25 cents per bushel. Was this duty imposed with an idea that because the figures appeared in the list, farmers would be deluded into the notion that they were receiving so much more for the contents of their granaries than they otherwise would? It cannot be that Canadian competition is feared from across the border, as it would be altogether too humiliating an admission that a wealthy nation of 70,000,000 of people could be beaten on its own ground by a comparatively poor neighbour not enjoying nearly the same natural advantages, and numbering all told some 5,000,000 souls. Nor does wheat stand alone,—barley, rye, oats, buckwheat, and maize all keep it company at rates which we might call prohibitive did they not merit a more derisive adjective. The duties on imported breadstuffs capable of being produced in the United States, added just $130,000 to the national revenue.

Butter and cheese at four cents a pound, reduced from six, eggs at three cents a dozen, and hay at two dollars a ton, potatoes at fifteen, and onions at twenty cents a bushel, are all in the same category. The M‘Kinley tariff, fearful no doubt of the competition of the British farmer, further rated fresh milk at five cents a gallon, and cabbages at three cents a piece. The German immigrant was more considerately treated, for his sauerkraut was admitted free, and he availed himself of the privilege by importing $7895 worth of it, about one fourth only of the year previous. But then it keeps for an indefinite period. A similar favour was extended to the Italian labourer, who was allowed to have his Bologna sausages (made by the way in Germany) free, and ate 359,260 pounds of that savoury article. But alas! the American sausage maker has captured the receipt, and has promised, with the assistance of a 25 per cent. duty, to capture the market too. The Frenchman was likewise encouraged to partake of his delicate dish of snails, but if he hankered after them there is no record of it. The Hebrew, safely established in the promised land, was invited to recall the wanderings of his fathers in the wilderness, by partaking of manna untaxed, but either on these liberal terms the price was still not sufficiently tempting; or he was otherwise occupied. And lastly, the English alderman was encouraged to spend his holidays and his money in the New World, whither his beloved turtle might follow him without fear from the sacrilegious hands of the custom-house official. Whether he himself actually arrived we do not know; if so, then judging from the absence of any return of imports, he must for once have been content to put up with the companionship of his turtle-dove.

In the taxation of foreign dried fruits there might be a little more sense were the Treasury very hard up for revenue, and the people unable otherwise to provide it. But apples, oranges, and lemons are scheduled no doubt to protect the home orchards from low prices, though judging from the rates at which American green fruits sell in England, the duty cannot do them much good.

Meat and provisions, fresh and preserved alike, receive the same grandmotherly attention. Live animals pay a duty of 20 per cent. *ad valorem*, and an agitation exists to increase it to the much higher M'Kinley rate of $10 per head, owing to incursions over the southern border. Yankee flesh and blood may be denied to Mexican skin and bone, though it is difficult to see how the immense and increasing meat and cattle trade with Europe is to be encouraged by the adoption of such a course. For once possibly, the United States Government may take a leaf out the book of its British rival, which in 1896 distinguished itself by passing a Cattle Exclusion Bill. But for a country which exports live cattle to the value of thirty-five million dollars a year, and fresh beef to more than half that amount in addition, a raid against foreign animals is utterly absurd.

The entire schedule was no doubt partly framed to blind the eyes of the suffering and depressed agricultural industry, which whatever may be said, does not flourish under protection. One of the first objects of the farmer who is thriving is to invest his capital in live stock; the surest sign of his decay is when he reduces the number, unless of course necessitated by scarcity of food, of which there has been no lack in recent years in the United States. In this respect the following official report issued on the 11th February 1897 tells its own tale:—

"The United States Department of Agriculture has to-day issued its annual report upon the number and value of domestic animals on farms and ranches in the United

# AGRICULTURAL STATISTICS

States in January 1897, of which the leading features are shown in the subjoined tables :—

### NUMBERS AND PRICES OF FARM ANIMALS.

| Stock. | 1897. No. | 1897. Value. | 1896. No. | 1896. Value. |
|---|---|---|---|---|
| Horses .... | 14,435,000 | $451,800,000 | 15,124,000 | $500,140,000 |
| Mules .... | 2,216,000 | 92,400,000 | 2,279,000 | 103,204,000 |
| Milk cows ... | 15,942,000 | 369,300,000 | 16,138,000 | 363,956,000 |
| Oxen and other cattle.... | 30,508,000 | 504,500,000 | 32,085,000 | 508,928,000 |
| Sheep .... | 36,819,000 | 67,500,000 | 38,299,000 | 65,168,000 |
| Swine .... | 40,600,000 | 167,400,000 | 42,843,000 | 186,530,000 |

| Stock. | Percentage decrease in No. | Average farm price. 1897. | Average farm price. 1896. |
|---|---|---|---|
| Horses....... | 5·0 | $31.45 | $33.07 |
| Mules....... | 2·3 | 41.70 | 45.29 |
| Milk cows ..... | 1·0 | 23.16 | 22.55 |
| Oxen and other cattle . | 4·9 | 16.54 | 15.86 |
| Sheep ...... | 3·9 | 1.83 | 1.70 |
| Swine ...... | 5·2 | 4.12 | 4.35 |

"The total value of all animals amounts to $1,652,900,000, against $1,727,926,000 in 1896, a decrease in round numbers of $75,000,000, or 4 per cent. This decrease in the total value has now been steadily progressing since 1893, when the total was $2,483,507,000, or over $830,000,000, or 33 per cent. more than now.

"The number of horses and mules has been increasing during the year in the South Atlantic and Gulf States, but decreasing generally elsewhere; milk cows have been increasing in the Rocky Mountain and Pacific States, while they have remained nearly stationary elsewhere; several Rocky Mountain States also show an increase in oxen and other cattle, and in sheep; the same region, and also the South Atlantic States, report an increase in swine. The great central States show a decrease in all kinds of stock, so that the downward movement in number reported a year ago still continues. The destruction of sheep by dogs was large in the South, and the percentage of loss from such depredations for the whole country, excluding the Rocky Mountain ranges, was 1·1 per cent., or about 250,000 altogether.

"In the average price there is a falling off of from 5 to 8 per cent. in horses, mules, and swine; but a further increase of 3 to 7 per cent. in cattle and sheep. The total value of horses, mules, and swine has declined 10 per cent. each during the year, while that of oxen and other cattle has declined 1 per cent. On the other hand, the total value of milk cows shows an increase of 1 per cent. and of sheep an increase of 3 per cent. since January 1896."

The reduction in the number of animals it will be seen, cannot be attributed to a fall in their value, for both cattle and sheep are steadily rising, while swine have been cheapened by the great fall in the price of their principal food,—maize. The industry is exhausted by the exactions made upon it from all quarters, for while it is compelled to sell its own produce cheap if it is to find a market at all, the commodities it requires in exchange are universally and artificially enhanced in cost. The manufacturer demands the straw as well as the wheat, and the agriculturist may go to the devil.

The great textile industries are amply provided for in Schedules I, J, K, and L. The raw materials used in them are mostly to be found on the free list. It would be ridiculous for cotton to be anywhere else, as the United States is pre-eminently the home of its growth and production. Yet an agitation exists to transfer it, because the sewing thread factories require the Egyptian staple, and some of the Southern planters think they ought to make the American answer the purpose. The great accomplishment of the Wilson Act was to place wool on the free list, whereas previously the duties had varied from 11 to 36 cents per pound on the better descriptions, and 32 per cent. to 50 per cent. *ad valorem* on the inferior ones. Nothing ever quite so much roused the ire of the American protectionist as this, and he threatens a terrible revenge. Wool growers indeed demand a bounty to assist them in rearing their flocks, and clothing their fellow-creatures. Why not gracefully round off the schedule, by making provision for a bounty to the owner of the happy mothers of puppies and kittens?

Raw silk has been free from duty under both tariffs, and the latest import exceeded $26,000,000 in value. Flax, hemp, and jute are not quite so fortunately situated, as if subjected to the slightest preparation, and technically known as "hackled," they become dutiable. The free imports reached $8,000,000, and the dutiable or hackled about $650,000. Mexican istle and sisal grass represented $4,000,000 more, also free.

It is of course the manufactures of these materials which come within the all-pervading arms of the custom-house authorities. No cotton goods whatever are admitted free, and the duties are calculated on a most complicated principle, though how these materials can enter the States at all is a mystery. Yarns commence at 3 cents per pound, for what are known as fifteens, and increase by ⅓ cent for every number of greater fineness, which makes the generally used or medium counts dutiable at about 6 cents. Under the M'Kinley Act the rate began at 10 cents, and went somewhere beyond the clouds. The present tariff is equal to an average of 40 per cent. *ad valorem*, yet admits of an import of about $1,000,000, principally very fine yarns for conversion into thread.

The value of cotton cloth depends largely upon the fineness or otherwise of its texture, and a system has been adopted of levying the duty in accordance with the number of threads found in the square inch. This will best be explained by reproducing clause 253 of the Wilson Act :—

"Cotton cloth, not bleached, dyed, coloured, stained, painted, or printed, exceeding fifty and not exceeding one hundred threads to the square inch, counting the warp and filling, and not exceeding six square yards to the pound, 1¼ cents per square yard; exceeding six and not exceeding nine square yards to the pound, 1½ cents per square yard; exceeding nine square yards to the pound, 1¾ cents per square yard: if bleached and not exceeding six square yards to the pound, 1½ cents per square yard; exceeding six and not exceeding nine square yards to the pound, 1¾ cents per square yard; exceeding nine square yards to the pound, 2¼ cents per square yard; if dyed, coloured, stained, painted, or printed, and not exceeding six square yards to the pound, 2¾ cents per square yard; exceeding six and not exceeding nine square yards to the pound, 3¼ cents per square yard; exceeding nine square yards to the pound, 3½ cents per square yard: *Provided*, That on all cotton cloth not exceeding one hundred threads to the square inch, counting the warp and filling, not bleached, coloured, dyed, stained, painted, or printed, valued at over 7 cents per square yard, 25 per cent. *ad valorem*; bleached, valued at over 9 cents per square yard, 25 per cent. *ad valorem*; and dyed, coloured, stained, painted, or printed, valued at over 12 cents per square yard, there shall be levied, collected, and paid a duty of 30 per cent. *ad valorem*."

Three similar clauses follow, stipulating the duties on cotton cloths exceeding 100 and not exceeding 150 threads to the square inch, exceeding 150 and not exceeding 200, and finally exceeding 200 threads, the rate rising as high as 6½ cents per square yard, and these charges, while much more graduated, are considerably lighter than under the M'Kinley Act. Were the funds of the United States Treasury at all redundant, a good round sum might be set apart towards founding a technical school where these intricacies might be studied, and possibly mastered. No doubt it is an interesting as well as highly intellectual occupation to count the threads in pieces of calico, particularly if in the end a dispute arises as to whether the hundred and fifty-first falls within or beyond the inch measure. And it is well paid for besides, so that the solution of the problem of the unemployed would be close at hand, if the United States would only import their prints and shirtings instead of making them at home.

Made-up clothing of cotton pays an even 40 per cent. Goods manufactured from cotton chenille, such as curtains, table-covers, etc., 40 per cent., likewise a considerable reduction on the former rate. Laces and embroideries pay 50 per cent. Stockings and hose, again, were beautifully graduated in the M'Kinley Act, by a clause similar to the one quoted, substituting dozen pairs for square yards, but in the later one are rated at 30 to 50 per cent. Despite these restrictions, the import of certain classes of goods is large, and the United States have not yet captured what may be described as the Nottingham trade. Laces, embroideries, window curtains, etc., figured for nearly $11,000,000, stockings and hose for $6,000,000 more, and their relative cost to the wearer will be appreciated when the enormous duty is taken into account. Bleached, dyed, etc., cloths were valued at $5,000,000, but fashion no doubt, had something to do with this item, while clothing amounted to $2,700,000, and miscellaneous goods to nearly $7,000,000 more.

The United States paid altogether in 1895-96 $32,500,000 for imported cotton goods, which must eventually have cost the wearer nearly twice as much as would have been the case in England, the

## THE WOOLLEN SCHEDULE

average duty upon them being estimated at nearly 50 per cent. If the same applies in any degree to goods of home manufacture, we gain some insight into the expense of living in that country.

English looms supply nearly half the American requirements of foreign cottons, Switzerland and Germany dividing most of what is left. France is only able to secure about 10 per cent. of the total. Most of the German trade is in knitted goods, such as stockings and hose, and of the Swiss in embroideries—in both of which England occupies a greatly inferior position.

The woollen industry has ever been the spoilt child of American protectionism, petted one day and whipped the next. The owners of woollen mills, we may rest assured, entertain no objection to free wool in its raw state, and are entirely out of sympathy with the demand for its taxation. They have no objection to clothing being dear, but they do draw the line at dividing the profit. When this commodity was placed on the free list therefore, manufacturers submitted with ill-concealed chagrin to a corresponding reduction in their own duties,

The clauses of Schedule K, numbering 34 in the M'Kinley Act, were reduced to just 19 in its successor. These figures are still out of proportion to the reductions made in the duties, the extravagant nature of which will best be illustrated by quoting one or two of the clauses of the former Act.

The M'Kinley tariff divided wool into three classes — (1) Merinos, etc.; (2) Leicesters, Cotswolds, etc.; (3) the commoner wools usually imported from South America and the countries of Eastern Europe, Egypt and Syria. And the duties imposed were—

| Class I. | Class II. |
|---|---|
| Unwashed, 11 cents per pound. | Unwashed, 12 cents per pound. |
| Washed, 22 ,, ,, | If scoured, 36 ,, ,, |
| Scoured, 33 ,, ,, | |

Class III.
32 per cent. *ad valorem* if value under 13 cents per pound, and 50 per cent. if over.

As the annual United States production of wool is estimated at over 300,000,000 pounds, an additional selling value of only 10 cents a pound given to it by these duties would mean a tax on consumers of $30,000,000.

Clause 391 of the tariff is as follows :—

"On woollen and worsted yarns made wholly or in part of wool, worsted, the hair of the camel, goat, alpaca, or other animals, valued at not more than 30 cents per pound, the duty per pound shall be two and one-half times the duty imposed by this Act on a pound of unwashed wool of the first class, and in addition thereto, 35 per centum *ad valorem*; valued at more than 30 cents, and not more than 40 cents per pound, the duty per pound shall be three times the duty imposed by this Act on a pound of unwashed wool of the first class, and in addition thereto, 35 per cent. *ad valorem*; valued at more than 40 cents per pound, the duty per pound shall be three and one-half times the duty imposed by this Act on a pound of unwashed wool of the first class, and in addition thereto, 40 per cent. *ad valorem.*"

Clause 392 reads :

"On woollen or worsted cloths, shawls, knit fabrics, and all fabrics made on knitting machines or frames, and all manufactures of every description made wholly or in part of wool, worsted, the hair of the camel, goat, alpaca, or other animals not specially provided for in this Act, valued at not more than 30 cents per pound, the duty per pound shall be three times the duty imposed by this Act on a pound of unwashed wool of the first class, and in addition thereto, 40 per cent. *ad valorem*; valued at more than 30, and not more than 40 cents per pound, the duty per pound shall be three and one-half times the duty imposed by this Act on a pound of unwashed wool of the first class, and in addition thereto, 40 per cent. *ad valorem*; valued at above 40 cents per pound, the duty per pound shall be four times the duty imposed by this Act on a pound of unwashed wool of the first class, and in addition thereto, 50 per cent. *ad valorem.*"

And a footnote adds :

"By an Act of Congress, approved 9th May 1890, the Secretary of the Treasury is authorised and directed to classify as woollen cloths all imports of worsted cloth, whether known under the name of worsted cloth or under the name of worsteds, diagonals, or otherwise."

Clauses 393, 394, and 395 deal with blankets, flannels for underwear, and women's and children's dress goods on the same principle, possibly with a few more complications, and need not be quoted. Clause 396 is as follows :—

"On clothing, ready-made, and articles of wearing apparel of every description, made up or manufactured wholly or in part, not specially provided for in this Act, felts not woven, and not specially provided for in this Act, and plushes and other pile fabrics, all the foregoing composed wholly or in part of wool, worsted, the hair of the camel, goat, alpaca, or other animals, the duty per pound shall be four and one-half times the duty imposed by this Act on a pound of unwashed wool of the first class, and in addition thereto, 60 per cent. *ad valorem*."

Clause 397 follows:

"On cloaks, dolmans, jackets, talmas, ulsters, or other outside garments for ladies and children's apparel, and goods of similar description, or used for like purposes, composed wholly or in part of wool, worsted, the hair of the camel, goat, alpaca, or other animals, made up or manufactured wholly or in part, the duty per pound shall be four and one-half times the duty imposed by this Act on a pound of unwashed wool of the first class, and in addition thereto, 60 per cent. *ad valorem*."

Carpets, druggets, mats, and rugs, are provided for in succeeding clauses, into which however we need not go in detail.

These clauses may mean anything or nothing to a careless and indifferent reader, but they suck the very life blood out of a people subjected to their operation. That clothing should be expensive to the wealthy is a hardship, though one they can very well put up with, but that it should be heavily enhanced in cost to the poor and needy, or even to the moderately well-to-do, is a crying iniquity and a scandalous abuse. And how dear it was in the United States under this Act we will now see.

We will suppose that the clothing of the working classes of America is made from yarn, which, on entering the country, would pay the lowest rate of duty, and in order that the calculation may be as favourable to the Act as possible, we will take the extreme price at which this could happen, namely, yarn at 30 cents per pound.

Cost of yarn at any United States port, 30 cents per pound.
Duty 2½ times 11 cents, . . 27.50 „ „
35 per cent. *ad valorem*, 10.50 „ „

Cost of yarn to weaver, 68 cents per pound.

Should foreign woven cloth instead of yarn be used, the cost would be

Value at United States port, 30 cents per pound.
Duty 3 times 11 cents, . 33 „ „
40 per cent. *ad valorem*, . . 12 „ „

Cost of cloth to clothier, 75 cents per pound.

Let the wearing apparel ready-made be now imported, in the shape of a suit of clothes weighing say six pounds, and costing forty shillings—a price at which an English working man would purchase articles of very good quality.

Cost of suit £2, or . . . . $10.00
Duty on six pounds at 4½ times 11 cents per pound, say 50 cents, . 3.00
60 per cent. *ad valorem*, 6.00

Cost of suit to wearer, . $19.00

Women's and children's outer garments it is difficult to illustrate, owing to the great variety of weight and value. Any reader may work out an example for himself, based on clause 397.

It cannot be supposed that the yarn merchant, the cloth factor, or the clothier would lie out of these heavy disbursements without ample recompense, and we are forced to the conclusion therefore that the M'Kinley tariff might have increased the cost of the cheapest clothing to at least two and a half or three times what it should be. Such an Act can only be fitly described by labelling it in the biggest type ever yet cast, "Cruel."

It must not be overlooked that duties on the raw material are infinitely more effective than when imposed on manufactured goods. Short of combination, which has not yet taken place in the American woollen industry, there is no limit to the number of manufacturers who can enter the business and thus create competition, which may, and as a rule does, keep the price of the cheaper sorts of clothing at a moderate level. But the moment wool itself is touched, the entire position is changed. The country has never yet produced sufficient for its own requirements, and as the deficiency must be imported, the price will be that ruling in the cheapest foreign market, plus the duty, which in turn will regulate the value of the home production as well. When it is maintained by protectionists, that the cheaper clothing did not sell at the outrageous prices which the M'Kinley tariff would have warranted, the only answer is, that it was an accident which that tariff did its best to prevent, though it failed in the attempt.

The Wilson Act, though instituting sweeping reductions, is still bad enough. The duties on yarn and cloth are mostly from 40 per cent. to 50 per cent. *ad valorem*, and on made-up clothing they are generally 50 per cent, and as at these rates Yorkshire is able to do a large and profitable business with the United States, it may be reckoned that the cost of clothing is now only about doubled. The difference between the two Acts is not of course additional profit or loss to the spinner and manufacturer, because under the M'Kinley the cost of the raw material was so much higher. And this is threatened once more.

The imports of women's and children's dress goods reached $20,000,000; of woollen and worsted cloths, $22,000,000; and of ready-made clothing, $1,250,000. The total value of dutiable woollens of all kinds was over $50,000,000, and the average rate of duty 48 per cent. This it must be remembered is with free wool, while under the M'Kinley Act it would have been almost doubled in price. Despite the enormous increase of cost that Act entailed, the import for 1892-93 was valued at $33,000,000, but in the year following, dry goods houses so restricted their operations, in view of the reduction of the duties, that the figure fell to

$16,000,000. Great Britain has by far the largest share of the trade,—only in dress goods are France and Germany serious competitors.

An enhanced cost of silk and silk goods is scarcely so objectionable as of woollens and cottons, and Schedule L may be allowed to pass with little comment. The rates, both under the M'Kinley Act and the Wilson Act, were and are undoubtedly excessive, the partially manufactured material paying 50 cents per pound, changed in the latter to 20 per cent. *ad valorem*, thrown silk being rated in both at 30 per cent. In manufactured goods little alteration has taken place, the rates being some 50 to 60 per cent. in the one, and 45 to 50 per cent. in the other. So popular however are foreign silks in the United States, that in spite of the heavy duties over $26,500,000 were imported, and were the rate only a little more reasonable this source of revenue would be perfectly legitimate. England of course makes a very poor show here, France doing about $11,000,000 of the trade, Germany and Switzerland another $10,000,000 between them, and Great Britain under $2,500,000.

Flax, hemp, and jute textiles, covered by Schedule J, are both numerous in quantity and in their uses. I have previously alluded to jute bagging for cotton baling, and grain bags made from the same material are likewise on the free list, though subject under the M'Kinley Act to a duty of 2 cents per pound. Hemp, twines, and cordage pay 35 per cent. against a former impost of 2½ cents per pound, and those made from grass fibres, such as Mexican istle, pay only 10 per cent. against 1½ cents. All these charges are more or less serious hindrances to important industries. Oilcloths and linoleums pay 25 to 40 per cent., against 40 per cent. and upwards under the M'Kinley Act.

It is of course under flax, that the greatest strain of this schedule is felt, and there is little to choose in this respect between the two tariffs. Collars, cuffs, and shirts made from linen now pay 50 per cent. of their value, against a graduated scale rising to a somewhat higher figure. Laces and embroideries, the product of Belfast and other linen weaving centres, pay 50 per cent. against 60 per cent., but the linen cloths which constitute the bulk of the imports are subjected to 35 per cent. only. Many of these goods, while not absolute necessaries, are scarcely luxuries, and if they are to be taxed at all, it should be on a greatly reduced scale. The import of these fabrics, principally linen, was $19,000,000; free goods, like grain bags and Calcutta and Dundee burlaps, representing $8,000,000 more. Great Britain, and of course India, almost monopolise the entire trade.

Schedule M devoted to pulp, paper, and books, is unwise as well as irritating, and amounts to a tax on knowledge, which was so objectionable a feature of the Middle Ages, and indeed until comparatively recent times. One would scarcely expect to see it adopted by a nation which prides itself upon its vast intelligence, and the encouragement it gives to learning. Yet all books printed in the English language are subjected to 25 per cent. duty, presumably with the object of compelling everything of interest to American readers to be printed in their own country. The United States have evidenced their sense of justice by their adhesion to the principle of international copyright, and they surely might go a step further and abolish the tax on it.

The paper trade is peculiarly international, as in almost every country there is some special manufacture which either cannot be made at all, or only at increased cost, elsewhere. This is illustrated by the fact that while the United States imported over $3,000,000 worth, they likewise exported $2,000,000, and it is evidently a business where exchange should be encouraged rather than repelled. Yet duties averaging 25 per cent. are still enforced.

At last we approach the end of our summary, thankful that the alphabet is not quite exhausted. The miscellaneous articles under Schedule N. include buttons and coal, corks and dice—not an unusual combination, dolls and jewellery—likewise sometimes observable in company, furs and feathers, pencils, photographic and smokers' materials. The principal item however is leather and leather manufactures, an industry in which the United States is supposed to excel, and for which it enjoys unequalled facilities. Yet 10 to 20 per cent. is not considered too much to demand on any goods that may find their way thither, though the M'Kinley Act thought 35 per cent. none too little on some. Gloves naturally fall under this heading, and are charged $1.50 to $4 per dozen pairs according to length, with $1 per dozen pairs extra if lined. The former tariff also imposed a dozen rate, but stipulated that in no case should the amount levied be less than 50 per cent. of the value, while in most instances it is now under 40 per cent. The glove import was valued at $6,750,000, and, as I have elsewhere observed, is a fair subject for reasonable taxation. Morocco leather or skins figured for $3,000,000 more, and other kinds for another $3,000,000. The exports of leather, naturally of a much coarser and cheaper description, fell just short of $13,000,000, while boots and shoes, harness, saddles, etc., were accountable for about $1,500,000 additional.

Notwithstanding duties averaging over 35 per cent. on so simple and usually inexpensive an article as buttons, the import of them reached nearly $1,500,000. Bituminous coal, though paying 40 cents a ton, figured for over $3,500,000—British Columbia supplying about 800,000 out of a total of 1,250,000 tons. The United Kingdom was responsible for 75,000 tons only, probably conveyed principally as ballast to Pacific ports. San

Francisco being the great consumer of foreign coal. As a set-off against the former item, Canada took 3,000,000 tons of coal from the United States.

Gunpowder and similar explosives, mulcted at 5 to 8 cents per pound, equal to 30 per cent., figure for over half a million dollars. Toys, including dolls, almost entirely from Germany, reached $2,500,000, but the jewellery was estimated at much more and came to nearly $8,000,000. This would be a fair subject of taxation were smuggling not so easily accomplished, and this fact must always render it difficult for honest people to prosper in the trade, though I do not mean to cast the slightest reflection on those actually engaged in it. The guilty do not openly associate themselves with the business.

And now, lest anything should have been omitted, clause 362 of the Wilson Act and 472 of the M'Kinley, stipulates for—

"Waste, not specially provided for in this Act, 10 per cent. *ad valorem*,"

while a special paragraph following the free list further provides,

"That there shall be levied, collected, and paid on the importation of all raw or unmanufactured articles, not enumerated or provided for in this Act, a duty of 10 per cent. *ad valorem*; and on all articles manufactured, in whole or in part, not provided for in this Act, a duty of 20 per cent. *ad valorem*."

Little comment need be made on the free list. It is remarkable rather for what is not on it than what is, and with this part of the subject I have just dealt. Several items have already been referred to, but there are at least two others calling for passing notice. Ploughs, reapers, and agricultural implements generally, are free of duty, and at first sight this might appear an important concession to the greatly oppressed agricultural interest. Not so however, because the United States manufacturers of these implements have long enjoyed a deservedly high reputation for the work they turn out, and the moderate price at which it is put on the market, so much so indeed that the export of these articles was valued at over $5,000,000, a fair annual average. Still it is rather hard that, unlike their neighbours engaged in other industries, they are not permitted to charge the domestic user 30 to 50 per cent. more than they can afford to sell at.

Wearing apparel, the property of citizens returning from a foreign shore, is also allowed free entry. It is sometimes said that a moderate-sized American family can spend a holiday of two or three months in Europe, and defray the greater part of the cost out of the saving they effect in stocking their wardrobes with British, German, or French clothing for the ensuing twelve months. It is quite certain that no sensible American ever returns home from Europe without a very complete outfit. The labourer, sweltering at the furnace or toiling at the loom, must pay the extravagant prices necessitated by extreme protection, while his employer can supply himself with better material at half the price. One would like to know whether the United States ironmaster, or even the cloth manufacturer, is so enamoured of the system under which he lives and prospers, as to be able to resist the temptation of employing the English tailor, or of allowing his wife and daughters to patronise the French costumier and milliner. There is an agitation certainly to put a stop to this abuse, and make wearing apparel dutiable, however imported, but inasmuch as it would solely affect the pockets of the rich, it is hardly likely to prove successful. The figures for two years under the M'Kinley, and two under the Wilson Tariff, are interesting, as showing the result of excessively high prices. The value of wearing apparel and household effects, entered as the property of tourists and travellers returning home, for personal use, was in—

| | | |
|---|---|---|
| 1892-93 | . $3,500,000 | M'Kinley. |
| 1893-94 | 2,750,000 | |
| 1894-95 . | . 2,250,000 | Wilson. |
| 1895-96 . | . 2,500,000 | |

Such then is protection, as illustrated in the United States of America. There is now and again a ringing of the changes, but what does it amount to? The Wilson Act reduced the M'Kinley duties in many instances by 50 per cent. or more, and in most others by 25 to 50 per cent. But it is much the same thing as offering a starving man, who has only ten cents in the world, a loaf of bread for twenty-five, and when he protests he has not got it, telling him he can have it at the greatly reduced price of twelve and a half. Still we must be thankful for small mercies, and a reduced tariff does benefit the consumer much more than appears on the surface. It may not greatly increase imports, and therefore has nothing tangible to show, but it does compel the home manufacturer to reduce prices; to sell his loaf in fact at twelve and a half cents instead of twenty-five, which is a distinct gain to those who have the money. That is why the cry of red ruin is raised whenever duties are reduced. It takes the manufacturer ten or twelve years to pile up the immense fortune to which he considers himself entitled in five or six, and he is consequently an aggrieved and injured individual.

We will defer to a later chapter consideration of the influences exercised by this system on the economic life and industry of the people who adopt it. That a liberty-loving and self-governing nation like the United States should so long have been content to live under it, is one of those things utterly incomprehensible. Possibly the rapidity of their expansion has blinded them to what has been going on, and the ease with which money has hitherto been made and accumulated, has resulted in some indifference as to the way in which it went. It says little for their political intelligence and economic knowledge, but speaks volumes for their untiring energy and daring enterprise that they have survived the ordeal. The check however has come at last. The eager rush forward has had to give way to a sudden standstill, prolonged beyond any former precedent, and if care is not taken, it will prove but the forerunner of a headlong descent. No nation, however industrious and determined, can survive the steady transfer of its wealth and influence to a limited and autocratic class, and any policy with such a tendency must be sternly repressed.

That the American people will extricate themselves before irretrievable ruin has overtaken them, nobody who knows anything of them or of their history will for a moment doubt. But there is only one way of effecting a thorough and radical reform in the system, and that is by sweeping it away entirely. Let warning be given, that two, three, four, or five years hence, as the people of the United States may themselves determine, protection shall cease, and those profiting so largely by it at present will be afforded ample time to readjust their respective industries on true and economic principles, and where that is not possible, to transfer their capital and energies to other spheres of labour where they will be assured of a reward. Then a tariff may take its place which shall provide ample revenue, without offending against righteousness and justice.

(*An Appendix to this Chapter will be found on page* 433).

# CHAPTER VI.

The Tariffs of France and Germany.

France :—PrevailingEconomic Conditions of the Country—Tariff as a Source of Revenue—The Nature of French Protection—Analysis of Foreign Trade—Export Statistics—Absence of Competition in French Products—National Character and Economic Policy—Tariff Rates—Textiles—Iron and Steel—Chemicals—Exemption of Raw Materials—Agricultural Products—Surtax on Indirect Imports—Colonial Tariff Policy—Reciprocity.

Germany :—Moderation of Tariff—Simplicity of Arrangement—Revenue Duties — Protective Duties — Chemicals — Iron and Steel—Textiles—Leather—Earthenware—Agricultural Products—Advantages enjoyed by Home Manufacturers—Retaliation and Reciprocity—Tariff Wars with Russia and Spain—Strained Commercial Relations with United States—The Denunciation of the British Treaty—Causes of Industrial Expansion in Germany.

The economic conditions in France are so totally different to those prevailing in Great Britain or the United States, that we could hardly be surprised to find the fiscal arrangements of these countries at total variance. The French are the most heavily taxed people in Europe, if not in the world, yet they carry their load contentedly, and even prosper under it. Important sources of revenue open to many other countries are however narrowed and rendered difficult in France. The production of wine is one of the most important of her industries, and a prolific source of wealth, and anything tending to check the consumption at home or the export abroad would be regarded as a serious blow at her prosperity. Neither does the moral aspect of the question count for much, as drunkenness or even excessive drinking is not a French vice, and the light natural beverages which are most popular are not in any way harmful. A French Government would no more think of imposing a heavy excise tax on light alcoholic liquors than an English one would on raw cotton. It is never safe to predict what a Government of the United States may or may not do, in that or any other direction.

Under such circumstances it is natural to find that commodities like tea, coffee, and cocoa are regarded as luxuries, just as wines and spirits are elsewhere, and are heavily taxed accordingly. Tea pays 208 francs per 100 kilos., coffee in the bean 156 francs, roasted or ground 208 francs, and cocoa in the bean 104 francs, equivalent respectively to about tenpence, sevenpence halfpenny, and fivepence per English pound; but as the ordinary drink of the people is free from such excessive burdens, there is little need to quarrel with these duties. Raw sugar likewise pays 60 francs per 100 kilos., and refined 68 francs, and not even French colonies and possessions are exempted or allowed any rebate on this tariff, though they benefit by a surtax recently imposed on foreign sugar. This is equal to twopence halfpenny and threepence respectively, and makes the price of sugar, which in moderate quantities is more a necessary than a luxury, considerably more than double, sometimes treble, what it is in the United Kingdom, and explains why French consumption per head is only about one-third of the British, and less than half the American. There is of course another aspect of the French sugar question, which does not concern us here. Most spices are rated like tea, one or two, mace and nutmegs for instance, 50 per cent. higher.

Tobacco and cigars do not fall within the same category as wines and spirits, and the manufacture of them is a government monopoly, private import of either the manufactured or unmanufactured leaf being strictly prohibited. Those who can afford something better than the State factories produce, are indeed permitted to import for their personal use up to 10 kilos., say 22 pounds per annum, on payment of 36 francs per kilo., or 13s. a pound. The tobacco *regie* is a most important source of revenue, of which I shall have more to say hereafter.

Were the entire French tariff framed on this principle, high though the duties are, we should have to regard it as levied for revenue only. But these items are only single stars in a vast firmament, and are so shut in by others created for protective purposes as to be almost lost. For protection is even more rampant in France than in the United States of America, and as one scans the 720 enumerated commodities, it is only now and again that the eye catches the word free. But protection in France has developed into a science, if not indeed into a fine art, and one does not find in its whole range, any clauses which enable special industries to accumulate rapid and enormous fortunes at the expense of the community at large. The design is to give everybody a little, and this has been accomplished so far as human ingenuity can effect it. If the peasant farmer has to pay somewhat more for his cotton blouse and wooden sabots than he would have to under a system of free trade, he is also able to get a rather higher price for his wheat, and rye, and barley. This equalises matters, or perhaps we should rather say neutralises them,—as how much better off is a man in the end whose receipts and expenditure alike are increased by fifteen or twenty per cent.? The Frenchman however believes that the system gives him full control of his own markets, and excludes foreign competition, and in that he is right, but it also shuts him out from other markets, and prevents him competing with the foreigner elsewhere. That he also recognises, and quietly submits, content to make the most of the unique position he occupies towards almost every other civilised and wealthy nation.

For France is to both Europe and America what Bond Street is to London, or Broadway to New York. Thither people with too much money in their pockets wend their way, and invariably succeed in lightening them. France is the purveyor to west ends, and inhabitants of these regions given to purchasing luxuries, do not as a rule enquire too closely into their legitimate value. They have one of their own, made up to a not inconsiderable extent by the pleasure they are supposed to afford. Frenchmen do not mix up in the vulgar crowd of Englishmen and Germans and Americans, struggling to sell a gross of thimbles, and would shrink from the idea of competing for a contract to construct a railroad across China, and equip it with rolling stock. They would gladly undertake the work if offered, but it would have to be in their own time and on their own terms. Until that happens, they are content to go on supplying the people who do take the contracts, and make money out of them, with the choicest of wines for their dinner tables, the loveliest of silks for their wives and daughters, and the most *recherché* articles in leather, in glass, in pottery, or in a hundred other materials for ornaments or presents. And on the whole they make a very decent living out of it without much worry.

French exports in 1896 were valued at fcs. 3,404,643,000[1] (£136,200,000). We have only to examine the details of the returns a little closely, to discover to what an extent this trade in luxuries reaches, and consequently how dependent France is on the prosperity as well as the goodwill of her neighbours.

[1] These figures, as well as those immediately following, are based on 1895 valuations, and will eventually be subjected to some slight alterations.

| | |
|---|---|
| Wines | £9,850,000 |
| Brandy and spirits | 1,950,000 |
| Silk | 3,850,000 |
| Silk yarns | 250,000 |
| Silk fabrics | 9,950,000 |
| Jewellery and plate | 1,000,000 |
| Toys and fancy goods | 5,250,000 |
| Millinery and artificial flowers | 2,800,000 |
| Table fruits | 1,100,000 |
| Ornamental feathers | 1,900,000 |
| Curios, books, and engravings | 1,900,000 |
| Perfumery | 500,000 |
| Olive oil, syrups, and jams | 450,000 |
| Carriages | 500,000 |
| Mirrors | 1,100,000 |
| | £42,350,000 |

Every item may be regarded as an absolute luxury, and they constitute almost one-third of the total exports. They are not things people who can afford to buy care to go without, but unlike the staple necessaries of life, most of them can easily be replaced without disturbing the regular flow of existence, or creating any keen sense of loss. But this list is by no means exhaustive, inasmuch as a great proportion of the goods included in the one immediately following also rank as luxuries, the woollen fabrics particularly being mostly high priced and of special quality :—

## DETAILS OF EXPORTS

| | |
|---|---:|
| Woollen manufactures | £11,600,000 |
| Cotton manufactures | 5,200,000 |
| Prepared skins | 3,600,000 |
| Leather goods | 3,300,000 |
| Porcelain, glass, and crystal | 800,000 |
| Musical instruments | 500,000 |
| | £25,000,000 |

In striking contrast to this are the exports of the principal food products and manufactures :—

| | |
|---|---:|
| Breadstuffs | £1,250,000 |
| Fresh vegetables | 850,000 |
| Salt and fresh fish | 1,200,000 |
| Cattle and dead meat | 1,250,000 |
| Butter | 2,150,000 |
| Eggs and cheese | 1,250,000 |
| | £7,950,000 |
| Raw and refined sugar | 2,750,000 |
| | £10,700,000 |

Sugar of course receives the stimulus of bounties, without which its shipment to foreign countries would be well nigh impossible :—

| | |
|---|---:|
| Iron and steel | £900,000 |
| Machinery | 1,900,000 |
| Tools and metal goods | 3,550,000 |
| Copper and copper goods | 1,700,000 |
| Tartrates and chemicals | 2,400,000 |
| | £10,450,000 |

Raw wool was exported to the value of £5,000,000, but, on the other hand, the import was worth nearly £15,000,000, or about treble. The remainder is made up of a miscellaneous collection of articles, rarely exceeding £1,000,000 in any individual instance, and they constitute the small change of a retail store rather than the big coin of a commercial bourse. The British trade returns, it is true, also show a good deal of this small change, but it is lost among the large money. It must further be borne in mind that the bulk of the cheaper and rougher manufactured articles which France does export are to her own colonies and possessions, and consequently as a competitor with the great industrial nations she is a nonentity.

France might of course, by charging extravagant prices, lose some of this special trade, but so long as she keeps within reasonable bounds there is little to be afraid of. Who would dream of drinking champagne "made in Germany" for instance. And though both England and Germany may turn out quite as good woollen fabrics, or distil equally delicious perfumes, the stamp upon them "made in France" at once enhances the desire of possession and the value with it.

All these things must be paid for, and paid for largely in other commodities. Raw materials not produced at home, such as cotton, jute, and copper ore, or tropical and semi-tropical produce like tea and coffee, are the first purchases made with the proceeds of exports. But when these are provided for, there remains a substantial balance still to be liquidated in some way or other. In recent years a great deal of gold has been taken, not direct into France, but by Russia, to whom it has been lent. Every country buying French luxuries however is not prepared to pay either in gold or raw materials, and France takes, though no doubt reluctantly, such things as coal, and cotton and woollen yarns, chemicals and machinery, all of which she can make herself, but it is better to receive it that way than not at all.

Certain industries are bound to suffer under such a system. Besides, with a population so stationary as that of France, and a country so well provided with railways and other public works, there is little scope for that expansion which manufacturers and traders are always pining for. Industries like iron and steel, earthenware, and even cotton, which is after all mainly concerned with the production of cheap and useful, rather than expensive and ornamental fabrics, find themselves restricted within the boundaries of their own territory, with little chance of making headway beyond. French manufacturers might it is true, like those of some other nationalities, produce more than is necessary for home consumption, and force off the surplus at best prices obtainable in foreign markets. But they do not believe in making deliberate losses, and are so far versed in the principles of political economy, that they prefer a small business with something to show for it at the end of the year to a large one with nothing. They have attempted to solve the difficulty in another fashion, and by opening up colonies and securing foreign possessions of their own, they obtain markets as secure as those of France itself. Algeria and Tunis, Tonkin and Madagascar, are not nursed as outlets for surplus population, but rather for the surplus products of that population. It matters little that the administration costs many millions of francs per annum, and is a heavy drain on the national exchequer; the taxes to provide it are paid with little reluctance, and the fact of being able to supply these countries with everything they want, and much that they don't, is regarded as ample compensation for the outlay.

This absence of growth of the population introduces us to another aspect from which to survey the fiscal and economic policy of France. That it is causing serious misgivings among French statesmen and thinkers is no longer concealed, and it is evident that if a change does not take place ere long, France must sink to a second or third rate European State, at anyrate where heads count. The causes are admitted with equal candour, and spring from an innate selfishness of national character, families being carefully restricted in size in order that each member may enjoy more of this world's goods. This carefulness is bound to reflect itself in commercial dealings, both among themselves and with foreigners, and is, as a matter of fact, at the bottom of the protective system. The French know what their own home trade amounts to, and are determined to keep it to themselves. If they gave part of it away, they might not get an equivalent in return. They might get more, but the risk is not worth running, particularly as they like to know the ground is quite firm before they tread on it. It is only in politics the Frenchman is a revolutionist, in every other walk of life he is the most conservative of his species.

When we take all these things into consideration therefore, protection for French industry seems quite as natural as free play and free trade for British. The Frenchman is under the paternal care of officialism from the moment of his birth to the day of his death, and interference with his trade and industry is rarely if ever resented, because he is convinced it is for his good. Nearly all Frenchmen are in consequence avowed and honest protectionists, the free traders of the nation are but a handful whose voices ring through the wilderness with scarcely a responsive echo. I have not the slightest desire to defend protection in France or anywhere else, but there are degrees even of heresy, and there are heretics whom one would hesitate about trying to convert, lest their new opinions made them worse instead of better. And it may be admitted that a nation situated like the French does reap the maximum of benefit with the minimum of drawback in an all-pervading and moderate measure of protection. Were she to relinquish it and step forth into the arena of commercial combat, her wits would be sharpened and her pockets more rapidly filled, but she does very well as it is, and it is just possible that were all the rest of the world to confess and recant the protectionist heresy, France would still cling tenaciously to her opinions.

A simple illustration will show that no detail is too minute for French protection to encompass. There is nothing extraordinary in a piano paying a duty of 50 francs, but a concertina is sometimes considered a musical instrument and pays 1 franc, while the humble tambourine or noisy castanets are charged 50 centimes. Anyone wanting a complete catalogue of musical instruments might do worse than turn up the French tariff, and there is no single instance of one appearing on the free list.

Regard is likewise paid to simplicity, and nearly everything is charged on gross or net weight, at a specified duty per 100 kilogrammes (220 pounds English).

It will be understood that all rates subsequently referred to are on this basis, and the English equivalent may be roughly arrived at by multiplying the rate of duty by the figure 10, which will give the amount chargeable on the English ton of 2240 pounds, and calculating the number of francs at ninepence halfpenny or even tenpence each. The exact equivalent is 1015 kilos. to the ton, and 25.25 francs to the £ sterling.

The United States tariff, as we have had occasion to observe, formerly reached the zenith of its oppressiveness in manufactured woollen goods, and may do so once more. It would be extremely bad policy on the part of the French government to place such duties on these fabrics as would materially enhance their selling price above that of other countries, which are such free and willing customers. As a matter of fact the rates vary from threepence to about ninepence per square yard according to the weight of the material, and as the price generally runs to some shillings the *ad valorem* rate is moderate. Still the very fact that it exists tends to increase the cost of production, whether destined for home or foreign use, and English and American wearers of French materials should bear in mind that when the British manufacturer can produce goods of equal quality and finish, the chances are they will be fully ten per cent. cheaper, and consequently better value for the money. This applies with even greater force to purely fancy articles such as embroideries, upon which the duties are considerably heavier, but there of course the French expect to profit by their superior skill of workmanship, real or supposititious. Woollen fabrics mixed with cotton are naturally rated at a lower, those with silk at a higher, level.

Cotton manufactures are treated on very similar principles, only each process they undergo adds to the weight of the impost. Yarns, for instance, are rated from a little over a halfpenny per pound on very coarse, to more than a shilling on very fine counts, the medium ones running from about three halfpence to threepence. When this is converted into unbleached calico, the duties are at once calculated on a more elaborate scale according to weight and the number of threads contained in a square of 5 millimetres, equal to about one-fifth of an inch. The coarsest fabrics weighing 4 ounces and upwards to the square yard pay about twopence halfpenny per pound, say a halfpenny per yard, while very fine ones weighing one ounce or less to the yard pay two shillings, which however is only equal to about three halfpence per yard, as there are so many more yards to the pound. If these goods are bleached the duty is at once increased 20 per cent., if dyed 30 per cent., and if printed, from rather more than a farthing to a penny per yard additional, according to the number of colours. These duties, from an *ad valorem* point of view, naturally vary in accordance with fluctuations in the prices of yarn and cloth, which in their turn are dependent on raw cotton, but in any case they lack the extravagance of the corresponding ones in the United States, the home of the raw material. The foreign trade in cotton tissues is of much less value than that in woollens, but the same remarks apply to the comparative prices of English and French goods.

The protection afforded to the French iron and steel industry is somewhat more on the American scale. Common pig iron at fcs. 1.50 per 100 kilos. is much the same as $4 per ton; iron and steel rails pay 6 francs, equal to about £2 10s. per ton. Steel ingots and billets are rated at 5 to 6 francs, sheet and plate iron 7 to 11 francs; tinplates at 12 to 13 francs correspond very closely to the 1½ cent. per pound in America, and is of course just half the rate under the M'Kinley tariff. There is however more justification for such duties in France, as the conditions of production are not so favourable. Steel rails cannot be rolled there at £3 to £3 10s. a ton, as ores are neither so profuse nor so rich, nor is the industry on anything like so gigantic a scale.

The total output of pig iron for 1896 was just 2,000,000 tons, that of wrought iron and steel together barely 1,500,000 tons, the values of the latter being estimated at about £4,500,000 and £7,500,000 respectively, or about one-half of the British export alone. The British consumption of coal, as we have already noted, was 150,000,000 tons, and the export another 45,000,000; but the total production of French mines was but 28,000,000 tons, while the import amounted to 11,500,000 more, or a total of under 40,000,000 tons. That in itself is ample proof of the limited scope of French manufacturing industry. France cannot construct a few thousand miles of railway every year, nor are Madagascar and her other possessions quite ripe for such extensive development. And not only does this apply to railways, but to almost every other undertaking in which large quantities of metal are absorbed. There is a steady demand for all sorts of finished iron and steel, but it is of miscellaneous character rather than of great weight.

Chemicals are far more generally subjected to duties than in the United States, and there is very little here on the free list. Nitrate of soda escapes, as does superphosphate of lime and most other chemical manures. Crude borax is free, but when refined, or partially so, pays 8 francs. Caustic soda at fcs. 6.50 is equal to £2, 10s. per ton against $11.20 in America; soda crystals fcs. 1.90, or 15s. against $2.80. Nitric and sulphuric acids are free, but hydrochloric pays 30 centimes or half-a-crown a ton. Most natural dyes, being largely used by the textile trades are free, but prepared colours are more or less heavily rated.

There would be little profit in going through the entire list, as we are dealing with the principles of the tariff rather than its details. And the treatment of the manufactured goods already referred to affords a fair index to all the rest.

Raw materials, when entering largely into manufacture, are rigidly maintained on the free list, even though they may be produced at home. Cotton, india rubber, gums, and dye-woods, we should naturally expect to find there, but flax, hemp, and silk can be and are cultivated in France, and as we shall see later on, are encouraged by bounties. Wool, hides, and tallow are likewise free, but receive no bounties, and cattle and sheep breeders have to be content with the protection afforded them on the carcases as dead meat. Some reference must however be made to agricultural products, as agriculture, represented by the army of small proprietors who cultivate her lands, is really the basis of the wealth and prosperity of France.

Where so large a proportion of the population is dependent on the land, and consequently produces much of its own food, a higher price is of less consequence than to a community engaged principally in industrial pursuits of another order. Dear bread in France is a much less serious evil than it would be in Great Britain, whose manufacturing supremacy depends so largely on the cheap cost of living. Nor is there the same hardship to the very poor, for while in one country they are congregated in large towns, where bread, however cheap, is almost unobtainable to those who cannot pay for it, in the other, they are more widely scattered throughout the rural districts, where food, because it has not to be bought by many who have it in abundance, is regarded as of less value. We see this amply illustrated in England, where tramps who devote their attention to farm houses and village communities wax fat, while their fellows in the towns are starving.

The tax on food in France is consequently less heavy than the tariff, taken by itself, would lead us to imagine, particularly as the selling price, both wholesale and retail, is often below foreign cost plus the duty. Wheat, which for a long time paid 5 francs per 100 kilos., was increased by a law passed in February 1894, and now stands at 7. Rye, the principal bread stuff of the poorer classes, pays 3 francs, equal to about five shillings per quarter, just the rate the English farmer sighs for to begin with. Barley, oats, maize, and rice, provided the last is in the husk, are rated the same, but in order to ensure employment for the home rice miller 8 francs is charged when imported cleaned for use. Potatoes pay 40 centimes only, between a farthing and a halfpenny the English peck of 20 pounds.

Fresh meat, which is much more of a luxury in France than in either England or America, is rated comparatively high, when the import and not the retail selling price is taken into account. 25 francs on beef and 32 on mutton is equal to a penny and three-halfpence per pound respectively, not very excessive perhaps on prime cuts which cost ninepence or a shilling to the consumer, but decidedly stiff on the cheaper products of the United States,

Argentina, and Australia, which can be retailed at threepence to sixpence. Hams and bacon likewise pay 25 francs, but the outcry raised some years ago about disease in American hog products, has led to a very rigid examination on debarkation, for which an extra 1.50 francs is charged. Tinned meats are admitted at 15 francs, but as the weight of the tin is included, the reduction is more apparent than real. Of animals, oxen pay 10 francs, sheep 15.50 francs, and pigs 8 francs per 100 kilos. live weight.

Dairy products, such as milk, butter, and cheese, escape much more lightly. Milk indeed at fcs. 2.50 per 100 kilos. is merely nominal, while butter and cheese at 6 and 12 to 15 francs respectively, represent a farthing and a halfpenny per pound. And here we witness the paternal care of the Government for its children dwelling on the frontiers of neighbouring countries, who are permitted to deal with them in perishable products in a retail way without let or hindrance. The trade in timber indeed is thrown open to forests and plantations within some miles of the boundaries, provided a like concession is made to France. Such friendly intercourse is in striking contrast to the hard and fast lines drawn between the United States and Canada.

Fruits, as might be expected, constitute an important section of the French tariff, and cultivators of the vine in particular clamour for heavy protection, not only against foreign wines and grapes, but anything capable of distillation, the plea being that wines prepared from foreign material are apt to damage the reputation of native liquor. Hothouse grapes and fruits pay about sixpence per pound, and common table or wine grapes at 8 francs per 100 kilos. are highly taxed when their actual value is considered. Formerly wines and spirits were largely distilled from dried currants and raisins imported from Greece and Spain, and the duty was 15 francs. In November 1894 this was raised to 25 francs, say a penny a pound, and has tended to check the consumption for this purpose, as the value of the fruit itself is often little more.

To such an extent does France carry out her protective policy, that she cares for the interests of merchants and importers as well as of cultivators and manufacturers. Foreign commodities imported from countries other than those of actual production, pay a surtax in addition to the ordinary tariff rate, and this precludes wholesale dealers from making purchases anywhere but in their own markets. In the case of wool an exception is made in favour of the fleeces of Australia, the Cape, and India, in order that manufacturers may obtain the benefit of the London sales, where the selection is the finest in the world. With cotton however it is otherwise, and the penalty of 3 francs, or nearly an eighth of a penny per pound, shuts French spinners off for six months in the year from the only large market, because by March or April little that is desirable is as a rule obtainable outside Liverpool. They must consequently either supply twelve months' requirements in six, or take their chance with whatever selection is offering in the much more restricted market at Havre. Coffee, spices, and tea are even more heavily surcharged, the last indeed to the extent of 60 francs, or nearly threepence a pound. Articles on the free list, even treated in the same manner, are chemical manures, and dyes must not be shipped in transit through another country if they are to enjoy the privilege of free entry. Were all French commerce carried in French ships, this enactment might be supposed to be entirely for the benefit of the shipowner, but as so much of the transport service is still effected in foreign bottoms, this can hardly apply.

The regulation often leads to serious dispute, as foreign raw materials may be prepared in a country other than that of their origin and then shipped to France. Elaborate distinctions consequently have to be drawn up as to what must pay the surtax, and what may enter free from it. As an instance, raw hides are free from duty if imported direct, but subject to 3 francs if through another country. Large numbers of foreign cattle are slaughtered at English ports, and consequently hides imported from Great Britain are charged 3 francs unless positive evidence is forthcoming that they are the skins of British cattle.

The rates which I have quoted are in every instance from the minimum tariff, which is applicable only to countries having commercial treaties or arrangements with France. These include most of the great trading countries, but Italy is markedly absent, not on political grounds, because Austria-Hungary and Germany, the other members of the Triple Alliance, are entitled to the privileges of the lower duties. Possibly the admission of Italy would remove some of the friction between the two peoples so constantly in evidence. Several of the principal South American Republics, Brazil and Chili for example, are likewise absent, and these must all pay according to the general tariff, which on many commodities, and especially on manufactured goods, ranges from 10 to 50 per cent. higher. Trade under such circumstances must naturally be greatly impeded.

Colonies and possessions are invariably subjected to the French tariff on all foreign imports, but treated as part of the country for all French goods. Free trade between the Colonies themselves is likewise permitted.

Protection in France goes much deeper down, and has many more ramifications than in the United States, yet there is something less incongruous about it. It is difficult to imagine an American citizen patiently looking on while the number of threads in his shirt are being counted. The Frenchman, after the process was completed, would be as likely as not politely to offer the rest of his garments for similar inspection. The foreigner journeying into France is rarely in a hurry; if he is, he will soon know better, and regards with more amusement than vexation the diligent search made among his baggage for soap and matches, the latter article being a monopoly. But the moment he lands at New York he feels as though he wants to be in San Francisco next day, and all his surroundings encourage the desire. That he should be hindered by having his trunks turned inside out, and all sorts of questions asked about his belongings is at least annoying, and he pines for the liberty of the British custom house, where, provided he eschews alcohol and tobacco, he may do much as he pleases and get away without demur. Nor is this contrast between France and the United States confined to so simple an incident. It permeates national character through and through, and because we find protection rampant in one country, is rather a reason why we should expect it to be absent in the other.

There is a widely prevalent opinion that Germany owes her industrial expansion and prosperity to protection. That can hardly have arisen from a study of her tariff, which an American protectionist would be apt to laugh to scorn for its moderation. That its object is largely protective is true, but the German manufacturer who wants to profit by it cannot afford to go to sleep. In most instances it just gives him a little advantage in the home markets and that is all, and it certainly offers no temptation to reckless extravagance in cost of production.

To begin with, the tariff aims at doing its work in the most practical way, and without annoyance or undue loss of time or money to anybody. With very few exceptions the rate is levied on 100 kilogrammes gross or net; in the latter case, fixed tares are allowed, subject to alterations, as the size or shape of the packages used in any particular trade may undergo change. Nor is there any counting of threads or measuring of yards and inches. The principal commodites are grouped into sections, and then usually into a few large subdivisions, so that the importer or merchant may be able to tell at a glance what the duty on any specific article is.

The heaviest duties, as in the case of the French tariff, are levied for revenue, and are to be found in the section devoted to colonial produce. The German imbibes his national beverage, lager beer, without feeling that he is being taxed for his indulgence, but when he wants the luxury of tea, coffee, or cocoa, he must pay for it. They are charged respectively 100, 40, and 35 marks per 100 kilos., about fivepence halfpenny, twopence farthing, and twopence per English pound, less than half the rates in France, and not much more than those in England. Sugar however, is again the prominent feature, and until recently was rated at 36 marks. But in May 1896 Germany, following the example of other beet-producing countries, increased the bounties on export, and at the same time raised the duty to 40 marks to compensate for it; so that now, sugar like coffee pays twopence farthing per pound, making its cost to the consumer fourpence or over, and materially checking the consumption, which is a few pounds per head less than in France. Tobacco on the other hand is very moderately rated, namely at 85 marks, or fourpence halfpenny per pound, against three shillings and twopence in England. Cigars and cigarettes pay one shilling and twopence, which throws most of the manufacturing into German hands, so that an excellent weed of German make may be had for fifteen or twenty pfennige, while a foreign one costs at least double.

Germany is also a wine-producing country, and the yield of her Rhenish vineyards is highly appreciated abroad. It is frequently strengthened to suit the foreign palate, and the importations for this purpose pay only a nominal duty. Wine in the cask, for consumption in the country, is charged 20 marks, weight being still preferred to liquid measure; bottled, it rises to 48 marks, and on sparkling wines to 80, while brandies and other spirits pass at 125, and liqueurs at 180. All alcoholic liquors are thus very lightly taxed. Dried fruits are also rated under this heading at 4s. per cwt., and green fruits, such as oranges and lemons, at 2s. Dates and almonds pay 5s., and spices of all kinds about threepence per pound.

The moderation here exhibited is characteristic throughout, and no German manufacturer will ever accumulate a gigantic fortune out of the high prices he is permitted to charge domestic consumers. Germany is the home of chemical research, and next to protection her success is attributed to technical knowledge and untiring patience in the perfecting of her products, though as a matter of fact, these should hold the first place. Under such circumstances heavy duties on chemicals and drugs would be grotesque, and Germany does not lay herself open to ridicule. The section is extremely short, and the most noticeable items are caustic soda and caustic potash, in which all foreign manufacturers apparently dread English competition, if the duties they impose are any criterion. The charge is 4 marks or £2 per ton, while bi-carbonate of soda is rated at 25s. There can be little objection to the taxation of ethers, chloroform, and volatile oils, but articles like artists' colours and lead pencils might well be exempted, especially as the Bavarian manufacture of the latter is in almost universal use throughout the world. No foreign Government is able to resist matches, which, whether of wax or wood, are rated at 10 marks, or 5s. per cwt. England barely escaped a similar tax many years ago, but the public protests against it were so vigorous and determined, that no statesman or economist has ever ventured to suggest it since.

It is the textile and iron and steel industries which are specially singled out as affording a powerful illustration of the ability of German manufacturers to make cheap sales abroad, on account of their large profits at home. Most heavy ironwork, such as rails and fish plates for railway use, bars and angles, tyres and axles, are rated at M 2.50, or 25s. per ton; plates and sheets 3 marks, or 30s.; tin plates 5 marks or 50s. Such duties are of course quite high enough, and represent 15 to 25 per cent. *ad valorem* at existing low prices, but are extremely moderate when contrasted with the 50 to 100 per cent. in the United States, where conditions of production are more favourable. The commoner and heavier sorts of tools, such as hammers, axes, scythes, and hayforks, pay 10 marks; the cheaper makes of Sheffield goods 15 marks; and the best cutlery, scissors and steel ware, 24 marks, which calculated on single articles is but a trivial impost. Sewing needles, steel pens, and clock movements however are more exacting, and at 60 marks are more than threepence per pound, though most of these articles are extremely light weight, and the difference in cost is hardly appreciable. Watches and watch-cases and movements are rated quite nominally, at only a few pence each.

In textiles, cotton yarns, singles of coarse counts pay 12 marks or just over a halfpenny per pound, starting at about the same level as in France. But there they part company, as the medium counts which are those most generally used are at 18 marks well under a penny per pound, and the finer ones which are often expensive, and in which English competition is most to be feared, are little over the penny. Doubled yarns are 10 to 20 per cent. higher, but so is their value, while if bleached or dyed the rates are nearly twice as much. Very fine and strong yarns for embroidery and thread making go as high as about threepence, but the *ad valorem* rate is no greater.

Unbleached calicos and fabrics of almost every description are charged 80 marks, or about fourpence per pound, equal to a penny per yard on coarse cloths, but not more than a farthing on the finer and costlier ones, in which there is greater risk of competition. Bleached goods are 25 per cent. more. Cotton hosiery and trimmings are 120 marks; curtains, laces, and embroideries 230 to 275 marks, but a considerable quantity and value of such goods often go to make up a pound or kilogramme in weight. Under this section the cheaper class of goods is undoubtedly well protected, the dearer and better ones scarcely at all.

Keen as is the competition between Saxony and Lancashire, the shipments of the latter to Germany are quite important, the yarn in 1896 having been valued at upwards of £2,000,000, and goods at £1,800,000, and the trade is steadily growing year by year. Germany on the other hand is only able to send us some £850,000 all told, and makes little headway. British exports to Holland are likewise greatly in excess of imports, and some, perhaps a great portion of this, is likewise destined for Germany.

Woollen yarns vary from 3 to 24 marks per 100 kilos., that is, from one-eighth of a penny to a little over one penny per pound, and the higher rate includes dyed material. Woollen fabrics at 135 and 220 marks according to weight is no more than threepence to sixpence per square yard, and in case of very light materials even less. Duties to be worth anything at all, either for revenue or protection, could hardly be fixed much lower.

Unbleached linen yarns made from flax, jute, or hemp vary from an eighth of a penny to a halfpenny per pound; dyed, printed, and bleached from a halfpenny to three-farthings; sewing thread three-halfpence to threepence. Ropes and cordage pay rather less than a halfpenny, and thin twines a little over a penny per pound. Linen fabrics are correspondingly reasonable. If unbleached, the rate varies from 12 up to 60 marks according to fineness, this being the solitary schedule in the German tariff in which there is any pretence at the enumeration of threads. Bleached, dyed, or printed fabrics are divided into two classes, those having less than 120 threads to 4 square centimetres (1½ inches) paying 60 marks, and above that number double, or threepence and sixpence per pound respectively. A good many pocket handkerchiefs and one or two shirts are required to make up this weight. Even damask and table napery are charged only at 150 marks, so that a handsome table cloth will pay no more than one or two shillings duty. The finest laces may be imported on payment of twopence an ounce, and everyone knows what a considerable value may be compressed into even this small compass.

Silks on the other hand are considerably enhanced in value by the time they have passed through the custom house. The unmanufactured article, like all other raw materials for textiles, is admitted free, but anything prepared or made up into fabrics is heavily weighted. Thread at 140 marks is less than a halfpenny an ounce, but fabrics pay 600 marks, or two and ninepence per pound, which is a premium on low bodices and short sleeves. Gauze and crape of the same material cost 1000 marks or threepence halfpenny an ounce; ribbons of pure silk threepence, and of half silk three-halfpence, which increases the cost per yard in proportion to the width.

Garments of silk are naturally more expensive still if imported ready-made. The suit of woollen clothing however, costing in England forty shillings, and which as we have seen if imported into the United States under the M'Kinley Act would have been quite doubled in price, has no more than five or ten shillings added to its value in Germany. Underwear of linen or cotton is still lower, and is allowed to enter at the rate of about eightpence per pound. The latest production of the Parisian milliners' art is charged something less than one shilling.

Among the coarser manufactured or partly manufactured commodities, leather does not figure quite so favourably. Dressed or half-dressed sheep and goat skins are scheduled at purely nominal rates. Sole leather, and Brussels or Danish glove leather are rated at 15s. per cwt., morocco at 18s. Belting leather at M 45 is nearly twopence halfpenny per pound. Gloves at 1 mark per kilo. represent but a very small charge per pair.

Common bricks, tiles, and earthenware pipes are on the free list, fire bricks at 5s. per ton, glazed and architectural building materials of similar character at 7s. 6d. Ordinary earthenware, burnt in one colour, pays 4s. per cwt.; white porcelain 5s.; coloured and ornamented 10s.; so that the cost of a single dinner or tea service is very little enhanced, though the coarser and heavier articles of domestic use are more heavily penalised in proportion. Vessels of common glass are rated at 4s. per cwt., window and plate glass is divided into three sizes, and rated accordingly at equal to three, four, and five shillings. Polished, ground, and mirror glass is charged 12s., and the most expensive decorated material pays no more than 15s. per cwt., the highest figure in the schedule. The contrast between these figures and those of the United States tariff is very striking.

Timber is likewise admitted at low rates, and for use in frontier districts free, provided it has been drawn by beasts of burden and not shipped by rail, the object of which is to prevent it being sent from any considerable distance. Brushes, which have occupied so much of the time and attention of the British Parliament of late years, are admitted in any quantity, with apparently no question as to how they are made or by whom, on payment of 1s. 6d. per cwt. up to 12s. for very fine materials, which do not come under any of the textile groupings.

Low as most of these rates are from the modern standpoint of protection, there does not exist any serious agitation for their increase. There is agitation for heavier duties it is true, but it proceeds from the agrarian and not the industrial party in the empire, and how sharply divided these two are recent events have abundantly proved. Not that agriculture lacks protection — indeed in that respect it is better off than anything else. Wheat and rye are rated at M 3.50, equal to 7s. 6d. per English quarter, which at the present price of the former cereal is high, and of the latter extravagant. Barley is only charged 2 marks, or 4s. 6d., the important brewing interest having no doubt to be considered, but prepared malt pays nearly double Fresh meat at 15 marks is equal to three farthings per pound, and pork fresh or cured at 17, to nearly a penny. On the grounds of disease, there has been a determined effort to exclude American bacon and hams entirely, and much friction has arisen with the United States in consequence. Vegetables at 4 marks per 100 kilos., or 2s. per cwt., would add somewhat appreciably to the cost of this nutritious and necessary diet were it enforced, but it is doubtful whether the German market gardener can often exact anything at all from his customers above the value of neighbouring countries. Butter and cheese at 16 and 15 marks respectively are increased in cost by nearly a penny per pound, so that on the whole the agriculturist is very well cared for. His grievances result from causes which protection will not cure, and are hardly therefore associated with the question of tariff, though we shall have something to say about them later.

The only important commodities remaining to be mentioned are oils, which play a most important part both in industrial and domestic life. As far as the former are concerned the duties are moderate, and no more than 2 to 4 marks or 1s. to 2s. per cwt. on such descriptions as palm, cocoanut, castor, linseed, and cottonseed oils, but it is somewhat surprising that anything should be levied at all, as they partake largely of the nature of raw materials. Tallow and beef and mutton fats come under the lowest rate; blubber and train oil at a middle one. Lighting and lubricating oils however are more unsparingly dealt with. Petroleum pays 6 marks, oils used in the manufacture of candles 10 marks, and lubricants the same. This schedule must on the whole be pronounced more unwise than any in the entire tariff.

Such then is the German tariff, and the British or other foreign manufacturer who imagines that were protection entirely abolished he could enter the markets of his rivals and undersell them, has seriously miscalculated the actual facts. The duties do afford an advantage no doubt, but in the language of the Stock Exchange or the produce markets it is more a jobber's turn than a dealer's profit. With the exception possibly of iron and steel, the rates are nowhere such as to enable the manufacturer to charge extravagant or even high prices to the domestic consumer, and it may be questioned whether in many instances he gets anything more than if protection did not exist. The average German, both in the shop and on the exchange, is fairly keen in striking a bargain, and if goods are to be had cheap he will try to get them. Besides, the British manufacturer himself has a very decided advantage in his own markets against his foreign competitors. He is on the spot and knows his customer's requirements, or at least ought to. Delivery can be arranged to suit, and when goods are wanted there are no awkward and unexpected delays of steamboats, or loss and damage through numerous transhipments, to say nothing of the added cost. The buyer has the seller within reach in case of inferior quality or other reclamations, and even should there be nothing of the sort, he will pay a little more for the privilege of grumbling, so dear to every Englishman. British manufacturers realise all this, and do not hesitate to quote higher prices to the domestic than to the foreign trader, particularly if they suspect the latter is receiving offers from elsewhere. It is because this principle—a perfectly legitimate one, if exercised in moderation—is pushed too far, that foreign rivals are often able to step in and pilfer trade, and not, as is sometimes supposed, because they are selling goods at a loss or can make them cheaper. Both they may occasionally do, but they are not the only culprits, and the British manufacturer could likewise tell a thing or two worth knowing in that way, were he only so disposed.

The tariff with which we have been dealing is a minimum or conventional one, applicable only to such countries as have commercial treaties or similar arrangements with Germany. There is another and much higher scale always kept in pickle for recalcitrant people who do not sufficiently appreciate the value of German manufactured goods, and when, as sometimes happens, they show a most determined preference for others, the brine is concentrated still more highly. A law promulgated on the 18th May 1895 enacts that—

"Dutiable goods proceeding from States that treat German ships or products less favourably than those of other States may, in so far as existing treaties are not thereby violated, be burdened with a surtax ranging up to 100 per cent. of the tariff duty imposed on such goods. Goods free of duty in virtue of the tariff may, under the same conditions, be burdened with a duty not exceeding 20 per cent. *ad valorem.*"

Nor is this an idle threat, for within recent years two European countries have come under the drastic regulation, or something akin to it, and both Spain and Russia have been engaged in tariff wars with Germany, in the latter instance with most disastrous consequences to their mutual commercial intercourse. An ordinance dated 29th July 1893 singled out commodities of Russian origin, and imposed on them a special tariff, the stringency of which may be judged from one or two examples. Wheat and rye are both cereals largely exported by Russia, and for which Germany was and is a good customer. The conventional duty is M 3.50, and the general 5 marks; but all Russian produce was condemned to pay M 7.50. The delicacy known as caviare, and almost entirely of Russian preparation, is ordinarily rated at 150 marks, but was raised to 225. Eggs paying 2 and 3 marks were raised to M 4.50. Pigs at 5 to 6 marks each could only change their nationality for 9; petroleum, in the production of which the wells at Baku lead those of Pennsylvania and the American oil regions a hard chase, was raised from 6 to 9 marks, no doubt with considerable regret that the United States should be permitted to enjoy such an advantage; tallow, instead of 2, paid 3 marks; and so on throughout the list, the trade returns between the two countries having been scanned with the utmost care, and every likely article of import subjected to the increased rates. And so hastily were they put in force, that the return of the Kaiser from his holiday could not be awaited, but were

"Given at Cowes, on board my yacht 'Hohenzollern,' 29th July 1893.
"WILLIAM."

This estrangement was entirely due to the convention entered into between France and Russia just at this period, under which the former guaranteed "most favoured nation" treatment, but the latter went one better, and made her new and wealthy ally concessions equal to 10 to 20 per cent. over all other countries. Eighteen months of this contest proved enough for both parties, and on the 29th January 1894 a treaty of commerce and navigation was concluded between them, breathing nothing but eternal amity and cordiality. Not only were the most favoured nation regulations restored in each case, but special protection was extended to the travellers and agents of firms domiciled in the respective countries in their endeavours to do business with their neighbours, and now all goes well again.

No sooner was the difficulty with Russia settled than a fresh one arose with Spain, and on the 25th May 1894 an ordinance was published surtaxing all Spanish products. Rye was once more rated at M 7.50. Iron ore was raised from 1 mark to 1.50. Dried fruits, upon which the conventional duty is 8 marks, and the general 24, were scheduled at the prohibitive figure of 36, or 18s. per cwt., and raisins form one of the most important crops of the Iberian peninsula. Similarly oranges, lemons, and citrons were raised from 12 to 18 marks. Wines and spirits suffered equally. Olive oil, at 3 marks conventional and 10 general, was rated at 15. Everything in fact was increased by 50 per cent. on the extreme duties. This state of affairs lasted rather over two years, and was eventually repealed on 25th July 1896.

The United States have been more than once threatened with something of the same sort, and there is constant exasperation over one dispute or another. Reference has already been made to the difficulties arising about bacon and hams, and by an ordinance dated 11th December 1895 all tinned meats were excluded from the benefit of the conventional duty 15 to 17 marks, and rated at the full one of 20, this being specially aimed at the United States. It is a poor game at best, and amounts to cutting one's nose to spite one's face, because as a rule German traders suffer quite as much as the offending foreigners. The possible consequences of the recent denunciation of the treaty of commerce between England and Germany are not altogether agreeable to contemplate on either side.

Germany is always active in framing and putting into operation commercial treaties, and all European States, with the exception of Portugal, now enjoy conventional duties. British and Dutch colonies are upon the same basis, by virtue of their connection with the mother countries. The South African, and most of the South American Republics, Brazil however again excepted, also come within their scope, so that the Imperial Zollverein may at present be said to trade with the whole world on equal terms.

The commercial policies of France and Germany afford a strong contrast, the one content to profit by the sale of what are practically monopolies, the other pushing and edging her way in everywhere. In one instance protection is a vital force, in the other almost a dead letter, except for purposes of retaliation. For plain living is as cheap, if not cheaper in Germany than in Great Britain, and that is the best proof that protection is inoperative. Food and clothing cost no more, though perhaps the qualities in each instance are on the whole a little inferior. But that is of small consequence, because if the people have as much as they want of good and wholesome diet, and are warmly clad, they can do their work efficiently. Nor are wages in the standard industries now much lower than in the adjoining island. The cause of British discomfiture, if such exist, must be sought in other directions than protection.

The principal one is close at hand, and is both natural and legitimate. A house furnisher going over a well appointed residence makes it his business to point out articles of his trade which would improve appearance as well as comfort. But set him in an empty country mansion of ample dimensions, and bid him "furnish it," and his heart leaps within him. At the conclusion of the Franco-German War, Germany was much in the position of the empty mansion, and her people have been engaged in furnishing it ever since. The energy induced by the work has commenced to overflow its former limits and to seek new channels, and the stubborn fact has to be faced, that the most dangerous rival to the commercial and industrial supremacy of Great Britain is not the nation that is the most protected, but the one that comes nearest to free trade.

# CHAPTER VII.

## Bounties.

Sugar :—Nature of Drawbacks—Tendency to develop into Bounties —Efforts to stimulate the Beet Industry—Continental Bounty Wars—Germany Antagonistic to the System—Cost to Consumers —Hidden Bounties—Surtax on Foreign Sugar in France— Futility of the System—Possibilities of Increased Consumption—Decline of the British and Colonial Industry—Fairplay but no Protection.
Shipping :—British Subsidies—Carriage of Mails—German Subsidies —French Construction Bounties—Navigation and Mail Subsidies —Other European Bounties—United States Shipbuilding— American Coasting Service—Mail Payments—The Canadian Subsidy.
Railways :—The German System—Cost compared with Great Britain—Watered Stock—Results of German State Control— French Subventions—Division and Remuneration of Capital— Total Cost to the Treasury—American Railroads.
Miscellaneous : — France — Canada — Australia—Sale of Surplus Products—General Influence on Trade.

WHENEVER a commodity is subject to an import duty, or an internal or excise tax on production, it is customary to refund it, or to discharge the owner from liability for payment on such portion as may not be used for home consumption but exported to foreign countries. The principle is just and equitable, though hardly in accordance with the popular idea of taxing the foreigner, which, carried to its logical issue, would impose the duty on everything belonging to him that could be laid hold of, irrespective of ultimate destination. This rebate or drawback is best known in Great Britain in connection with the export of beer, which is about the only dutiable commodity shipped abroad to any value. Most beer-drinking countries brew their own, but there are certain English specialities known all over the world, and the land which had never seen the black bottle with Bass's label would hardly be counted civilised. Any general export trade in English beer however is quite out of the question. Some half-million barrels only are exported out of a total production of nearly thirty-five millions.

Now although the drawback may be the full amount of the duty chargeable, the very fact that there is a duty at all enhances the cost of production, which on export really amounts to a small tax. The restrictions which are necessary for carrying on the trade, whatever it may be, are always more or less costly, both by the presence and supervision of revenue officials, and the more involved and often more expensive routine necessary to clear the goods, whether for a home or a foreign consumer. It follows that it is unwise for a country desirous of encouraging an export trade in any particular commodity which is not a monopoly, to impose any tax or restriction, external or internal; either upon its manufacture or free movement, and this applies equally to such articles as spirits and tobacco, though the moral phase of the question, in the former case at any rate, is of so much importance that a Government is amply justified in departing from the strict economic principle.

Let us apply this to sugar. Most countries place it in the category of luxuries, and regard it as a taxable commodity. A certain quantity of it is as necessary to a healthy individual as salt, but beyond that it may be regarded as a luxury, and the principle of taxing it moderately is therefore legitimate enough. The beet-growing countries of continental Europe act on this, and impose a duty, not only on all foreign sugar imported, but on all sugar grown at home. It was found however, many years ago, that opportunities offered for building up an export trade, and in connection with this the question of drawback had at once to be considered. The disadvantage to which I have referred no doubt occurred to those who were interested in the matter, and a small bonus in addition to the drawback was granted as compensation, to enable dutiable sugar countries to compete with those in the East and West Indies where there was no such restriction. And thus we get at the principle of the sugar bounties, which, once admitted, were capable of expansion in all directions, and as far back as the beginning of the present century, attempts were made to give an artificial stimulus to the cultivation of sugar by money premiums and reduced rates of transport to the seaboard, when the ultimate destination was a foreign country.

Had it gone no further there would have been little ground for complaint. But there is nothing in this world quite so greedy as protection. It is always wanting more. Beet growers and sugar manufacturers, having once inserted the wedge, were always on the alert to drive it home. The trade grew, and they kept urging on their respective governments to increase the bonus, in order that eventually they might capture, if not the whole, at least the greater part of it, and this they have now succeeded in doing. The governments concerned appear to have been on an inclined plane, and quite unable to resist the pressure put upon them, yielding inch by inch until the bounties have assumed their present magnitude—M 2.50 per 100 kilos. on raw, and M 3 to M 3.55 on refined in Germany, and fcs. 3.50 and fcs. 4.50 respectively in France. Austria-Hungary is second only to Germany in extent of production, and likewise grants bounties, but owing to isolation from the seaboard the sugar is exported through other countries, and the general public hear less about it. Russia is likewise a great producer, but requires most of it for home consumption. Holland and Belgium carry on the industry very extensively, and of course grant bounties too. But it will be sufficient for our purpose if we confine our attention to Germany and France, as all the others are on more or less similar lines.

Germany is at least honest with regard to these bounties. Her Government does not like them, and frankly says so, and the last ordinance issued regarding them expressly stipulates the right of instantaneous repeal provided other countries are willing to lead the way, or follow, unlikely events at the moment. It likewise publishes annually the amount of drawback paid to exporters, while the French Government returns are complicated, and the actual payments difficult, if not impossible, to estimate. Nor do German exporters get more than they are openly entitled to, and the rates of M 2.50 to M 3.55, equal to about 1s. 3d. and 1s. 9d. per cwt. respectively, may be regarded as operative.

France, on the other hand, works the machine more scientifically, and though she has been the last of the beet-growing countries to raise officially the rates of bounty, it was undoubtedly her unfair competition which led the others to act. The fcs. 3.50 and fcs. 4.50 per 100 kilos. are the direct rates now paid, it is true, but how much more is there behind? The tax on sugar is fcs. 60 per 100 kilos.; but partly to stimulate the extraction of the utmost possible quantity of juice from the root, and partly to assist the export of the product, half only of the nominal duty is charged on the yield between $7\frac{3}{4}$ and $10\frac{1}{2}$ per cent., while anything above the latter figure is divided into two parts, one paying the full, the other half duty, or an average of 75 per cent. Thus when the sugar is exported, and the drawback or credit claimed at the full rate, a bonus of 50 per cent. is given on one portion of it, and very often 25 per cent. on another.

The burden of these bounties is transferred intact to the shoulders of the home consumer, and a portion at anyrate of the import and internal duties levied are meant to pay for them. We have a means of estimating what this amounts to. The German bounty has recently been raised from M 1.25 to M 2.50 on raw sugar, and from M 2 to M 3 on refined, and, at the same time, the import duty was increased from M 36 to M 40. Now from this it is evident that the Treasury authorities consider a tax of 4 marks per 100 kilos. necessary to compensate them for an increase of M 1 to M 1.25 in the bounty, and in proportion to this the amount of the tax equivalent to the M 2.50 and M 3 would be M 10 to M 12, that is, German consumers pay at least 10 marks per 100 kilos. more than they would be called upon for, did the bounties not exist. It is all very well to point out in the official returns of national expenditure the amount paid for these bounties, and expatiate upon it as a wise incentive to agricultural and manufacturing industry; but if every time the German *hausfrau* poured a pound of sugar into the domestic basin she would only say to herself, "On that sugar I made a present of 5 pfennige to my English sister, who is also at this moment pouring a pound into her basin," the phrase would soon grow monotonous, and she would want to know what her English sister had ever done for her, that she should be so generous. Then the matter would assume an entirely different aspect.

In addition to this it must not be overlooked that the price of sugar in Germany is the market value, plus the duty, *plus the bounty*, as if the domestic consumer did not pay the last item as well as the other two, the owner would export it to secure the extra allowances.

France, for reasons already stated, makes the English consumer a much handsomer present still. The *Economiste Français*, probably the highest economic authority in that country, recently published an estimate of what the indirect or hidden bounty amounts to, that is, the sum the French exporter receives in drawback, over and above what he originally paid or was liable for. In the year 1886 it had reached the extravagant figure of over 15 francs per 100 kilos., or about six shillings per cwt., owing to the much greater quantity of juice extracted from the root than the excise officials calculated and charged for. Steps were taken to reduce it to something more reasonable, and the present law and method of levying the duty was the outcome. Since 1890 it has fluctuated round

6 francs, say about half-a-crown per cwt., but has again shown a tendency to increase, owing to improvements in manufacture, every nerve of course being strained to extract additional saccharine matter, because each extra ounce means so much additional bounty.

With the direct bounties now given, the total amounts once more to fully 10 francs, or over four shillings per cwt., and the tax paid by French consumers to meet it must be at least a penny per pound. A refining tax of 4 francs on all sugar for home consumption has been openly imposed to pay the direct bounty, with the stipulation that should it prove insufficient in any one year the bounties in the year succeeding are to be reduced to cover the deficiency, but if that ever happens it is much more likely that the French Chambers will vote a supplementary credit rather than risk the angry protests of the refiners. Provision for the hidden bounty is made in the ordinary excise tax.

Nor is this all. Factories for extracting the juice are invariably in close proximity to the beet fields, but the refineries are often at considerable distances. When the raw sugar destined for eventual exportation is shipped from one port to another where the refinery is situated, or conveyed overland a minimum distance of at least 250 kilometres, a reduction of duty of 2 francs is granted, equivalent to a further bounty. Added to all this are the galling restrictions imposed on foreign sugar. We have already had occasion to notice the surtax on commodities imported from other than the country of origin, but in the case of sugar this is levied indiscriminately at the rate of 9 francs on raw and 10 francs on refined, though if after refining the product is re-exported, this surtax is refunded, but without the addition of the bounty. These complicated regulations require all the intellectual faculties of an expert to grasp, and the attitude of the French Government towards the sugar industry more nearly resembles a gambler throwing his last stake, than a common-sense man of business endeavouring to make ends meet and earn a livelihood.

From whatever point of view these bounties are regarded, they have been a failure. That they have helped to destroy West Indian sugar plantations, and ruined British sugar refiners, and shut up the refineries is certain, as thousands of people interested know to their cost. That of course might be a matter for congratulation rather than otherwise in the beet-growing countries; but how have they benefited themselves? The growers complain that they are ruined because prices have declined so heavily; and despite the tremendous falling off in the production of cane sugar in Cuba owing to the revolution, the crop of 1895-96 having totalled only some 300,000 tons against over 1,000,000 in the preceding year, the value has dropped to the lowest ever recorded. Consumers, though unable to act together, are a powerful body, and have in this instance at anyrate captured the bounty for themselves at an even greater ratio than it has been granted. On the other hand, the temptation of the bounty has stimulated producers, who, in their reckless competition against cane, have grown more than sufficient for the world's requirements.

More than sufficient that is, in a relative sense, because the possibilities of increased consumption must be enormous, when the 30 lbs. per head in France or the 27 lbs. in Germany are contrasted with the 88 of Great Britain, or even the 68 of the United States. Not only is there room for expansion in its domestic use, but in those numerous industries into which it so largely enters in England. The difference is more than half a hundredweight per inhabitant, and were only half this made up the requirements of the populations of France and Germany alone, with their 100,000,000 of population, or close upon it, would be 1,250,000 tons per annum. There is no natural commodity in the world which requires less stimulus to encourage its use than sugar, and wherever it has been made cheap its consumption has steadily increased. But most governments, with a perversity worthy of a better cause, continue to make it dear. Great Britain is the only country in Europe which exempts it from taxation, and in most of the others the national revenue derived from it, together with the sums paid in bounties, are far in excess of the prime cost. Only Denmark, Switzerland, and Turkey, the last, in fiscal matters, far in advance of any of its continental neighbours, subject it to a moderate exaction,—nowhere else is it less than 15s. per cwt.

The argument that bounties stimulate production and provide employment for the industrial population of the country paying them, is utterly fallacious. Abolish them and give the industry fair play without let or hindrance, and the world's consumption, which is now no more than 10 to 12 pounds per head of the entire population, will double itself in the same number of years.

The real boon required then by cane and beet growers alike is not bounties, whether great or small, but the adoption of measures which will materially cheapen the cost of the article to the consumer. The British Government is at present in a position to give a helping hand in this direction, such as nobody else can.

A word of warning is however necessary. Sooner or later the British public will be roused against the manifest injustice of these bounties, and West India planters and British refiners would be more than human did they not take advantage of the circumstance to get a little more than they are entitled to. And there is another side to the question which must not be overlooked. The depression of the sugar industry is not by any means due entirely to the operation of continental bounties. Economy in production and utilisation of waste-products have more to do with it than anything else. The sugar cane after the juice is extracted is cast aside as worthless. All beet-growing are likewise cattle-raising districts, and the green tops as well as the pressed pulp are used for food. The British industry which suffered most and is now practically extinct, was that devoted to the production of loaf or lump sugar. It has been almost entirely replaced by crystals, and a well-known English firm has had quite as much to do with that as the French bounty.

Moreover, Germany and not France has been the keenest and most successful competitor, and until lately the bounties granted by that country were little more than nominal. Neither the West Indian nor the British industry can have been possessed of much backbone if they were to be ruined by sevenpence halfpenny, or even a shilling per cwt. Now that the rates have been doubled, prompt and energetic action is called for. Not on the lines of the absurd convention of 1889, which placed the English supply of sugar entirely at the mercy of one or two continental countries—Germany among them, and which would have prohibited the import from any country paying bounties, whether large or small. There is another and simpler way of coping with the difficulty, and the motto of any government which seeks to put it into operation must be "Fairplay, but no Protection."

In the public mind at any rate, bounties are generally associated with sugar, but they are an economic evil which is rapidly growing, and they assume no more insidious form than when applied to shipping. There are so many different ways of granting them without detection, and of making extravagant payments for services rendered, or supposed to be rendered, to the State. Several of the great British lines receive a small annual subsidy from the Government, in return for which their best steamers are held at the disposal of the Admiralty as fast cruisers in case of an outbreak of war, in which Great Britain is involved. But for that purpose costly additions are made in their original construction which would not be necessary were they only required for the merchant service, and welcome though the subsidy no doubt is, part of it is only interest on the extra capital outlay. On the other hand, the Government is assured of a splendid addition to its navy in an emergency, without prolonged negotiation, and the risk of being squeezed financially.

The total amount of these subsidies is under £50,000 per annum, of which the two great Transatlantic Companies receive about £15,000 each, the Peninsular and Oriental Company £11,500, and the Canadian Pacific Railway Company £7,500 towards the fast service between Vancouver and Australia.

The number of steamers actually subsidised is eleven, but the Admiralty has a further right of call upon four of the Cunard and ten of the Peninsular boats for transport service, so that as a matter of fact the payment is less than £2000 per vessel.

There can be no economic objection to an arrangement of this sort, provided it is moderately and not extravagantly paid for. There are many advocates of its extension, but unless restricted within very narrow limits, and to the best and newest ships, it would speedily lend itself to jobbery and favouritism. There is another way however of subsidising, namely, by contracts for carrying mails, which is such an important function of all fast steamers. The British lines are paid, and paid well for this service, but not more than they are entitled to, considering all the circumstances of the case. There are season trades to every part of the world, times of the year when the great steamship companies strain every nerve for the quickest and most efficient dispatch possible, and times when they would rest on their oars, and only work their slower and less expensive boats. But by their contracts they are compelled to run the best available all the year round, and they loyally adhere to them, though the New York correspondent of the "*Times*" never fails to let the world know when a slow steamer has taken the place of a quick one, altogether ignoring the fact that vessels, like journalists, require an occasional rest and overhauling. There is no doubt whatever that all the mail lines run some of their steamers at one time or other during the year without any profit, if not at an actual loss, and are fairly entitled therefore to a liberal scale of remuneration. There is no secret about what is paid for these services, and the companies naturally make the best terms they can for themselves.

That is all the British Government does for British shipping, and it is all that can fairly be asked on strict economic lines. Other Governments however go a great deal further, and Germany is usually singled out as an instance of stimulating her shipping trade, like orchids, in a hot-house. But in this, as in direct protection, Germany is by no means so great a sinner as she is represented. One line, the North German Lloyd, which now possesses a greater tonnage than any other company in the world, is subventioned to the extent of about £300,000 per annum, but this was to enable it to establish a regular service with the Far East and Australia, and as it has now accomplished it and is making it pay, the probability is that ere long the subvention will be withdrawn.[1] This concern in its former history overreached itself and got into financial difficulties, but in 1894 it was reorganised and a heavy loan raised for that purpose. But the fact that it was able to borrow M 35,000,000 at 4

[1] I notice the North German Lloyd has recently demanded an additional £75,000, to enable it to add to the number of ports of call in the Far East.

per cent. interest with a capital of M 40,000,000 already in existence, proves that confidence was felt in it. Its adverse balance, after writing off large sums for depreciation, was that year upwards of M 4,500,000, and was drawn from a reserve fund which had been specially constituted, but that gave it a fresh start, and for 1896 it declared the fairly substantial dividend of 4 per cent.

The other great German Line, the Hamburg Steam Packet Company, is not believed to be directly subsidised at all, but is less handicapped than many of its British rivals. It is not, for instance, compelled to run its fast boats through the winter months, nor does it even lay them up; for availing itself of the magnificent accommodation they afford, these steamers are dispatched on pleasure trips to the Mediterranean and southern climes, and earn on these voyages a very fair dividend on the entire capital of the Company. German merchants and correspondents are not inconvenienced, because they can still address their mails by Southampton and Queenstown, and have them delivered as quickly as by their own fast boats. A Company which has for several years increased its dividends, and for 1896 declared the handsome one of 8 per cent., after writing off a large amount for depreciation, needs no subsidies.

At what rates the conveyance of mails is paid for is not so definitely known, and here at least the German lines may have an advantage over their British competitors. The postal and telegraph service of the German Empire is a big thing, but it pays, and if the steamship companies do get more than they are reasonably entitled to, it is only out of the profits of the entire system. The estimate of the Imperial Budget for 1896-97 reckoned upon a gross profit of over thirty millions of marks, or about £1,500,000, which was just a little more than the realised surplus of the two previous years; but against this there is a charge for central administration, so that the net income is about £1,000.000 sterling. If German steamers are heavily subventioned therefore for mails, it is not directly at the expense of the taxpayers.

But with France it is far otherwise. She, as we have already seen, is the real delinquent over the sugar bounties, and does nothing to atone for it in the treatment of her shipping. From the time the keel of a vessel is laid on the stocks, to the moment she is broken up for old iron, her owners are squeezing the Government, and draw gold rather than blood at every pressure. A tonnage bounty is given on everything built in French shipyards, the rates being 65 francs per gross ton on iron and steel ships, 40 francs on wooden vessels over 150 tons gross, and 30 francs on smaller ones. Further bounties are given on the engines of steamers ; but inasmuch as British marine engineers are able to do the work so much cheaper than French ones, the question was raised only quite recently, whether a vessel built in a French yard might not be fitted out in a British one without foregoing anything more than the bounty on the machinery. French engineers naturally protested, and won the day, so that British work does not desecrate ships which fly the tricolour from their mast heads.

The moment the bounty-constructed vessel gets up steam or sets sail, she becomes the recipient of a navigation subsidy. This is calculated at the rate of fc. 1.70 per ton for every thousand miles covered during the first year, with a reduction of 6 centimes for every subsequent year. A new French steamer of say 5000 tons, would consequently earn a bounty of about £2000 for every voyage to New York and back, irrespective of what it received for freight and passengers. An instance has lately been recorded of a large iron sailing ship making a voyage round the world which occupied just twelve months, and resulted in a subsidy of upwards of fcs. 100.000, or £4000, in addition to another fcs. 3000 paid as a premium for apprentices. The speed may be fast or slow, the payment is the same, only there is a strong incentive to cover as great a distance as possible, particularly in the early years of a vessel's life. Still the only result is that France keeps some of her shipping, as she does most of her trade, in her own hands, and makes little or no attempt to compete in foreign ports. If the Government is good enough to provide ship-owners with dividends, why should they throw them away by carrying goods at low rates for foreigners?

The French budget for 1897 makes provision for these bounties to the extent of fcs. 11,000,000, say £450,000. This is certain to be an underestimate, as the Government does not care to make the figures appear too large, and for 1896 a supplementary vote of fcs. 2,750,000 was required, bringing the total payment for the year up to fcs. 14,250,000, or £570,000.

But French shipping bounties do not end here, and further heavy allowances are made under the guise of mail service. How excessive these are, we will best ascertain by contrasting them with the amounts disbursed by the British post-office for similar services.

|  | France. | Great Britain. |
|---|---|---|
| New York & West Indies, | £450,000 | £245,000[1] |
| India, China, & Japan, | 240,000 | 435,000 |
| Australia & New Caledonia, | 125,000 | |
| East Africa & Indian Ocean, | 75,000 | 30,000 |
| West Coast of Africa, | 20,000 | |
| Mediterranean, | 55,000 | |
| Algeria, Tunis, Tripoli, & Morocco, | 35,000 | 25,000 |
| Corsica, | 15,000 | |
| Calais and Dover, | 10,000 | |
| | £1,025,000 | £735,000 |

[1] Including Canada, £60,000.

The demands on the carrying capacities of British mail steamers are certainly much greater than upon French ones, yet they are only paid three-fourths of the amount, of which moreover the colonies contribute £200,000. It must be remembered too that the greater part of the correspondence of the United Kingdom with Europe, and a good deal of that with the East, passes through Dover and Calais. One half at least of the French payments must be regarded as a direct bounty, so that French shipping is subsidised to the extent of one to one and a quarter millions sterling per annum.

Other European countries follow this vicious example. Denmark, for instance, with its small merchant fleet, allows a payment for every ton of dairy produce or fish landed by a Danish steamer at a British port. The Netherlands Royal Steam Packet Company, trading principally with the Dutch possessions in the East Indies, draws an annual navigation bounty of £50,000. Italy does her utmost to encourage shipbuilding and shipping, and would pay the owners of a 5000 tons steamer of 2000 horse power, £13,000 if constructed in an Italian shipyard, while for every voyage she subsequently made, say to or from New York, they would receive about £500. Austria-Hungary offers more extravagant inducements still, but until she reaches Salonica, she can make no pretence to being a maritime power, her single port of any importance at present, namely Trieste, being too far out of the way.

It is terribly hard for the British shipowner to compete against wholesale subventioning of this sort, which permits of low freights. Foreigners however, are sharp witted enough not to give the British merchant the advantage of them, and their steamers do not cross to English ports and offer to carry cargo for next to nothing. But the English owner is omnipresent, and there is no port in the world open to him where he does not try to capture a freight, and usually gets it on some terms or other, not it is to be feared always profitable. Complaints are often made by British shippers of what looks very like discriminating rates against them, as a steamer will partially load in a foreign port at a low freight, and fill up in a British one for the same destination at a considerably higher rate. To procure the first at all they must cut low, though it may not pay, and it is rather creditable than otherwise that they should beard the lion in his den, and carry off some of the spoil.

German steamers do make regular calls at English ports like Southampton and Plymouth, and get whatever share of the mails is addressed specially for them, receiving payment in accordance with the weight carried. This concession of the British post office is naturally objected to by British companies, but it wisely declines to cancel any facilities of which English correspondents may be able to avail themselves. Nobody addresses letters by a German liner unless they know there is likely to be a saving of time in delivery, and whenever that is possible it should be conceded. Besides, the summer calls of these steamers is a decided benefit to English trade, as many American tourists are enabled to spend the last weeks or days of their holiday in England, who would not do so were they compelled to embark at Hamburg or Bremen, from one or other of which ports their return tickets are available.

It would be strange indeed if the bounty system had not crept, surreptitiously or otherwise, into the United States. The M'Kinley tariff, as we have had occasion to observe, did nothing by halves, and when dealing with sugar did not confine itself to the miserable 1s. 3d. or 1s. 9d. per cwt. prevalent on the continent of Europe, but boldly marked it at 2 cents per pound, or 9s. 4d. per cwt. That the Act of 1890 did not include shipping within its scope, and make some extravagant provision for it as it did for tinplates, its authors have never ceased to regret, and if recent declarations are to be regarded, they mean to make full atonement for the omission. For all that a very costly experiment was made, and two steamers were constructed and launched at Philadelphia, which could have been better built at little more than half the money on the Clyde or Belfast Lough. These, together with two others transferred from the British to the American flag, now constitute a heavily-subsidised American Line. It takes the form of a payment for mails, and amounts to over £3000 for every voyage from New York to Southampton, whether they carry one bag or a thousand. As one thousand bags is a somewhat high average, and the weight will vary from 80 to 100 tons, the payment is thus at the rate of £30 to £40 per ton. British steamers are paid only for what they carry, and it requires a big mail to earn £1000. As the four American liners manage to put in about 55 voyages per annum among them, the difference is equivalent to a subsidy of £110,000, a dividend of over 5 per cent. on the £2,000,000 of capital sunk, or which would have been sunk had they all been built in the United Kingdom. The United States post office is not worked at a profit, and this money consequently comes out of the pockets of the taxpayers, or rather, as American finance is worked at present, is added to the national debt. The £400,000 granted to the North German Lloyd has to be distributed among about sixty steamers, the £110,000 of the American line is absorbed by four.

But the M'Kinley Act did not entirely neglect shipping. It provided in one of its clauses that,

"Material for building vessels for foreign account may be imported in bond, and no duty charged, provided the purpose is fulfilled, and the ships do not engage in the coastwise trade."

It forgot one important provision however, and did not stipulate that American mechanics were to be compelled to labour in American shipyards at a wage of a dollar a day, and consequently the world did not rush eagerly to seize the privilege of having its fleets built in United States harbours.

But it went further, and in the succeeding clause enacted that articles needed for repair of American vessels in foreign trade were to be admitted free of duty. Even this was ineffective, and one of the American liners has been known to cross the Atlantic propelled by one screw, in order that the damaged machinery connected with the other might be repaired in England; while certainly one, if not both American-built boats have in the course of their short lives paid private visits to English graving docks. The stipulation in the next Act must be more rigid, and forbid any vessel sailing under the American flag to be repaired in a foreign port, while it can reach one in the United States either under steam or under sail.

In spite of all this, the United States possess a very considerable merchant fleet, but it is engaged almost entirely in the coastwise service. As no foreign-built vessel, even if owned by an American, is permitted to enter into competition, American shipbuilders enjoy a monopoly, and charge what they please for the tonnage engaged exclusively in the Atlantic, Pacific, or Gulf Service, or on the great lakes. As these vessels carry principally agricultural produce, and the freights are naturally enhanced by their extravagant cost, a fresh burden is imposed on the unfortunate southern planter or western farmer, who has to carry the shipbuilder as well as the woollen and iron manufacturer on his shoulders.

Hitherto shipping bounties have only indirectly affected British owners. They have not had to compete against them in their own ports, because the foreign ships which do bid for British trade are of an inferior class, and owe the advantage they possess to the less stringent regulations under which they are navigated. When shipowners send their craft to foreign ports however, they cannot expect to have quite so much their own way, particularly in these days of high protection, and must simply take their chance. But vague threats are beginning to be whispered of a determined and wholesale effort to call into being a United States merchant fleet which is to monopolise as far as possible the foreign trade of United States ports. This can only be effected under existing circumstances by enormous subventions. The American people are perfectly at liberty to build as many ships as they like, how they like, when they like, and with whatever money they like ; but when the American Government steps in and begins to pay a portion of the freights of exporters to British ports, it will be time for the British Government to follow and claim it for the relief of the British taxpayer. The American Government may pay the freights of British exporters, and consequently of United States consumers if it likes, that is entirely its own affair.

The results of a subsidised American line so far as they have been experienced are not of a very satisfactory nature, and the mail service, if not disorganised, becomes occasionally something of a scandal, in the creation of which the British postal authorities are to blame quite as much as the American. It seems absurd that with three fast steamers sailing nearly every week, it should sometimes happen that two or three mails are delivered one on top of the other, and then for nearly a week to elapse without one. The United States post office naturally reserves everything it can for the steamers sailing under the American flag, and consequently another steamer as fast or faster sailing the same day gets nothing. Though as a rule compelled to ship one portion of a week's mail by a British steamer, it is invariably the smaller half (if there be such a thing), while the British post office in self-defence adopts the same tactics on the reverse route. Not a very sweet taste of protection and bounties this! Surely it is possible to arrange between the three lines for sailings every other day, and for all mails on both sides of the Atlantic to be despatched with equal regularity. Then with few exceptions there would be as regular a service as between London and Edinburgh, or New York and Chicago.

The most important subsidy ever countenanced by a British Government has just been conceded for a fast service between the United Kingdom and Canada. The amount is $750,000, say £150,000 per annum, two-thirds of which is to be contributed out of Canadian, the remaining third out of British revenues. How totally different in principle this bounty is to the foreign ones we have just been discussing will be apparent at a glance.

To begin with there are weighty political grounds for the establishment of rapid intercourse between Great Britain and the largest of her self-governing colonies. Such intercourse has hitherto been provided through the United States, but the hostility of certain sections of the people of that country as well as of foreign nations generally, makes a more direct route advisable, if not absolutely necessary. The geographical situation of Canada, with its ports closed against navigation for several months in the year, renders a fast service on ordinary commercial conditions an impossibility; consequently, to ensure it, monetary concessions must be made which would otherwise be unnecessary.

Besides, Canada now offers an alternative route to the Australasian Colonies, which is absolutely under British control. Were Great Britain involved in hostilities with a continental power, the probability is that the Suez Canal would no longer be available for the intercourse of her ships with either the East or the Antipodes, and there would remain the route round the Cape of Good Hope, or across the United States and from San Francisco. It is of course highly improbable that both these would be blocked at the same time, but sentiment as it exists at present, demands a highway through British territory in preference to any other.

The necessities of the case being conceded, the conditions under which the subsidy is granted must be considered. In the case of France and the United States the services which are so exorbitantly paid for are not unique, they admittedly could be, and are actually performed for very much less, and the bounty is given principally to stimulate the construction of tonnage which may or may not be required. In the Canadian contract, competition has been allowed full play; the firm which has hitherto enjoyed the monopoly of the mails finds itself shut out in the cold, and an untried and comparatively unknown opponent occupies its place. In either of the countries alluded to the new departure would have been made the occasion of a handsome concession to some favoured individuals. Possibly the same thing might have happened in Canada had there not been a radical and altogether unexpected change of government, for whatever else may be said of the political party which so long enjoyed the upper hand in the Dominion, it cannot be accused of having forgotten its friends. As those friends are often the openly avowed enemies of the party which has suddenly come uppermost, they can hardly expect a continuation of the favours to which they had grown so accustomed.

It is stoutly maintained by the former contractors, and those associated with them, that the service cannot be carried out for the subsidy agreed upon, and that the arrangement is bound to end disastrously for one, if not both parties to it. Only time can prove the correctness or otherwise of this contention, but it may at once be admitted that the conditions appear unduly onerous. It is not the size and speed of the vessels which are too exacting, as similar ones already sail the ocean. Possibly however the difficulties of navigation have been underrated, and the penalties for non-performance are extremely severe. There may be no actual intention of enforcing them when every precaution has been taken to ensure the fulfilment of the contract, but there is just the risk that political animus may some day take unreasonable advantage of them. There can be no guarantee against anything of the sort while great industrial corporations identify themselves with party rather than with national interests. Whatever happens to the subsidised, the subsidisers will receive full value for their money, and the word bounty in its stricter meaning, is consequently hardly applicable in the present instance.

Closely allied with the shipping trade is inland transit, whether by rail or canal. Here at least is a preponderating advantage enjoyed by German over British traders. The German railway system, or more than 90 per cent. of it, is owned and controlled by the State. Acquired originally for strategic purposes, it has been converted into a mighty engine for the promotion of trade. The Government can and does, facilitate certain industries at the expense of others, and in this way grants what is fully equivalent to a bounty. But there are natural advantages without the necessity of creating artificial ones. The total mileage of the German system is about 28,000 English miles, that of the United Kingdom just over 21,000. But while the former has cost to construct some £560,000,000, the latter stands capitalised at rather more than £1,000,000,000, that is, whereas the German system has cost some £20,000 per mile the British works out at £47,250, so that a British railway must earn nearly two and a half times as much as a German one to make the same return. True the £1,000,000,000 is not all genuine capital, £90,000,000 being watered or duplicated stock, for which no consideration has ever been paid. It is high time indeed that this process was stopped, if British trade is not to be permanently injured. One great English company is at the present moment seeking to double its ordinary stock,[1] and enormously increase its preference, and if successful, others will want to follow, with the result that in a very few years the capital will be swollen to £1,500,000,000, or even £2,000,000,000.

This may appear a matter of small consequence in itself, but there is a deep policy actuating it. When dividends are good, traders are apt to agitate for reductions in rates, but by artificially increasing the capital the dividends may be nominally, though not actually, reduced, and this circumstance used as a buttress against concessions. The excessive cost, in the first instance, of building British railways was not the fault of the companies, but due entirely to the rapacity of landowners who regarded themselves as entitled to any exorbitant demand they liked to make, and unfortunately were only too often able to enforce. But that is no reason for making bad worse, and in face of the serious competition of foreign railways nothing must be permitted which will tend in the least to extravagance of management, or even of demand.

It is evident that all other things being equal, German rates of carriage should be no more than half those in the United Kingdom, but on the other hand distances are much greater, which tends to

[1] The Midland Railway Act of 1897 has now accomplished this. The ordinary stock has been converted into equal amounts of preferred and deferred, and by a stroke of the pen the capital of the English railway system has been increased by this one item alone by £34,500,000.

equalise matters somewhat. But the German Government takes neither distance nor anything else into consideration when bent on assisting a new or struggling industry. Shipbuilding on the Baltic for instance, has lately sprung into great activity, and the State railways convey all materials required at a greatly reduced rate. Cotton-spinners in Saxony receive their raw material at less than the normal charge for freight. Exporters are likewise specially favoured, and have their goods conveyed to port of shipment often at merely nominal rates. This is undoubtedly unfair to other German interests, but it is equally disastrous to British competition, and this fact is a strong inducement to continue the policy, though some day perhaps the German sufferers may successfully protest against it. Meantime British trade has to struggle against a bounty far more wide reaching than that on sugar.

Again, this is done without any levy on the German taxpayer. For the year ending 31st March 1895, the working of the State railways resulted as follows :—

| | |
|---|---|
| Gross receipts, . . | £70,500,000 |
| Working expenses, . . | 43,000,000 |
| Net receipts, . | £27,500.000 |

For the year ending 31st December 1894 the returns from the railways of the United Kingdom were :—

Gross receipts, .    .    £84,311.000
Working expenses, .       47,208,000

Net receipts.       £37,103,000

The net receipts for the United Kingdom for 1895 amounted to £38,046,000, or nearly a million increase, but as I have no official returns of the German State system for the corresponding period I cannot compare them. No doubt they increased likewise, as greater briskness in trade was characteristic of both countries.

We thus see that upon a considerably greater system the net returns were nearly £10,000,000 less. Had the German gross traffic equalled the British, the corresponding net receipts would have been increased by about £5,000,000, and the difference between them would have been but £5,000,000. There would have been no reason however for any such increase, as the amount is more than sufficient as it is to meet the interest on the obligations pertaining to the railways, and any further profits arising from a growth of traffic would be applied to a reduction of rates. In other words, the German Government is able to grant a substantial bounty to industrial interests, which in Great Britain would be divided among railway shareholders, and as the trade of the country increases, this bounty will increase with it.

The net receipts of British railways were equal to $3\frac{3}{4}$ per cent. on the entire capital, or to rather more than 4 per cent., if the watered stock is taken into account, whereas the Imperial German Government is able to borrow all it needs at 3 per cent., while the capital itself is so much less. It is true the German railway loans are mostly State loans, and pay a somewhat higher rate of interest, but all that will some day be needed to reduce it is the Imperial guarantee. Meanwhile the net return of the system works out at nearly 5 per cent., so that over and above the concessions and bounties, a substantial sum accrues in mitigation of taxation.

After the payment of all interest for the year 1896-97, there is an estimated balance carried to the credit of the Imperial revenues on the railways for which it is directly responsible, of over M 23,000,000 or £1,150,000 sterling, reduced somewhat by extraordinary expenditure estimated at M 7,000,000. But the fact nevertheless remains, that after all liabilities have been discharged and an important stimulus given to industry, there is still a balance of over three quarters of a million sterling for the relief of the Imperial German taxpayer.

Here then British traders suffer under a disability which must remain permanent, and can only be combated by increased energy and vigilance. The transfer of the railways to the State would not obviate it, because it would be unfair to demand for £550,000,000, or even £750,000,000, what had cost shareholders nearly £1,000,000,000 to construct, and which upon an earning capacity of 3¾ to 4 per cent. has a market value of some £250,000,000 more. Besides, there are many and perhaps insuperable difficulties connected with State management in Great Britain which do not exist in Germany. In the latter country the Government is almost despotic, makes whatever regulations it likes, and defies public opinion as reflected in the Reichstag. But in England, where the popular voice is supreme and makes and unmakes ministries, there would be a constant, and, it is to be feared, disastrous struggle between different sections of the industrial community for special rebates and other privileges. Still, the day is probably not far distant, when other interests than those of shareholders will have to be represented on the boards of the great railway companies, and when management will be devoted to something more than the earning of increased dividends.

While Germany can offer such a substantial and legitimate bounty as this to her manufacturing industries, we need not fly to protection nor to steamship subsidies for reasons why she has become so keen a rival to Great Britain.

Railways in France, though nominally the property of companies as in Great Britain, are actually under state control and management. A process of consolidation of all the minor companies has gone on, until the entire system has been absorbed into five, or at the most six great undertakings, the dividends upon the capital stock being guaranteed by government. Of the five important ones, the Northern, Southern, Eastern, Western, and the Paris-Lyons and Mediterranean Railways, only the first earns sufficient net income to meet the whole of its obligations to its shareholders without dipping into the national purse. The capital arrangements of French railways, moreover, differ widely from the English ones. The ordinary stock of the former constitutes only a small percentage, of the latter considerably more than a third of the total. In France the indebtedness is mostly in the form of obligations bearing 3 per cent. interest, but issued in days gone by considerably below par. They partake too of the character of lottery loans, as fixed amounts are drawn annually and repaid at par, the difference between that and the issue price constituting the prize. With the growing cheapness of money these obligations have naturally increased in value, and while many were originally issued at less than fcs. 400. some indeed below fcs. 300 per 500 franc bond, the market value of most of them is now about fcs. 470 to fcs. 480, and all new issues are upon this basis.

These obligations bear some resemblance to the debenture and preference stocks of British railways, and the earnings of the companies are amply sufficient to meet them. The ordinary stocks however are much more favourably situated than the preference, inasmuch as they enjoy an absolute government guarantee. The Northern Railway, for instance, is guaranteed a dividend of fcs. 54.10 per 500 franc share until the year 1914, but as a matter of fact earns over fcs. 60 on an average. All the others fall short of the guarantees, which, from an English point of view, are excessive, that of the Paris-Lyons and Mediterranean being fcs. 55 or 11 per cent., the Southern, fcs. 50 or 10 per cent., the Western fcs. 38.50 or $7\frac{3}{4}$ per cent., and the Eastern fcs. 35.50 or 7 per cent. Needless to say the market price of these shares is very high, the average yield being barely 3 per cent., as the Government rigorously fulfils its engagements and disburses many million francs per annum to make up the dividends. Should it ever happen that the actual earnings of any of the companies are in excess of the sums required, the surplus will go, not to the shareholders, but to the Government, in reduction of what is somewhat facetiously termed a debt.

The total outstanding ordinary stock of these companies is little over fcs. 1,000,000,000, or £40,000,000, yet provision is made in the Budget for an estimated expenditure of fcs. 55,250,000 to cover the interest guarantee upon it. The Government claims as a set-off, a very large figure for taxes and for postal and military facilities, all of which are more sentimental than real, as it cannot be supposed, for instance, that were the railways privately owned they would be allowed to escape their proper share of taxation. British companies at any rate enjoy no such immunity. Military and strategic considerations no doubt compel France, like Germany, to keep a tight grip over the railway system, but the advantages, whatever they may be, are scarcely calculable in francs and centimes.

These shares, like the obligations, are subject to annual drawing and redemption at par. There would be manifest hardship however in paying off at fcs. 500 what sells in the open market at 1000 to 2000, and though the stock is cancelled, the holder receives an *action de jouissance*, or profit share, which entitles him to any annual dividend in excess generally of $3\frac{1}{2}$ per cent., so that he is in reality no worse off. These railway concessions, it must be borne in mind, are all terminable sooner or later, when it will be open to the Government to make fresh and perhaps less exacting conditions. When the time arrives the stock itself will have been redeemed, and it will be the *actions de jouissance* which have to be dealt with.

Interest payments on ordinary shares constitute only a small portion of the obligations of the State to the railways. Under a law of the 17th June 1873, for instance, the Minister of Finance has to provide an annuity of fcs. 20,500,000 to the Eastern Company, while there are a number of others amounting to fcs. 50,000,000 additional.

The Minister of Public Works is responsible for further annuities amounting to fcs. 40,000,000, the total sum which the Treasury has to find being close upon £7,000,000. Whatever name may be given to it, this is really a bounty, and though Government may juggle the figures and claim to be recouped by services rendered, the fact remains that the money is found and the trade and industry of the country directly relieved to a proportionate extent, though eventually it has to be refunded in the form of taxation.

In the United States the railroads, with one or two notable exceptions, are entirely free from Government control. No systems in the world however have been the recipients of such enormous bounties as some of the great trunk and trans-continental roads. They have had literally millions of acres poured into their lap, acres which are to-day worth untold millions of dollars. True, it was the only way in which the country could be developed, and for that reason little objection can be taken to it. But the treasure has been squandered, and the roads themselves wrecked and thrown into bankruptcy. Had American railroads been honestly financed and economically managed, they might have been worked to-day at rates which could not have been touched by any other country, and the advantage would have been such that no system of protection could possibly afford. Little wonder that the industrial population rises in revolt against the exactions, and protests against providing money for dividends on stock which represents nothing but the booty of manipulators. But what American agriculturists and European investors have lost, European industries have gained, as they are not called upon to compete against rates which could not exist in the older continent. The question of American railroads is however far too big to be dealt with casually in a work of this sort.

Bounties are paid on commodities other than sugar, and again France leads the way. There is no need to go into detailed particulars, and it will be sufficient to state the amounts provided in the Budget for the industries participating, and which appear partly in the estimates of the Ministry of Commerce and partly in that of Agriculture :—

| | |
|---|---|
| Deep Sea fisheries, | £140,000 |
| Breeding of silkworms, . | 180,000 |
| Silk spinning, . . . | 120,000 |
| Flax and hemp cultivation, . | 100,000 |
| Viticulture. . . | 20,000 |
| Mineral Oils, | 10,000 |
| | £570,000 |

Again these figures fall considerably short of the payments actually made, and supplementary estimates were voted in 1896 of £80,000 on fisheries and £50,000 on silk spinning, and will, as likely as not, be repeated in 1897.

While France adheres to protection and admits raw materials free, it is perhaps only consistent that bounties should be given to the producers of such commodities as silk, flax, and hemp.

Sugar bounties are not unknown in Australia, and in Canada iron manufacturers receive substantial payments on all they produce. The new tariff provides for $3 per ton on all pig iron smelted from native ore, and $2 if from foreign ores. Puddled bars, if made of Canadian iron, receive $3 per ton, and steel ingots, if containing at least 50 per cent. of native iron, also get $3. The principle of these and all similar subsidies is utterly indefensible.

There is another form of bounty still to be dealt with which is not direct, but springs from, and is provided for by protection. When a protective duty is imposed which is really effective, that is, enables the native producer to make all that is required for home consumption, his first aim is to take care that the market is kept fully supplied with the domestic commodity, so that the foreign one may be excluded. It is however utterly impossible to gauge the demand in a country so wide, say, as the United States, particularly if it be of a fluctuating nature, and dependent upon prosperous or adverse seasons in other industries. Moreover, where protection ensures large profits, the tendency is to over-produce, in the hope of additional sales being effected. This means that more actually is produced than is required for home consumption, and a surplus remains on the hands of the producer. It could be disposed of no doubt at a reduction, but to make it would be bad policy, because that might necessitate a reduction in the price of the bulk as well as the surplus.

The only alternative is to export the latter, and sell it in a foreign country at the best price it will fetch. Great Britain being the only large free market in the world, most of these stocks are diverted thither, and British buyers are offered bargains unobtainable anywhere else. How often do we hear the remark, "I do not know how such a thing can be made for the money." It cannot be, and never was, and the purchaser is getting it for less than cost price, in order that a buyer in another country may be compelled to pay for the same article 50 per cent. more than its value.

That such competition is unfair there can be no question, and it often bears hardly on small manufacturers engaged in the industries liable to be affected. Like many other evils however, it has its compensations, in this instance the advantage gained by the consumer. When a great store is opened in the midst of a number of small traders, whom it undersells, and perhaps in the end ruins, the law does not step in and compel it to close its doors or raise its prices. Low prices are regarded as for the public good, and the public is always on the lookout for a bargain. Underselling cannot be restrained by legislation and must work its own cure, which means collapse and bankruptcy if carried too far. The extent to which it can be carried on is therefore limited, and not even American manufacturers go on deliberately making goods to sell below cost in England or elsewhere. They would rather sell all they produce at a profit at home, than export a portion abroad at a loss; but it often happens that in the determination to keep ahead of the home demand, there is a regularly recurring surplus, which keeps a foreign, and generally a British market, slightly but regularly supplied. Nor must it be forgotten that there is another side to the question, for such goods must be paid for, and almost invariably are in commodities sold at a profit, so that while the producer is selling to the foreign consumer at less than cost price, he is probably purchasing from the foreign producer what he might not otherwise require, at a reasonable profit. On which side of the account the ultimate balance is to be found need hardly be pointed out.

Protectionists are well aware of this, and in order to blind the eyes of the victims of the system, exhibit apparent exultation over their ability to undersell foreigners in their own markets, without explaining the cause. No man who is not a lunatic or a criminal sells goods at a loss for which he can realise a profit, and few men deliberately manufacture goods on those terms either. So far from protection in this instance meaning the taxation of the foreigner, it amounts to a bounty, granted him at the expense of the home consumer.

There are times, even under sound economic conditions, when such sales may be necessary. Over-production is not confined to protected countries, and is an evil well known, though not so widely diffused, in Great Britain. The British manufacturer, under such circumstances, often recognises the inadvisability of flooding his own markets with cheap commodities, which they will require time to digest, and defer the period when he can supply them again profitably. It is then the consumer handicapped by protection has one of his few opportunities of striking a bargain, and it is then the wail of the protectionist is heard demanding higher duties.

Against the operation of bounties of this sort no country is able to protect itself, as when a sacrifice is decided on, duties, while intensifying, will not prevent it. But every Government can and should protect its people and its industries against deliberate payments, granted to enable cheap sales to be made in foreign markets. By all means encourage foreign Governments to grant these bounties, but let them be attached for the relief of the general taxpayer, and not confined to the individual consumer.

# CHAPTER VIII.

## TARIFF AND TAXATION.

Sources of Indirect Taxation—Proportion to Direct—Distribution of Taxation in Great Britain—Taxation in United States—Revenue Derived compared with Actual Burdens—Cost of Collection—Effect of Protection on National Finances—Taxation in France—Sources of Revenue compared with United Kingdom—National Expenditure—Cost of Debt—Why France is able to prosper under it—Taxation in Germany—Imperial and State Systems—Moderation of Debt and Taxes—State Contributions—Prussian Budget—Immense Advantages enjoyed by Germany over her Industrial Competitors.

THAT the incidence of taxation exercises immense influence on trade is an axiom which nobody would care to contest. Free traders and protectionists alike, subscribe their respective creeds, because they believe the system they support throws national taxation on the shoulders of those who ought to bear it, in the latter instance erroneously supposed to be the foreigner. We cannot do better therefore than inquire as closely as possible how the various revenues bear upon individuals and communities, according as they live under a stringent or a moderate tariff.

To begin with, let us acquaint ourselves with the amounts actually received from indirect taxation in the countries whose tariffs we have been considering. The years are not always identical, because I have chosen the latest for which I have been able to obtain the fullest and most reliable details, but as there have been no radical changes in taxation in any of the States for a year or two, the differences between one and another will not vary greatly.

From customs duties there was received, or estimated to be received, by

| | |
|---|---|
| Great Britain, 1895-96 | £21,040,000 [1] |
| United States, 1895-96 | 32,000,000 [2] |
| France, 1897 | 16,400,000 [3] |
| Germany, 1896-97 | 17,800,000 [4] |

Tobacco, included in the British Customs returns, falls largely under the head of internal or excise revenue in the United States and Germany, where the plant is cultivated, and in France it is a strict Government monopoly.

From excise revenue on commodities there was received during the same period by

| | | |
|---|---|---|
| Great Britain—Spirits and Beer | | £27,530,000 |
| United States—Spirits and Beer | £21,700,000 | |
| Cigars and Tobacco | 6,150,000 | |
| Oleomargarine | 190,000 | |
| | | 28,040,000 |

---

[1] Actual. The returns for 1896-97 show some increase, but as it is an all-round one, the proportions will not vary appreciably.

[2] Actual at $5 to £.

[3] Budget estimate at fcs. 25 to £.

[4] Budget estimate at M 20 to £.

## REVENUE FROM COMMODITIES

| | | |
|---|---:|---:|
| France—Alcoholic and other liquors | £18,600,000 | |
| Tobacco Regie | 15,250,000 | |
| Sugar, Salt, etc. | 8,650,000 | |
| Matches and Gunpowder | 1,600,000 | |
| | | £44,100,000 |
| Germany—Spirits and Beer | £7,140,000 | |
| Sugar and Salt | 6,230,000 | |
| Tobacco | 560,000 | |
| | | 13,930,000 |

Now we will contrast these sums raised from the taxation of commodities, with the total revenues of the respective countries—

| | | | Percentage. | Excluding Postal Revenue. |
|---|---:|---:|---:|---:|
| Great Britain, | £48,570,000 | £109,530,000 | 44 % | 51 % |
| United States, | 60,040,000 | 81,900,000 | 73 % | 92 % |
| France, | 60,500,000 | 133,250,000 | 45 % | 49 % |
| Germany, | 31,730,000 | 62,770,000 | 51 % | 52 % |

Great Britain, the United States, and France each include the gross revenue received from postal and telegraph service, amounting respectively to £14,300,000, £16,500,000 (the telegraphs are private property in the United States, and are therefore not included), and £9,000,000 (inclusive of telephones). Germany merely brings into account the net revenue out of gross receipts amounting to £14,700,000. In the first three cases therefore the percentage of indirect to total taxation is materially increased; in fact, in the United States practically the whole revenue is derived from commodities.

Most reasonable men will concede that the principal burden of taxation ought to fall on the shoulders of the wealthy, and that labour and industry should be as free as possible, and only contribute on acquired results. We will endeavour to find out to what extent this operates in the four countries we are dealing with.

The simplicity of British taxation enables us to arrive at fairly definite conclusions. There are but few commodities liable to duty, and the direct taxes are limited in number, so that if we can draw an equitable line between poor and rich, we may be able to apportion the respective payments of each.

A large proportion of the wealth and annual income of Great Britain is drawn from trade and industry, and by means of the income-tax returns we can form an estimate of the number of rich people in the kingdom. An annual return is made of the number of persons assessed under Schedules D and E, which include all profits earned in trades and professions, and incomes received from employment and pensions. Parliament in its wisdom has decreed that those in receipt of an income of £400 a year, or under, shall be entitled to a rebate of £160, and at this point we may fairly draw the line. It would of course be absurd to class people in receipt of £400 per annum as poor, many such, where they have only themselves, or at the most one or two others to support, may live on this amount in comparative luxury, and might well afford a liberal contribution to taxation. But most people with incomes below this cannot afford a considerable outlay in any one direction, and a certain amount of discretion is necessary in their expenditure. An additional payment, say in taxation, precludes them making an outlay on something else, and in this sense at least taxation becomes an important question.

On the other hand, there are many persons with incomes of over £400 per annum who find it difficult to make ends meet. Their families may be large and expensive, and they may be compelled to maintain a position in society which strains their resources to the utmost. They are consequently less able to bear taxation than others in the enjoyment of smaller incomes, but we may here reasonably set one off against the other, and class all under £400 as poor, and all over as rich. The former will include the vast majority of the middle class of the community.

For the year ending 5th April 1895,[1] there were assessed to the income tax in the United Kingdom of Great Britain and Ireland some 64,000

---

[1] This was the culminating year of a prolonged and severe trade depression, and the number of persons assessed at £400 per annum and upwards fell off to the extent of 10,000, showing how dependent the country is for its income on good trade. The figures under Schedule E were more extraordinary still, and exhibited the heavy fall that had occurred in the market value of clerical and similar highly paid labour. In 1894, upwards of 32,500 persons reported themselves as in the enjoyment of salaries or pensions of £400 per annum and upwards, a year later the number had fallen to less than 19,000. This represented a drop of upwards of £6,000,000, against which however there was, by way of set off, an increase in assessable salaries of under £400 per annum of nearly £2,500,000.

persons in receipt of £400 per annum and upwards under Schedule D, and 19,000 more under Schedule E, or together 83,000 persons. They contributed about £4,000,000 out of a total of £15,600,000, but for all that they constitute the majority of the income tax payers of the kingdom. The remainder of Schedule D, for instance, contributed to the revenue upwards of £5,000,000 on railway dividends, and profits from foreign, colonial, and British joint-stock undertakings, the great bulk of which is drawn by the trading and professional classes. Schedule C, under which another £1,200,000 was contributed, also falls largely upon this class, both directly and indirectly, as it represents dividends from consols and any other Government stocks and annuities, large amounts of which are held by banks, insurance companies, and other undertakings assessed under Schedule D. It owns too a great deal of property, both in land and houses, upon which the tax is paid under other schedules for which it is impossible to make any return of persons. There are numerous incomes, both large and small, enjoyed by persons not in any trade, profession, or employment; but if we state the number in receipt of over £400 at another 40,000, we are probably going beyond the mark. On the other hand, the 64,000 assessments referred to, included firms and private companies, embracing in many instances more than one individual. If then we say that the number of individuals in the

United Kingdom in the enjoyment of an annual income of £400 and upwards is 150,000, we are probably not very far wrong. Possibly in years of great trade activity there may be ten or even twenty per cent. more.

These 150,000 persons have many others dependent on them. A family is generally supposed to average five persons, but in the case of rich people there are invariably a number of relations desirous of being included within the charmed circle. But again, many such families include more than one income tax payer. As if I err at all, I am desirous of doing so by over- rather than under- estimating the numbers of the wealthy, I will assume that each income tax payer represents nine others besides himself, from the new-born babe to the centenarian, and that consequently the wealthy people in the kingdom in the classification I have adopted number 1,500,000. As the total population is now about 40,000,000, that would leave 38,500,000 to come under the head of the other classification of poor, that is from the pauper to the recipient of a competency of £400 per annum. The percentages are $3\frac{3}{4}$ and $96\frac{1}{4}$ respectively.

I will now allocate in tabular form the £92,550,000 actually raised by taxation in 1895-96 between these two classes, and then state the reasons which have induced me to divide the total amounts in this particular way:—

|  | Rich. | Poor. |
|---|---|---|
| Imported Spirits—Rum, | £50,000 | £2,030,000 |
| Brandy, | 500,000 | 875,000 |
| Gin, | 10,000 | 160,000 |
| Unenumerated, | 50,000 | 700,000 |
| Liqueurs and perfumed Spirits, | 35,000 | ... |
| British Spirits, | 800,000 | 15,580,000 |
| Beer, | 300,000 | 10,850,000 |
| Wine, | 1,000,000 | 250,000 |
| Cigars, | 450,000 | 100,000 |
| Tobacco, | 350,000 | 9,850,000 |
| Customs Sundries, and Warehouse Charges, | 25,000 | 50,000 |
| [1] Licences — Brewers, Distillers, and Tobacco Manufacturers, | 35,000 | ... |
| Liquor Retailers, | 1,500,000 | 500,000 |
| Tobacco Retailers, | 10,000 | 70,000 |
| Auctioneers, Pawnbrokers, and Plate Dealers, | 150,000 | 30,000 |
| Hawkers, | ... | 20,000 |
| Gun, Game, Servants, Carriages, Armorial Bearings, etc., | 930,000 | 80,000 |
| Dog, | 100,000 | 400,000 |
| Tea, | 150,000 | 3,600,000 |
| Coffee, Cocoa, and Chicory, | 175,000 | 175,000 |
| Dried Fruits, | 200,000 | 200,000 |
| Estate, Legacy, & Succession Duties, | 13,600,000 | 500,000 |
| Income Tax, | 14,000,000 | 2,000,000 |
| Land Tax, | 1,000,000 | 20,000 |
| Stamps, | 7,000,000 | 340,000 |
| House Duty, | 1,000,000 | 490,000 |
| Railway Passenger Duty, | 260,000 | ... |
|  | £43,680,000 | £48,870,000 |

[1] Practically the entire revenue derived from licences is devoted to the relief of local taxation, the Imperial Exchequer having benefited to the extent of less than £250,000 of the total.

This is fairly equally divided, the proportions being respectively 47½ per cent. and 52½ per cent.; that is, some 4 per cent. of the population pay rather less than half the total taxation, and the remainder is contributed by the other 96 per cent. It is worth noting that this 52½ per cent. corresponds very closely with the 51 per cent. derived from indirect taxation, as shown on page 239. So that it may be said roughly that the poor pay now all the indirect, the rich all the direct taxes.

There can be no doubt that the 4 per cent. possess more than half the accumulated wealth of the kingdom; a very large part of the 96 per cent. has none at all, and lives simply from hand to mouth. If we turn again for a moment to income tax assessments, we find that about 570,000 persons were scheduled under D and E, as in receipt of incomes between £160 and £400, and the great majority of all such are in trade or employment. At the outside therefore this class will embrace and represent 5,000,000 of people, leaving considerably over 30,000,000 of the population receiving or dependent on £3 per week and under, and it is not easy to accumulate wealth on that. In strict proportion to their means, the rich are still under taxed, but this is less open to criticism in view of the fact that what is paid by the poor is principally on beer and spirits. The inequality may be rectified to some extent by the reduction of the tobacco duty already advocated.

Reverting now to the table, rum is essentially a poor man's drink, and I have charged barely 3 per cent. in the first column. Brandy, on the other hand, is an expensive liquor, and of the two and a half million gallons consumed, I have placed the large proportion of about one million to the account of the rich. Foreign gin occupies much the same position as rum, but the consumption of it is trifling. The unenumerated is principally cheap stuff, worth less than a shilling a gallon, imported from Germany, but sweetened spirits and liqueurs are specialities of the wealthy.

A man does not as a rule indulge more largely in alcoholic drinks because he is wealthy, his greater responsibilities and probably superior education teach him rather to be abstemious. In charging under 4 per cent. of the population then with 5 per cent. of the spirit duties, I am making allowance for hospitality they may extend to poorer friends and neighbours, and not supposing that they themselves consume more than a fair average. Wine and cigars however are such decided luxuries, that I have charged them with by far the larger portion, though cheap wine, and particularly cheap cigars, are indulged in by the poorer section.

Tobacco, on the other hand, is the refuge of the poor, and in allowing the 150,000 highly rated income tax payers some 12 pounds per annum in addition to their cigars, I am probably providing them with as much as they ever smoke. Of the large number of retail licences throughout the kingdom, I have assumed that three-fourths of the payments are drawn from wealthy brewers, distillers, and property owners, or that the tenants are themselves men of substance. These fees are individually too small to be transferred to, or recouped from, the consumer.

Brewers, distillers, and tobacco manufacturers are invariably wealthy men; the great majority of tobacco retailers are poor ones. Gun, game, and carriage licences are indulged in almost exclusively by the rich, but a few of the poorer class own guns, and there is a licence on hackney carriages of 15s., the whole of which is not paid by wealthy car proprietors. The rich own more dogs in proportion to the poor, but the canine friends of the latter are very numerous.

For reasons which I have stated elsewhere, the tea duty is likely to be paid in somewhat greater proportion by the larger than by the smaller class, but I have contented myself by dividing it in their respective ratios. The remaining duties on consumables I have distributed equally, as with the exception of currants, on which the charge is only 2s. per cwt., they are only very sparingly used by the poorer classes.

Passing now to the direct taxes, we deal first with the estate or death duties. These were instituted specially as a charge on accumulated wealth, and payments on small bequests such as the poorer class are likely to make are calculated upon a very low percentage. The estates of deceased persons under £300 pay a nominal registration only, from £300 to £500, thirty to fifty shillings, and from £500 to £1000, two per cent. Most individuals possessing private estates of much over £1000, draw very rapidly towards the class enjoying over £400 per annum. On the other hand, small legacies are often received, which, owing to distance or absence of consanguinity, pay a heavy rate. The £500,000 placed in the second column will represent a very large capital sum passing every year in small amounts by death.

With the income tax we have again reliable figures to work upon. The 570,000 persons assessed at under £400 per annum, actually paid £1,550,000, and they undoubtedly constitute the great majority of all who are liable. I have added about a third to the amount for those who pay under other schedules either as agriculturists, or on investments and real estate.

Land is not often owned by poor people, and I have placed a merely nominal sum of the tax against that class. Great numbers of them likewise escape house duty, while those of moderate means pay on a more moderate scale. Mansions, especially if situated in the country, escape far more lightly than they are entitled to, otherwise this tax would be much more productive.

Stamps cover a very wide area, but the bulk of the revenue is collected from transactions more germane to the wealthy than the poor, or even the well-to-do. Bill stamps, for instance, form a very small tax on commerce, far too insignificant to be passed on, and besides, foreigners are charged with a considerable proportion of it on foreign bills of exchange. The Stock Exchange and public companies contribute largely, and transfers of real estate account for much more. I have charged but 5 per cent. therefore to one class, and the remainder to the smaller one.

These divisions are, of course, more or less despotic, but if they err in occasional instances to the extent of 5 or even 10 per cent. from the real facts, they still present us with a fair idea of the incidence of British taxation. It has been the consistent policy of successive Governments, for at least two generations, to lighten the burdens on the poorer classes, so far as they are not connected with the drink traffic, and to transfer them to the wealthier. The first serious departure from this was made by the Agricultural Rating Act of 1896, for though there are many persons connected with the landed as with every other interest requiring relief, this Act dealt it out in inverse ratio to as it was needed. The reversal, or even the suspension of the principle is however only temporary, and the political party which has been mainly responsible for taxation reform in the past will one day again be in the ascendant, and able to carry it in directions where there is still ample room for it to work.

In the meantime, the vast majority of the British population have but little to complain of on the score of taxation. A reference to the table will be convincing, that a man who is satisfied with mere existence need pay nothing at all. It is only when he begins to grope after comforts, or to plunge into dissipation, that he feels the hand of the tax-gatherer intruding more or less deeply into his pocket.

Far different is it in the United States of America, where an individual desirous of living in any kind of decency finds it almost impossible to escape the net, or to creep through the meshes when he is in. Practically the entire revenue is collected from taxation on commodities. The amount received from customs and internal revenue was upwards of $306,000,000. Included in the latter however are the licence duties paid by distillers, brewers, and liquor dealers, amounting to $6,000,000, and a similar tax upon oleomargarine of $265,000. This is the nearest approach to a personal tax, as the amount is too small to levy on consumers, the licence of a retailer costing only $20 to $45, and of the biggest rectifiers, $200. Consular and other fees amounting to another $3,000,000 are invariably added to invoices, and become as much a charge on the consumer as the duty. $3,000,000 profits on coinage, $2,000,000 from sinking fund on Pacific railroads, and $1,000,000 from the sale of public lands, cannot be regarded as taxation at all, and the $1,750,000 derived from a tax on national banks can hardly be called direct. Nor do the few remaining and insignificant items fall under that heading either. In the previous year's return of internal revenue there was, it is true, an item of $77,130.90 for income tax, but the Supreme Court promptly put the extinguisher on that, and the only practical attempt to tax acquired wealth was thus for the time defeated.

It is utterly impossible to tabulate and analyse the incidence of American taxation as we have done British. It might not be difficult to allocate the $12,000,000 paid on silks, or even the $22,500,000 on woollen manufactures. Nor, on the other hand, would it require much effort to distribute the $30,000,000 on sugar; but on what principle is the $4,000,000 on chemicals or on earthenware, or the $10,000,000 on iron and steel, to be divided? It is necessary therefore to proceed on more general principles. We may however divide the population of the United States into two classes much in the same way as with the United Kingdom, drawing the line perhaps a little higher up, owing to the greater cost of living, and making it $2500 per annum instead of £400. The percentages falling on either side would probably not now greatly differ.

Were we to distribute the taxation between the two classes on the basis apparent in the United Kingdom namely, the direct to the rich, and the indirect to the poor—we should arrive at the startling result that the latter provided fully 90 per cent. of the revenue, and the former nothing at all.

It may be fairly conceded however that some of the $160,000,000 of customs revenue was paid by the well-to-do and the wealthy. Imported articles are, as a rule, too expensive for the poor to indulge in, as the extravagant duties, particularly where they are specific and not *ad valorem*, shut out most of the cheaper goods, which the domestic manufacturer is prepared to supply at just a trifle less. But the duties actually paid at the custom house form an infinitesimal part of the taxation imposed on the American people. It may be that the small rich class contributes about half as much as the large poor one, against about equal proportion in the United Kingdom, but it certainly recoups itself many times over out of the protection afforded it.

The internal revenue of $146,000,000, derived almost entirely from beer, spirits, and tobacco, falls like similar taxes in England, principally upon the poorer class. These duties are lower, in some instances very much lower—on beer, $1 per barrel of 31 gallons; on spirits, $1.10 per gallon against 10s. 6d.; on tobacco, 6 cents per pound against 3s. 2d.; on cigars, $3 per 1000, taking 80 to the pound, equal to 1s. per pound against 5s.;

and on cigarettes weighing under 3 pounds per 1000, 50 cents. The consequence of these light duties on tobacco and cigars is that the revenue received is almost equally divided, and the number of cigars and cheroots which paid the $3 rate was 4,237,755,943, and of cigarettes at 50 cents 4,042,391,640, the manufacture of which must have afforded employment to an enormous number of hands compared with the similar industry in Great Britain.

But having said this much about the customs revenue, it is about all there is in its favour. It is not absolutely compulsory, but it is the millionaire, and not the pauper, who can escape it if he will. The former may carefully eschew imported articles, and when he wants an outfit go to England for it, and pay his expenses out of the difference in the cost. He may confine his drinks to tea and coffee, and sweeten them with Louisiana sugar, and may otherwise evince his patriotism by using only domestic goods when he cannot import foreign ones as personal effects, and at the end of the year, when he has contributed his mite to the national exchequer, he will take $4.90 change out of a $5 bill. The workpeople he employs may neither smoke nor drink nor purchase imported articles, but they cannot go to England for their clothing. They have consequently to pay the prices demanded by the home manufacturers and clothiers, which, as we discovered, would under the M'Kinley Act have cost very much more than abroad. Whenever a working man buys a suit of clothes therefore, or his wife a new dress, he may reckon that quite one-half of the amount is taxation. Did the money go to support and carry on the government of his country, there might have been a little consolation in it, but it was divided between the wool grower and the cloth manufacturer, and helped to make one, if not both, rich at his expense.

That is where taxation falls in the United States, and its amount is incalculable. What is the good of cheap tobacco, and cheap drinks, and free tea and coffee, if everything else a man touches is taxed over and over again to its utmost capacity? For it is rarely a single tax on any one commodity. As in clothing the wool is taxed, then the yarn, and finally the cloth, so in other things, the component parts which make them up have all to bear their share. We saw how far-reaching the chemical schedule was for instance, consequently most things into which chemicals enter are taxed through them. If any United States citizen is really anxious to know how much a year he contributes in this way, let him find out how much everything he purchases, except ordinary foodstuffs, would cost in England, add 10 per cent. for legitimate difference in price, and then deduct the total from what he actually pays, and he will arrive at something like the result.

Some things of course, are rather cheaper, particularly to the Western citizen. Breadstuffs and animal food are obtainable at prime cost. A well-known American ironmaster, a short time ago addressed a letter to a London journal, in which he referred to the *cheap* cost of living in the United States, and claimed that a pound sterling went further there in the purchase of necessaries than in Great Britain, and singled out items of food and drink which cost less. That is all very well as far as the particular commodities are concerned, but is poor consolation to the producers of them. There was no mention made however of sugar, enhanced to begin with by a 40 per cent. duty, since raised to 75 per cent., and then by an extravagant dividend for the Sugar Trust, nor did he refer even to that natural product, so necessary in so many households where neither gas nor electric light can be turned on at will, petroleum, charged for at any price his friends of the Standard Oil Company like to fix. Clothing of course is not food, neither are steel rails, and besides, the pool only collapsed after the letter was written.

Nor have we yet exhausted the evils of the system, for the cost of administration is in itself a grievous burden on the revenues of the Republic. To collect $146,000,000 of internal taxation, with its complex requirements of gaugers, brewery, distillery, and factory superintendents, and stamp distributors cost just $4,000,000, but $11,000,000 more of customs revenue added over $3,000,000 to the charge, and brought it up to nearly $7,250,000. The total expenditure on the customs service is returned as $17,969,000, and on internal revenue $4,203,000, but these figures are inclusive of drawbacks. The result is that the net revenue received from both sources is about equal, the cost of collection about double.

There are some most extraordinary details connected with this. At Natchez in Mississippi, the total revenue received in 1894-95 was $1.10. It took two people to gather it in, and cost $500. The same persons received their $500 for 1895-96, but on the last day of the fiscal year they were still whistling for the one dollar and ten cents. Two people at Annapolis, in Maryland, bagged between them in 1894-95, $28.45, and only charged $956.25 for their trouble. No doubt out of consideration for the fact that in 1895-96 they had no sport at all, they reduced their demand to $825.75. Teche, in Louisiana, however, enjoys the record, having had expended upon it $2624.50 without collecting a cent, though it is only fair to add that about 300 coastwise vessels touched at the port, and required some official attention. There was a slight amount of work at the other two of the same sort, but Galena, in Illinois, and Paducah, in Kentucky, each received $350 without apparently having done a stroke of any sort to earn it. There were fifty customs ports in which the aggregate duties did not reach $50,000, and there are innumerable instances where the amount expended was far in excess of that received.

New York is the great centre of the import trade, and there the percentage was reduced to a minimum. But 1932 persons were employed in dealing with the revenue of $109,000,000. The officials of the custom houses in London and Liverpool occupy a few moderate-sized apartments, and have plenty of elbow-room. The New York staff, with their wives and families, would found a colony which would make German mouths water. The M'Kinley Act provided for the appointment of nine appraisers at an annual salary of $7000 each, whose duties, no doubt, partly consist of superintending the counting of threads in tissues and fabrics; but to prevent so splendid a piece of patronage being made the cause of too much jobbery, it was stipulated that only five were to be selected from one political party. The post is no sinecure however, if we are to judge from the fact that for the last financial year over 20,000 protests were lodged by importers against the classification of their goods, and on the 30th September 1896 there were no fewer than 43,420 cases awaiting final decision, affecting some 200 classes of imports.

The manipulation of direct taxes for a like amount would cost less than half the money, as the machinery is already largely in existence for State and municipal purposes.

And what has high protection resulted in? Up

to and inclusive of the year 1890, there had been for many years a constant surplus of revenue over expenditure, and the national debt had undergone rapid diminution. It was necessary to put an end to that, and the ordinary way of doing it was to reduce taxation. That was not the protectionist's method of going about it however. In the first place, the country was searched high and low for the sisters, the cousins, and the aunts, of anyone who had supplied the federal troops with groceries during the civil war, and when found they were rewarded for the patriotism of their relatives by a more or less substantial pension. In a country where everybody is supposed to work and earn their living, the pension list for 1894-95 amounted to $141,395,228.87, and for 1895-96 $139,434,000.98, nearly half the taxation of the country. The recipients of over $100,000,000 are classed simply as "invalids," a very convenient designation, which might easily be made applicable to fully 99 per cent. of the human race.

The next process was to pass an "Act for reducing the revenue," but had the tariff of 1890 been termed "An Act to create annual deficits, and increase the national debt," the United States Congress would have had to be congratulated on the most successful legislation it ever achieved. The $85,000,000 [1] surplus of 1889-90 dwindled to

[1] The gross surpluses were larger still, the expenditure including the premiums paid on redeemed government bonds. The actual difference between ordinary revenue and expenditure this particular year was $105,000,000.

$27,000,000 in 1890-91, to $10,000,000 in 1891-92, to $2,500,000 in 1892-93, and then finally disappeared. The results for the succeeding years were—

| | | |
|---|---|---|
| 1893-94 | . . . | $69,803,260 deficit |
| 1894-95 | . . . | 42,805,223 ., |
| 1895-96 | . . . | 25,203,246 ., |
| | | $137,811,729 |

while for 1896-97 there will be a further one of many million dollars,[1] so that in four years, budget deficiencies will have been created amounting to some thirty to thirty-five millions sterling, without any practical attempt to stop the drain.

Such a state of things would be a disgrace to a semi-bankrupt South American Republic, how much more so to one of the richest nations on earth, counting seventy millions of people, and requiring not much more than half the revenue of many European countries with only half the population. Nor will posterity record any blame against the administration of ex-President Cleveland, during whose term of office this happened. It struggled manfully to impose a just and equitable tax to cover the deficit, but was defeated by those who will live in America, make money in America, accept all the protection

[1] In consequence of the enormous sums paid in customs duties in order to forestall the new tariff, the deficit promises to be under $20,000,000 against the original estimate of $64,500,000. What influence this will have on the finances of 1897-98 remains to be seen.

the American Government affords to life and property, and then resolutely refuse to contribute directly a cent towards the cost. Besides, no stretch of the imagination can bring the year 1893-94, when the greatest deficit occurred, under the Wilson Tariff, which only came into operation on the 28th August of the latter year. The forces which led to the disaster had been steadily accumulating, and it was only the old story of one man sowing the wind, and leaving his successor to reap the whirlwind. And now, almost identically the same Act, enacted in 1890 to reduce the revenue, is to be re-enacted in 1897 to increase it. We have had the result in practice, and no theory is ever likely to reverse it.

The moment we touch the subject of French taxation, we stand in amazement and awe at its amount as well as its ramifications. The Budget Estimate for 1897 is fcs. 3,331.902,951, or at 25 francs to the £ sterling £133,276,118, only a trifling portion of which is derived from sources other than taxation. No wonder the French people groan under the weight, though so far they have shown no signs of rebellion, and their prosperity is marvellous considering the absence of growth in the population.

The principal business of a French Minister of Finance is naturally to invent new taxes, and not to remit old ones. The laws under which the revenue is collected are consequently innumerable, and incredible though it may appear, money is still gathered into the Treasury under edicts passed during the Reign of Terror a century ago. One item is levied, for instance, under the law 27 Vendémiaire an II., another under those of 13 Fructidor an V., 19 Brumaire an VI., and 9 Frimaire an VII., a third under 22 Frimaire an VII., and 22 Ventose an VII., and so on. Indeed there is scarcely a year since the great upheaval of 1789 which has not provided fiscal legislation still operative. It can well be imagined therefore what a complicated machine French taxation is, and how it permeates the social and political system of the country and people.

The recapitulation of the anticipated budget receipts gives the income as follows :—

| | | | |
|---|---|---|---|
| Taxes and other revenues | Fcs.2,497,403,325 | say | £100,000,000 |
| State monopolies | 658,499,524 | ,, | 26,350,000 |
| State domains and forests | 50,620,750 | ,, | 2,000,000 |
| Miscellaneous receipts | 57,320,535 | ,, | 2,300,000 |
| Exceptional receipts | 265,000 | ,, | 10,000 |
| Revenue in repayment of expenditure, or for local purposes | 67,793,817 | ,, | 2,700,000 |
| | Fcs. 3,331,902,951 | ,, | £133,360,000[1] |

As these figures will convey little or no idea as to how the money is raised, I have for purposes of comparison with taxation in England prepared the following table :—

[1] Totals will vary slightly where the English equivalents arrived at by different methods of distribution are given in even money.

| DIRECT TAXES. | FRANCE. | UNITED KINGDOM.([1]) |
|---|---|---|
| Land occupied by houses and buildings | £3,200,000 ([2]) | £7,500,000 ([3]) |
| Landed estate | 4,800,000 ([2]) | |
| Property in Mortmain, and mine royalties | 370,000 | ... |
| Personal property, and door and window tax | 6,000,000 ([2]) | 11,800,000 ([4]) |
| Income tax on dividends, etc. | 2,630,000 | |
| Trade licence tax | 5,000,000 ([2]) | |
| Transfers of real estate | 5,700,000 | |
| Transfers of personal estate | 2,400,000 | 4,200,000 |
| Property dealt with judicially or extra-judicially by way of mortgage hypothecation, etc. | 4,500,000 | |
| Life settlements and donations | 900,000 | |
| Death duties | 7,750,000 | 2,500,000 ([5]) / 11,200,000 ([6]) |
| Stamp duties on insurance and transport contracts, cheques, receipts, and business documents and securities | 6,750,000 | 2,650,000 |
| Bourse tax on contracts | 350,000 | 150,000 |
| Horse, mule, and carriage tax | 500,000 | 500,000 |
| Dog tax | ... | 500,000 |
| Bicycles, billiards, and clubs | 200,000 | ... |
| Hunting licences | 300,000 | 300,000 |
| Drink licences | 550,000 | 2,000,000 |
| Military tax | 200,000 | ... |
| Verification of weights, measures, etc. | 200,000 | ... |
| Sundry excise dues and licences | 1,475,000 | 550,000 |
| | £53,775,000 | £43,850,000 |

# SOURCES OF FRENCH AND BRITISH REVENUE

| INDIRECT TAXES. | FRANCE. | UNITED KINGDOM. |
|---|---|---|
| Customs, statistical, and navigation dues | £16,400,000 | £21,750,000 |
| Proceeds of tobacco monopoly | 15,250,000 (²) | |
| Sugar tax (after deducting bounties) | 7,750,000 | ... |
| Match and gunpowder monopolies | 1,600,000 | ... |
| Salt, oils, candles, and vinegar | 900,000 | ... |
| Alcoholic liquors and beverages | 18,600,000 | 28,400,000 |
| Taxes on locomotion | 2,275,000 | 250,000 |
| Playing cards | 150,000 | 20,000 |
| | £62,925,000 | £50,420,000 |
| Postal and telegraph service | £8,600,000 | £15,180,000 |
| Telephone | 400,000 | ... |
| Railway receipts | 440,000 | ... |
| Domains and forests | 2,030,000 | 420,000 |
| Miscellaneous | 2,400,000 | 2,500,000 (⁸) |
| Reimbursement of expenditure | 2,700,000 | ... |
| | £16,570,000 | £18,100,000 |
| Total Revenue | £133,270,000 | £112,370,000 |
| Grants in aid of local taxation | ... | 9,000,000 |
| Net estimated national revenue | £133,270,000 | £103,370,000 |

(¹) Based on Budget estimates 1897-98. (²) These are the State proportions only. The gross produce is nearly twice the amount, the difference, together with the octroi duties, constituting the main part of local taxation. (³) Land Tax, Inhabited House Duty and Income Tax, schedules A and B. (⁴) Income Tax, schedules C, D, and E, (investments, trades, professions, and employments). (⁵) Real estate. (⁶) Personal estate. (⁷) Cost of material and labour must be deducted to arrive at net taxation ; upon a similar gross return in 1895 the actual profit of the *régie* was £12,500,000. (⁸) Inclusive of £750,000 interest Suez Canal shares and advances to Egyptian Government.

As this is not primarily a work on taxation, the figures for the United Kingdom require no comment at all, and those for France very little. In its licences to traders, the French Government endeavours to carry out its policy of protection for the small as well as the great, and does not, like that of the United States, favour the huge monopolies. A separate tax is charged on every group of articles dealt in, rental and number of employees are likewise taken into account, so that the universal provider gets in this respect no advantage over the small draper or grocer who confines himself to his own trade. The two great retail establishments in Paris, known to every frequenter of the city, contribute between them something like £70,000 per annum to this fund.

In the raising of fresh revenue, increased protective duties are out of the question, as they would tend to diminish imports and reduce the taxation already derived from them. Of late years therefore French Ministers of Finance have paid increased attention to securities dealt in on the Bourse, and a great outcry has been raised in consequence. Bourse operators complain that in one way and another they now contribute at least £6,000,000 per annum to the National Exchequer, though probably this is not excessive when compared with the United Kingdom. It is largely a tax, equal to about 4 per cent., on profits as well as dividends,—for instance, when railway obligations or shares are drawn for payment, the Treasury claims its percentage on the difference between the original price of issue and the par value. It is probably the constant increase of these taxes rather than their aggregate amount which causes friction and annoyance.

Though the manufacture and sale of tobacco is a government monopoly, the tax per pound is somewhat less than on the other side of the Channel. But the quality is so inferior, that foreigners accustomed to smoke the product of other countries rebel against using it. It is likewise retailed under State regulations and supervision, and the vendors are practically civil servants, who retain during good behaviour a position regarded by those fortunate enough to secure it as a pension for life.

The tax on locomotion is a levy on fast trains and other conveyances, whether for goods or passengers. Those content to travel or to send their merchandise by *petite vitesse* escape it,—it is the express, or *grande vitesse*, that provides this revenue.

To those acquainted with the political history of France, the smallness of the revenue derived from State domains must be a surprise, when it is borne in mind that at one time and another, nearly the whole of the landed estate of the country has been confiscated. Yet it is nearly all back again in private hands, and in no country in the world are the rights of private property held more sacred.

The communes also possess some landed estate, but it consists principally of forests.

The other side of the account does not really fall within our province, but having discovered how the revenue is raised, it will be interesting to gain some idea of its expenditure in the various departments of government to which it is allotted. We can do this in two ways, first by applying it to its actual purposes, and second, to the various ministries responsible for it.

I.

(1) Ministry of Finance,
 for Public Debt,
 pensions, etc.        . Fcs. 1,250,331,061 say £50,000,000
(2) Ministry of Finance,
 for maintenance of
 Service of President,
 Senate, and Cham-
 ber of Deputies   .      13,183,720  „        525,000
(3) Departmental Ser-
 vices           .    .    1,635,756.820  „   65,430,000
(4) Cost of administra-
 tion of taxes and
 other public rev-
 enues           .    .      374,017,993  „   15,000,000
(5) Reimbursements, re-
 stitutions & bounties       41,069,162  „     1,600,000
                          ─────────────    ─────────────
                          Fcs. 3,314,358,756   £132,555,000

II.

(1) Ministry of Finance Fcs. 1,508,647,807 say £60,350,000
(2)     „     Justice
 and Public Worship        78,055,086  „      3,120,000
(3) Ministry of Foreign
 Affairs      .    .       15,049,800  „        600,000

| | | | | |
|---|---|---|---|---|
| (4) Ministry of Interior | | Fcs. 76,629,262 | „ | £3,060,000 |
| (5) „ War | | 622,551,397 | „ | 24,900,000 |
| (6) „ Marine | | 258,167,273 | „ | 10,330,000 |
| (7) „ Public Instruction and Fine Arts | | 211,675,532 | „ | 8,450,000 |
| (8) Ministry of Commerce and Industry | | 26,624,244 | „ | 1,060,000 |
| Posts and Telegraphs | | 175,950,347 | „ | 7,050,000 |
| (9) Ministry of Colonies | | 83,874,840 | „ | 3,350,000 |
| (10) „ Agriculture | | 28,822,173 | „ | 1,150,000 |
| Domains and Forests | | 13,778,745 | „ | 550,000 |
| (11) Ministry of Public Works | | 214,532,250 | „ | 8,580,000 |
| | | Fcs. 3,314,358,756 | | £132,550,000 |

Neither of these divisions afford us a very clear idea of how this vast sum of money is expended, as comparisons with similar departments of the British Government would be altogether misleading, because both the duties and the expenditure involved are different. The pension list, for instance, amounting to over £9,000,000 in France, is under the Ministry of Finance, in England most of it is accounted for in the separate services. In the army and navy this is quite proper, because most of those receiving allowances constitute a reserve force, which would become active if needed. On the other hand, in the revenue departments and civil service, pensioners are not likely to be called upon for further duty, and the inclusion of their allowances makes the cost of working the departments in one sense appear greater than it really is.

Again, the Minister of Public Works in France is concerned almost entirely with the management of roads, bridges, rivers, canals, and harbours, work undertaken and paid for in England by local authorities. Half the expenditure of the department, moreover, is for payment of guaranteed interest and annuities to railway companies. The function of the corresponding minister in England is the care of all royal and government buildings, the cost of which in France is borne by the separate departments instead of being lumped together. The same remark applies to all stationery used.

The administration of justice in the two countries is totally dissimilar, though curiously enough the cost is almost the same. The Minister of the Interior is a more important official, and has much more far-reaching duties than even the Home Secretary and President of the Local Government Board combined, as the Government of France is essentially beaurocratic. Most of the expenditure for prisons is charged to this department, but some fcs. 10,000,000 is debited to the Ministry of the Colonies for the penal settlements there. There is no poor law in France as in England, and charitable relief has consequently to be controlled by the Minister of the Interior. Bounties and technical education are provided at the cost of the Ministries of Industry and Commerce, and of Agriculture.

Though the total revenue of France is only some 20 per cent. greater than that of the

United Kingdom, the cost of collection is about double, due principally to the multitude of indirect taxes, which are always expensive to work. The administration of the French custom house alone, with its army of officials, and laboratories so indispensible where the tariff is so far-reaching, costs just twice as much, though the duties paid amount to 25 per cent. less. The benefit of direct taxation can hardly be better illustrated than by the low figure for which it is worked.

There is no greater contrast between the two countries, than in their methods of Colonial administration. France has no self-governing colonies, and her foreign possessions are exploited for the benefit of home manufacturers and traders. They are, it is true, represented in the Chambers like any Department of the Republic, and rejoice further in separate budgets,—that of Algeria, for instance, is for the current year estimated to yield a revenue of fcs. 53,802,194 against an expenditure of fcs. 71,008,728, a deficit of nearly £700,000, which wipes out the apparent surplus at home. This is a fair illustration of the price paid by France for her colonies, more than compensated for however in the eyes of the people, by the trade actually done, or in prospect at some future time.

The military expenditure directly incurred in this department is £2,350,000, and every reader must decide for himself the equivalent paid by Great Britain. An appendix to the British Army

Estimates calculates the cost of the Colonial and Egyptian services at £2,545,415, but then large repayments are made, and there are many involved accounts to take into consideration. One thing however is practically certain, that but for the possession of India and the colonies, the military and naval expenditure of Great Britain would be but a very moderate percentage of what it actually is.

Assistance to primary education in France is only given largely in country districts and the smaller towns. The limit is fixed at a population of 150,000, and all places having a greater one than this receive only a small grant in aid, amounting in the aggregate to £175,000, a very different state of affairs to that prevailing in England, where the great centres of population absorb the bulk of the money. France, on the other hand, spends much more on higher grade education, and in the promotion of the fine arts, not excluding the drama.

The real difference between the expenditures of the two countries is to be found in the cost of the national debt, and the acquisition and control of the railways, as the following figures will show at a glance :—

| | |
|---|---:|
| Consolidated Debt . . . . . | £27,750,000 |
| Redeemable and Floating Debt . . | 10,250,000 |
| Railway Annuities and Guaranteed Interest | 7,000,000 |
| | £45,000,000 |
| Interest and Sinking Fund, British Debt . | 25,000,000 |
| | £20,000,000 |

This is amply sufficient in itself to account for the much heavier taxation necessary in France, compared with the United Kingdom.

Would any other nation in the world submit so patiently to so permanent as well as tremendous a burden of taxation? Yet the people thrive under it, and no Panama collapse can affect them for any length of time, and we have lately seen them busily occupied in putting Russia on her financial legs. Whatever general discontent may exist, there is little cause for specialising it. No one industry in France can say it is being ruined in the attempt to make another prosperous, and no individual can complain of being heavily over-taxed, while his neighbour goes scot free. If protection imposes a burden on industry, all suffer from it, if it really does stimulate home trade, all benefit by it. If the economic law of not imposing any restraint on production is broken, the other one of levying revenue on acquired wealth is rigidly put into operation. The entire fiscal arrangements of France are made up of apparent contradictions, and still from so many negatives, a positive is evolved.

The incidence of taxation in France is in fact much more analogous to Great Britain than the United States, and despite protection, the wealthy bear a fair, if not a full share of it. Civilisation is supposed to travel westward, so apparently do political and economical revolutions, for it is democratic America that, finding itself in the grip of a new tyranny unknown to past ages, is making desperate efforts to regain the control of its affairs in the interests of the great mass of the population.

There is a lesson to be learned from all this, and it is that tariff, and trade, and taxation are not everything. Civil and religious liberty have always counted for much, and are likely to count for more as the world grows older. France rests content, because her people control their own destinies. They can abolish protection tomorrow if they like, and whenever they choose to do so, the tens of millions of dollars or francs of industrial magnates will not divert them from their purpose. They are a liberty-loving, and law-abiding, though much official ridden people, but the officials are their own, and not a tyrant's. They have consequently relinquished the overturning of dynastic and political systems, and indulge only in the milder and more innocent dissipation of overthrowing ministries. Their steadfast adherence to their present form of Government has astonished their friends and confounded their enemies. Socialism does exist, but it has not permeated the body politic, and few deputies professing the creed find their way to the people's Chamber. Yet across their frontier, where taxation is lighter, trade expansion more rapid, and industrial prosperity apparently at high-water mark, political and social discontent is eating into the vitals of the nation. The moral is obvious.

With a debt of but slightly over £100,000,000, and an Imperial revenue of about £60,000,000, Germany appears to be more highly favoured than any other country in Europe. But the German Empire is but a congeries of states, kingdoms, grand duchies, and duchies, each with its own budget, and most of them with separate national debts. Any specific allocation of taxation is therefore an utter impossibility, as while the Empire presents an appearance of unity to the outer world, it is internally administered in its component parts, and in their financial arrangements many curious anomalies are presented. There is one settled principle however underlying all, and that is, the exclusion of indirect taxation on commodities. Within the Zollverein, which now embraces all the States and Free Towns alike,—the city of Hamburg having been the last to succumb so recently as the year 1888,—there is absolute free trade, the Imperial Government being the sole authority, and maintaining entire control in all questions relating to tariff. Whatever indirect taxation there is, it is responsible for, and the moment any commodity has passed the frontiers of the Empire and paid the toll demanded, it may be conveyed without let or hindrance through the length and breadth of the land.

The event which caused an immense increase in the national debt of France, enabled the German Empire to commence its financial operations with practically a clean sheet, and without in any way burdening the States. We find that the debts of the latter are very moderate, Prussia as might be expected leads the way with about £320,000,000; Bavaria follows a long way behind with £70,000,000; then Saxony with £36,000,000; Würtemburg with £23,000,000; Baden with £17,000,000, and the others with gradually decreasing sums, often less than a million sterling. The entire indebtedness of Germany is not greatly in excess of £600,000,000, and even this is more apparent than real, for it is largely a railway debt, and the interest upon it is met out of the net earnings of the State system. We can appreciate therefore what an immense advantage Germany has in taxation, and consequently in trade, by having little or no debt charge to provide for.

Despite her protective tariff, Germany draws in reality considerably less from indirect taxation than any of the other three countries. Her customs revenue was expected, according to the budget estimate for 1896-97, to yield £17,800,000. The percentage of duty on the total imports we can best see by going back a little. In 1894 the duties actually collected amounted to £18,400,000, and imports to £198,165,000, so that the rate was under 10 per cent. Of course there was a large amount of raw material included in this, about £84,500,000, little of which paid any duty at all, but food and live animals represented £71,850,000, and manufactured and partly manufactured goods the remaining £41,815,000. If we apportion the duty to the two last items, it is still barely 15 per cent., and as commodities like tea and coffee are rated heavily, the comparison, if these are deducted, would be still more favourable. We see again how comparatively slight protection in Germany really is.

The fact is, as I have previously stated, German protection is almost non-effective, except in special and retaliatory instances. Agriculture is more favoured in this way than any other industry, but that bone having been flung to it, it is left to take care of itself. All the choice pickings of railway privileges and reduced rates fall to the share of the manufacturing industries, and the agrarian party is furious in consequence. But hitherto it has howled in vain, and the German Government has refused to make food dear in the industrial districts of North Germany. True, the £70,000,000 worth is increased in price by the duty imposed on it. But one may travel a whole day through North Germany, and outside the towns see little else than wastes and sandheaps. We must go to South Germany and the Rhine provinces for the smiling cornfields and terraced vineyards, and the conveyance of their produce to the territories adjoining the Baltic and the North Sea would add considerably to its cost. Food therefore, after paying the duty, is not much dearer than if it had to pay inland carriage, and the imports through Hamburg and Bremen, and across the Russian frontier, go merrily on.

Of the excise taxes on internal production those on tobacco and beer are merely nominal—the latter pertains more to the individual states—and except spirits, sugar is the only commodity rendered dear by them. This is due more to the vicious bounty system than anything else, and must sooner or later come to an end.

Of the remaining Imperial taxes, stamps contribute about £3,000,000, a very moderate sum compared with either England or France. Posts and telegraphs yield a profit of £1,700,000, which is not taxation; neither is the £800,000 net railway revenue, nor the £75,000 profit on State printing, nor in the real sense of the word the charge of £280,000 on the State banks. The balance of slightly over £20,000,000 is made up by what are called matriculatory contributions from the States.

To consider these would plunge us in the deep water of what is really local taxation, which lies quite beyond our inquiry. Local taxation, whether heavy or light, devolves in almost every country on real and personal property, and is direct; even wealthy protectionists in the United States have not yet been able to devise means of getting out of that, and are compelled to pay it like their poorer neighbours. So that we see at once the taxation of Germany is, with the exception of a small amount, direct, and must fall on acquired wealth rather than upon industry in its incipient stages. Particular communities may be heavily burdened, but the burdens must be paid in cash by those who have it, and cannot be deducted from wages, or added directly to the price of commodities, though of course taxation, whatever form it takes, must eventually increase the cost of living.

It may be interesting to glance for a moment at the Prussian budget, which is the most important of the subsidiary ones. Its total in fact reaches £97,000,000, or fully 50 per cent. more than that of the Empire. But this is inclusive of upwards of £51,000,000 raised from railways and other public works, and after deducting £29,000,000 for working expenses, there is a balance to the good of £22,000,000, while the total charge for the debt, including sinking fund, is under £14,000,000. State domains and forests yield £4,000,000, and lotteries another £4,000,000, but in each instance the net revenue is only moderate. Direct taxation produces £8,000,000, and indirect £3,500,000 only, while the department of commerce and industry draws upwards of £6,000,000 from mines and salt works, but parts with most of it again in working expenses. The net burden of taxation is extremely moderate, and in this respect Prussia is but an example of the sister States.

Again we see the immense advantage enjoyed by Germany over her competitors, and the wonder is, not that she forges ahead so rapidly, but that she has not long ago left all her rivals in the rear. Great Britain got a long start and owns the capital, and above all, the Almighty has placed her in a geographical position, and provided her with natural resources unequalled in all the world. But these will not avail if energy and intelligence are not brought to bear in every occupation and almost every pleasure, for if the latter is allowed to undermine the physical or mental constitution, activity is an impossibility. Germany is still a long way behind in the race, and is handicapped by that most terrible and exacting of all taxes, the conscription, which withdraws her youth from active industrial and business life for the three years when they should be learning most. And she is honeycombed with discontent, created by her repressive political system. With these shackles struck off, Germany might surprise the world far more than she has ever done yet.

Tariff is the most potent of all influences in taxation, and probes to the quick the industrial life of a nation. Where it lies heavily on the poor, whether directly or indirectly, the struggle may be of long duration, but exhaustion is certain in the end. When it falls on the rich, or the surplus revenues and pleasures of the poor, it will be of less hindrance, and progress need not be impeded. But beyond the taxation necessary to secure the moral welfare of the people, the pith and marrow of true economy is to draw on abundance and reverence penury.

# CHAPTER IX.

## IMPERIAL CUSTOMS UNION.

Discovery of America — Spanish Colonies — Portugal and her Possessions—Germany in Africa and Oceana—French Colonies — Extent of Trade — Algeria and Tunis — Madagascar — The Egyptian Question — Relationship between France and her Colonies. GREAT BRITAIN :—Crown Colonies—Colonial Tariffs —Colonial Trade—The Basis of Union—Schemes Propounded.— Proportion of Colonial to Foreign Food Supplies—The Canadian Preferential Tariff—Distribution of Canadian Trade—Origin of Dutiable Imports—Analysis of Canadian Exports—Possibilities of Canadian Expansion—The Belgian and German Treaties— What their Denunciation may mean—Constitutional Aspect of the Question—Australasian Trade—Australian Federation—Free Trade in Agricultural Products—Australasian Loans and the British Trustee Act—The True Basis of Imperial Federation— Phœnicia and Greece.

IT is customary to draw the dividing line between the Middle Ages and modern times at the year ever famous for the discovery of America by Columbus, and in truth, 1492 did witness a new force introduced into human affairs which has altered and shaped the destinies of many nations. For nearly three centuries the Spaniards monopolised the American continent south of Virginia, with the exception of the Brazils, occupied and administered by Portugal, upon the double claim of prior discovery— accidental though it was—and the papal bull which granted her all territories east of a line drawn from north to south 370 leagues west of the Azores, within which part of the Brazilian coast actually falls.

From the first moment of the dissemination of the startling news that a new world had been discovered, or rather, as was then believed, that a new way had been opened to the uttermost parts of the old, which was in a sense true, the Spanish monarchy and the Spanish people alike regarded the territories they were so prompt in annexing as the special gift of Providence for their exclusive joint and individual benefit. And it was upon this basis that the administration was conducted, for while Government claimed a heavy royalty on the production of the colonies which proved so rich in gold and silver, it transferred to the merchants and manufacturers of the Peninsula the sole rights of trading—rights which after a while the rest of Europe challenged, but for a long time only defeated by surreptitious and contraband intercourse with the colonists.

We need not here go into the story of how Spain lost her colonies, or even how she manages to retain a fitful grasp over the one or two remaining. She has learnt little by experience, and that little grudgingly, and to-day does her utmost to render trade with the outside world as difficult as possible. In Cuba, Porto Rico, and the Philippine Islands, she imposes a heavy tariff on all foreign imports, while permitting almost all goods of Spanish origin to enter free, so that the cotton spinners and iron-founders at home are still able to keep some control over the markets. The duty on steel rails, for instance, is $16 in the Philippines, and $17.50 in Cuba; but then who ever dreams of railway enterprise under present conditions? Cotton fabrics are rated almost as elaborately as in the United States, and at almost prohibitive rates as far as the outside world is concerned. And if the Spanish crown no longer draws vast net revenues, it is because rebellion after rebellion has loaded the colonies with debt, for which Spain is ultimately responsible, and they have to be unmercifully bled to provide the interest.

Going back to 1894, previous to the outbreak of the recent troubles, and while trade was still in its normal channels, we get an idea of how the colonies discharge this indebtedness. It is not by sending their produce to Spain, because their exports thither were only 77 million pesetas,[1] while their imports amounted to 175 millions, a difference of nearly £4,000,000 due to the mother country on trading account alone. But these same colonies shipped to the United States, produce worth $86,000,000, and only took in return $23,000,000, though there was then a special convention with Cuba under which many United States productions

---

[1] The Spanish peseta is the same value as the franc, though the paper currency is now somewhat depreciated.

were accorded free entry, and others privileged to the extent of 25 to 50 per cent. below the minimum tariff rates.[1] From this source consequently there was £12,500,000 to pay the £4,000,000, and leave a very large sum for interest. The United States paid Spain £2,000,000 or £3,000,000 [2] of this direct, by sending more goods than received, and the balance formed a credit for Spain to draw on in any way she pleased. Cuba is responsible for the greater part of this sum, her balance due to the mother country being only some fifteen million pesetas less than the total, while the balance due to Cuba by the United States, principally for sugar and tobacco, was £11,000,000.

Portugal likewise retains a fragment of her once glorious colonial empire, as a reminiscence of the days when Lisbon was by far the wealthiest capital in Europe. Her hold on Eastern Africa, we know, is retained merely because the cession of the little strip of territory to any other power would be the signal of a conflagration, such perhaps as the world has never yet seen, and Lorenzo Marques owes its fame and vitality to rivalry and jealousy among other nations. But she still owns two little islands off the West African coast, St. Thomas and Princes

[1] These valuations are according to United States returns for 1893-94, and do not therefore quite correspond with the Spanish year. But the trade of 1894-95 was already affected by the revolution.

[2] Spanish returns say 79,689,000 pesetas, those of the United States 88,858,000. There is the same overlapping of years, but even allowing for that, the figures do not tally.

Island, and the tariff applicable to them is, in one sense, a curiosity. Nations, as a rule, like to retain the colonial markets for their home producers, but are less particular as to how colonial produce is distributed. An export tax of 16 reis per kilo. upon coffee, and of 12 reis on cocoa, equal to rather less than a halfpenny per pound, is increased to 30 and 25 reis respectively, if exported to foreign countries in Portuguese ships, and to 45 and 40 reis if in foreign ships. Other governments are satisfied to encourage colonial industry by opening the home markets, either free of duty, or at reduced rates; it has been left to the pioneer of modern colonial enterprise, to restrict as far as possible dealings of every description with foreigners.

Spain and Portugal, like the Netherlands, which also have important colonies in the east, fall beyond the range of our enquiry, and their systems have been introduced merely to provide us with the key necessary to unlock doors of more modern construction. For if some of the Powers which are to-day anxiously seeking to extend their foreign possessions and influence, have not entirely appropriated the antiquated ideas of these two monarchies, they have at least borrowed a good deal from them.

Of the two countries which now vie with Great Britain for colonial empire, France has been by far the longest in the field. Germany indeed only entered the lists so recently as the year 1884, and her exploits are soon enumerated.

She has acquired plenty of territory, but that is about all. If square miles counted for anything, then would Germany be an African as well as a European power. But at the end of 1895 there were fewer than 3000 Germans and all other Europeans combined, out of a total population of over ten millions, to be found in the German possessions, or spheres of influence as they are sometimes designated, throughout Africa. The latest estimated revenue from all sources is M11,000,000, or a little more than half a million sterling, and of this sum M 8,000,000 is contributed by the Imperial Government. The imports into the West African settlements reached in the year 1894, the latest for which returns are available, M 9,500,000, and the exports M 7,500,000, about £475,000 and £375,000 respectively. East Africa falls within the ivory region, and this valuable commodity constitutes the bulk of the export trade, rubber occupying the second place. The Asiatic element is strong among the native traders, and the currency of the country is the rupee. Imports in 1895 were valued at Rs. 6,750,000, and exports at not quite Rs. 3,000,000; but the value of the coin differs so materially in the various continents, and fluctuates so widely in its exchange value as well, that it is difficult to express these figures in the European equivalent.[1]

[1] The German returns give them as M 7,600,467 and M 3,247,485 respectively.

One thing is clearly evident, that a large portion of the import into these colonies is paid for by subventions from the Government.

The story of German settlement at the Antipodes is sorrier still, and notwithstanding the high-sounding designation of important territories, as Kaiser Wilhelm's Land, and Bismarck Archipelago, only some 280 Europeans have so far been attracted thither.

Whatever the German colonial system is going to produce therefore, it has accomplished little yet, and as an economic force may be dismissed. With its political aspect we have here nothing to do.

France has done much more than found a territorial empire beyond the seas, and it would be astonishing were it not so, considering that she began to build it up long before England became merged into Great Britain, and was her keenest rival.

She is impartial in her favours as far as locality is concerned. Algeria and Tunis on the Mediterranean coast of Africa, Senegal and Dahomey on the west, Madagascar and Réunion on the east, Pondicherry in India, and the great territories known as Indo-China beyond, Tahiti in the Pacific, Guadeloupe and Martinique in the West Indies, and French Guiana on the mainland of South America, are fairly distributed. Her hold on North America is lost, French Canadians are loyal to the British crown, and Newfoundland is only useful as an occasional bone of contention when a French statesman wishes to make himself particularly disagreeable, and takes as a basis the little islands of St. Pierre and Miquelon.

Self government is about the last thing France thinks of conceding to her colonies. They are supposed to exist solely for the benefit of the mother country, and to afford that outlet for the productions of French industry, which, as we have already seen, is denied them elsewhere. The colonies therefore, are not run for the advantage of the Government as such, as in the case of Spain. They are indeed costly luxuries, the Algerian budget alone having last shown a deficit of nearly twenty millions of francs, which had to be defrayed by the taxpayers at home. The vote for the Ministry of the Colonies, other than Algeria, is fcs. 84,000,000, although of that upwards of fcs. 9,000,000 is expended on the penal settlements, and must hardly be regarded as colonial expenditure. But, as I have remarked elsewhere, all this is supposed to be amply compensated by the commercial and industrial activity which it produces.

And what does this amount to? Leaving out the semi-European possessions of Algeria and Tunis, the imports of all the French colonies generally for 1894, the latest year I have been able to obtain them, were £9,000,000, while exports were

£10,000,000. But of these France provided only about £4,000,000 and took £5,000,000 respectively, the rest of the trade being done with foreign countries. That does not mean England or other European rivals, as in many places there is considerable local trade. Especially is this the case with Indo-China, for of the fcs. 77,000,000 of imports, France shipped but fcs. 17,000,000, and took only fcs. 28,000,000 out of total exports of fcs. 104,000,000, most of the remainder having been with China, Siam, and other surrounding territories, and consisted largely of rice, the staple product and diet of that part of the world. The commerce, as far as France is concerned, was consequently under £2,000,000, or less than 25 per cent. of the total.

British exports to these countries amounted to £195,000 or fcs. 5,000,000, principally cotton goods, but as the wall of protection is built higher, the trade steadily diminishes, and for 1896 was valued at £110,000 only, or little over fcs. 2,500,000.

From a French point of view nothing else is quite so bad as the foregoing. Nearly the whole export of Martinique and Guadaloupe, for instance, is shipped to France, and in the year 1896, for which unofficial returns are available, only fcs. 1,000,000 out of a total of fcs. 21,000,000 for the former, and a merely nominal amount out of fcs. 19,000,000 for the latter island, were shipped to foreign countries. But even here the import trade is only supplied by the mother country to the extent of about 50 per cent. of a total of some fcs. 45,000,000. Of the other half Great Britain has to be content with a beggarly fcs. 4,500,000, and the United States walk off with most of the rest. It consists principally of phosphates and other manures, and complaints are made that British shippers think anything good enough, while their United States rivals don't. Lancashire at anyrate maintains her share of the trade with the French West Indies.

All this is materially altered when we come to Algeria and Tunis, the former practically French territory, the latter controlled by France much in the same way as Great Britain controls Egypt. We have the complete figures in these instances for 1895; the imports into Algeria were valued at just over £10,000,000, of which £8,000,000 were of French origin. The exports were £11,500,000, and France took nearly £10,000,000 of them. Tunis is not quite so favourable, but then there are commercial treaties which prevent the exclusion of other countries from trading. Some of these have been got rid of, and the only serious rival France now has is Great Britain, and she is very anxious to induce the latter to relinquish her rights, so that Tunis may be as close a preserve as Algeria. Of £1,700,000 of imports, France shipped little more than half, and of nearly £2,000,000 of exports, took

£1,250,000, so that the influence or protectorate was worth something.

What I may have to say regarding the French possessions in West Africa will be more appropriate in a later chapter. I pass on therefore to Madagascar, and the principal business so far effected by the latest possession, seems to have been to borrow a considerable sum from the Comptoir National d'Escompte de Paris, with which to pay her conquerors part of the cost of subverting her liberties. Up to now there have been no returns from Madagascar as such, because the island has only quite recently been formally included among French possessions, and trade with the principal port, Tamatave, would be classed as foreign. Diego Suarez in the extreme north, and the little island of Nossi Bé, off the north-west coast, have however been classed as French for some years, and their trade in 1893 amounted to fcs. 9,000,000 of imports, and about fcs. 3,000,000 exports. These figures may form no criterion of the volume when the country becomes settled, and in course of time France no doubt hopes the trade of Madagascar will become worth a few millions sterling per annum; but has not the price paid—we will not say for the goodwill—been somewhat excessive?

The sum total of the whole is, that France exports to all her foreign possessions about £13,000,000 worth of goods per annum, and receives in return about £16,000,000 of colonial and other produce. Not very large amounts, but a fair percentage of the foreign trade of the country. We can understand what wistful glances she turns towards Egypt, of which she would like to make another Algeria. The imports and exports of that country for 1895 were £8,600,000, and over £13,000,000 respectively, but of these France only benefited to the extent of £1,000,000 in each instance, the United Kingdom of course absorbing the lion's share. But the present difference between Egypt and Algeria is, that France is as free to trade in the former under British protection as in the latter under her own. How long the British would enjoy the same freedom were the protection transferred, is not very difficult to predict.

There is no such thing as customs union between France and her colonies, the only phrase applicable is customs subjection. Every possession, whether near or distant, is under the French tariff, with often enough a special one of its own for the purpose of providing revenue for carrying on the Government. This however is generally light, and is frequently an export, not an import tax. French manufacturers want the full prices obtainable for their goods, and object to duties on them within their own territories. Thus in Madagascar there was a duty of 10 per cent. *ad valorem* imposed on all imports, but in August 1896 this was declared applicable only to foreign goods, those of French origin to be admitted free. All exports are likewise subjected to a tax of 10 per cent., except such as are specially scheduled to pay fixed rates,— wax, for instance, fcs. 20 per 100 kilos., and coffee fcs. 16, whatever their destination, this being supposed, as it undoubtedly is, a tax on the native producer, who receives so much less for what he sells. Similarly in Tunis, the revenue, raised principally from the monopolies of tobacco and salt, is augmented by duties of fcs. 12 per 100 kilos. on unwashed, and fcs. 20 on washed wool, of 2 to 6 francs on dates, and of fcs. 12.37 on olive oil. The import tariff is light, 8 per cent. on nearly everything, and 10 per cent. on wines and spirits. France in short tries to run two tariffs, and recognising that protection and revenue are strange bedfellows, keeps them separate.

Totally different is the system adopted by Great Britain towards her colonies. When dependent directly upon the Crown, a tariff is fixed to provide revenue, and is enforced against all countries alike. When self-governing, they may do as they please. In many of the Crown colonies the tariff is far-reaching, and few imported goods escape it, but it is light, and certainly not protective. Most of them are plantation colonies, yielding but one or two products, which it would be foolish for any other country to ship thither, and most of what they want beyond the natural foods must be imported.

A customs duty is therefore an easy way of raising the revenue, and not an unfair one. The number of people upon whom direct taxation would fall is generally extremely limited, and were it possible to collect it from the natives, the expense would often be greater than the income derived. Not even Great Britain runs her colonies as philanthropic institutions, and she wants her subjects of whatever creed or colour to contribute something towards the cost of the civil protection they enjoy. Many of them expend part of their savings on imported articles, and are therefore readily reached in this way. As a rule nothing is materially enhanced in cost except alcoholic drinks, which is as it should be.

But the great colonies of English-speaking communities frame their own tariffs to suit their own purposes, whether protective or otherwise. Foremost among them is the Dominion of Canada, and the pernicious influence of its great neighbour had until quite recently a most demoralising effect. Whether or not there is anything in the atmosphere of North America which disseminates the contagion of protection, all the people inhabiting it fall at one time or other victims to the disease. A cursory study of the old Canadian tariff is sufficient to show that it was a more or less faithful copy of the worst enforced across the frontier. True, there is nothing so utterly extravagant as 100 to 300 per cent. on woollens, and

100 per cent. on tin plates, not to mention other things. The supreme height to which the Canadian protectionist attained was 35 per cent., with now and again a higher rate concealed under mixed specific and *ad valorem* duties. The average on all dutiable goods imported in 1895-96, was just 30 per cent., but this is somewhat reduced if allowance be made for alcoholic liquors, tobacco, and other luxuries. The average upon woollens however was 32 per cent., while on silks it was only 30, and on linens 22. Cotton goods averaged 28, and iron and steel 25 per cent. No doubt the patriotic Canadian frequently gazed up with admiration and longing at the greater flights possible across the border, but with clipped wings these have now passed beyond his reach.

Moreover, the most obnoxious features of the United States tariff were reproduced in the Canadian, and the result was a childish battle. which grown-up men ought to have had too much dignity to play at. It is absurd enough for the United States to impose a tariff on Canadian cheese, but it attains the sublimely ridiculous for Canada to mulct the United States product at 3 cents per pound. If there is anything in which the Canadian agriculturist excels, it is cheese, and the export, steadily increasing year by year in quantity, though not in value, reached upwards of $14,000,000, occupying second place only to timber and its products, which must, as civilisation advances and population increases, become a decaying industry. In the same category we find apples at 40 cents per barrel, another production in which a little interchange would do no harm to either side, while the climax is reached in strawberries, raspberries, gooseberries, and blackberries at 2 cents per pound. As the last-named fruit is generally gathered in no-man's land, one wonders if it pays two duties when picked from the bushes growing just on the frontier; or is one side of them supposed to be Canadian and the other American? On the other hand, if there be anything in which United States craftsmen excel, it is in the production of bank notes, and forms for bonds, bills of exchange, and similar instruments; and well they may, for no nation has ever created more of the finished article. Yet they are taxed on entering Canada to the extent of 35 per cent. But if wanted in moderate quantities, surely it will be less expensive to have them mailed in small parcels under the ordinary postal arrangements.

Protection to manufactured articles was aimed against Great Britain quite as much as the United States, for it is very difficult for the latter to compete, when the cost of production has already been so greatly increased by their own tariff laws. Still Canada takes payment for the produce she ships to the mother country in manufactures, augmented in price though they are by 25 to 30 per cent. Woollen goods, and iron and steel, are the largest items in her import list, cotton and other miscellaneous goods follow, and made up a total value in the year 1896 of $110,000,000 from all sources, against an export of $121,000,000. Canada is not greatly indebted either to Great Britain or the United States, hence the fairly equal balance of her trade account. When the Grand Trunk Railway Company considers the time ripe to resume dividends to its shareholders, the farmers of the Dominion will have some new customers, and that should be an inducement for them to hasten it on.

Canada maintains a strict customs federation between all its separate provinces, and in that respect is at total variance with the great territories of Australasia. On the Continent itself, there are five separate Governments, and each goes its own way, totally independent of, and indifferent to its neighbours. Western Australia, as the most progressive just at present, owing to the recent discoveries of gold, has many wants to be supplied, and raises the means by a very general application of a stiff tariff. Butter pays 2d. per pound, cheese, bacon, and hams 3d., hay 30s. per ton, wheat 6d. per bushel, tobacco 2s. to 3s. per pound, cigars 6s., wines 6s. 6d. to 10s. per gallon, and spirits 16s. The rougher manufactured goods are admitted at 5 per cent. *ad valorem*, gradually mounting to 20 per cent. as they approach or become luxuries. But most kinds of iron and steel, and implements and machinery, are wisely admitted free, and the moment the Government of the colony can see its way to mitigate the full force of taxation, there are a number of other things which should be transferred to the same list. It is a tariff for revenue rather than protection, and a financial equilibrium is difficult to establish while a country is being rushed.

But to know what free trade really is, one must turn to the tariff of New South Wales. It contains just five items—spirits, wine, beer, tobacco and cigars, and opium—and few people would suggest that one of them should be eliminated. The duties on alcohol are high, but not excessively so, on unmanufactured tobacco 1s. per pound, and on cigars and cigarettes 6s., an example which the mother country might well follow. There are one or two other items the duties on which are not yet totally abolished, but on candles, oils, sugar, biscuits, and various other confections, are gradually reduced, until the last fraction disappears on the 1st July 1900. The only other instance of such simplicity within the British Empire, if not indeed in the whole civilised world, is the Straits Settlements, where duties are imposed on nothing but alcoholic liquors, and the bulk of the very moderate revenue required is raised from licences of various kinds. Singapore is the great clearing house between East and West, and its prosperity is bound up in the cheap facilities it can afford to its transit trade.

Queensland has lately followed in the footsteps of New South Wales, but still at a very respectful distance. By an Act passed as lately as the 5th October 1896, a great sweep has been made from the dutiable to the free list, which now includes agricultural implements and machines, as well as machinery of almost every description, iron and steel manufactures, drugs and chemicals, and raw materials of various kinds. There does not remain a great deal after this, and the rates do not in many instances go beyond 15 per cent. Alcoholic liquors are an exception, and unmanufactured tobacco pays 2s. per pound, but 6s. for cigars. The least satisfactory feature is sugar at 5s. per cwt. on raw, and 6s. 8d. on refined, and this is protective, because Queensland is a sugar-producing country. Tea and coffee at 4d. to 8d. per pound are less objectionable, but there are other comestibles which should receive the attention of the Colonial Legislature the moment there is a budget surplus to dispose of.

After Canada, Victoria is the most persistently protective of the British colonies, for while New South Wales does not consider the items of its tariff worth numbering, the dutiable ones in that of its neighbour run up to 321. Nor are they by any means light. If free trade between the colonies should exist in anything, it surely ought to be in live animals, for which the market should be made as wide as possible. Yet cattle pay 30s. per head, pigs 10s., and the great backbone of the industry of the continent, sheep, 2s. Breadstuffs fare no better, wheat, maize, beans, and peas are rated at 2s. 11d. per cental, oats and barley at 3s.—quite prohibitive. Dead meat pays nearly a penny per pound in a country where it is an important article of export; pork is 1¼d. There seems to be quite an Hebraic animosity against the unclean animal. Sugar is charged 6s. per cwt., but if it has had the misfortune to be brought up in a beetroot instead of a cane, it pays 12s.

Nor do manufactures escape any more easily. Boots and shoes run up as high as 5s. per pair; the carriage builder is particularly cared for, broughams, landaus, and, of all things, victorias, pay £40 each. Hats, caps, and gloves are all more or less heavily rated, glass and earthenware share the same fate as iron and steel, much of the latter being charged £3 per ton, or 25 to 30 per cent. *ad valorem*. The line is drawn however at machinery, most of which is admitted free. Wearing apparel of all kinds naturally suffers, materials being rated at 15 per cent., and made up and finished goods from 25 to 35 per cent. *ad valorem*. Truly, the schoolmaster has not been much abroad in Victoria, or if he has, it has been to little purpose.

Though New Zealand is nominally included in Australasia or Oceana, the great distance separating it from the continent, renders it practically independent of the fiscal and economic conditions prevailing there. It is perhaps sufficient to say that it maintains a tariff more akin to that of Victoria than any of the other Australian colonies.

Questions relating to their own tariffs do not greatly trouble British possessions in South Africa at the present moment. The colonists there may have much to say about that of the South African Republic, and some of the serious problems now pressing for solution have undoubtedly been intensified, if not originally created, by hostile fiscal laws and regulations. But where political excitement runs high, economic principles are cast to the winds, and there is little use discussing them while it lasts. It will be time enough to consider the fiscal union or otherwise, of South Africa, when the smoke has been cleared away, and race animosities allayed. A tariff war is bad enough, but one in which shot and shell play the most important part will be infinitely worse. Let every effort be made to avert that, and the other will some day right itself.

The same policy of free trade prevails in British India as in the United Kingdom, but opium and salt take the place of tobacco, and tea and coffee. The necessity arose a short time ago, to increase the revenue by other means than the sources usually appealed to, and at the end of 1894 an almost universal duty of 5 per cent. *ad valorem* was imposed on imports. The agitation among

British cotton spinners was so great, that at first cotton textiles were excluded, but soon after treated in the same manner. Almost the only exceptions are living animals, admitted free, machinery the same, and most descriptions of iron and steel manufactures at 1 per cent. Gold bullion is likewise free, silver pays 5 per cent., but to discuss this would lead us into an immense question. As a temporary expedient, nothing could be much wiser than to place a small tax upon everything, and there can be no pretence to any protection, though cotton spinners and manufacturers, believing their interests imperilled, succeeded in getting an excise duty imposed on the native production of certain qualities. But the classes of goods made are on the whole so totally different, that competition between them can hardly be said to exist.

Such, then, is a brief summary of the various British colonial tariffs as they are now, or have been until lately, and they present a chaos, out of which it appears utterly impossible to evolve order, or perhaps we ought rather to say uniformity. Nevertheless there is a strong sentiment in favour of federation, to be preceded and based upon a customs union, in which all the colonies, great and small alike, shall be linked together, and around the mother country. The importance of the trade between them cannot well indeed be urged too strongly, but after all it comprises but a fourth of the total foreign trade of the United Kingdom, and the last thing in the world likely to benefit either the colonies or the mother country is to place that in jeopardy.

The trade returns for 1896, combined with more recent events, may afford stimulus to those who favour such a scheme, without knowing exactly how it is to be brought about. Exports to British possessions increased from £76,070,000 in 1895 to £90,650,000 in 1896, the difference representing more than the total augmentation of British exports in the latter year, so that trade with foreign countries was actually less. On the other hand, imports decreased from £95,530,000 to £93,210,000, a percentage ratio in the one case of very nearly twenty, and in the other of barely two and a half. The whole of the increased imports, and some £2,000,000 in addition, were therefore drawn from foreign sources.

These figures are on the face of them extraordinary, and demand some explanation. That however is easily forthcoming, and when we find that the imports from Australia alone fell off by £3,960,000, while exports thither increased by just £5,000,000, the balance is at once largely redressed. The Australian continent has lately passed through the unfortunate experience of a severe and protracted drought, which not only prevented the grain crops from growing, much less maturing, but destroyed sheep literally by the million. Instead of exporting wheat, Australia was compelled to import it from the United States to feed her own people, while there was at the same time an enormous falling off in the shipments of wool and tallow, the two most important commodities of the country. These three products account for about £1,000,000 each, the remaining million being distributed over the various commodities more or less dependent on the same climatic conditions.

On the other hand, mining activity in Western Australia has made large demands upon British manufacturers for machinery, apparel, and the thousand other articles required by an almost entirely new country, and a few of the many millions sterling invested in this enterprise have been spent in this manner. And then, despite the unfavourable climatic influences, Australia is slowly recovering from the financial collapse of a few years ago, and filling up the gaps which are so apparent. Possibly she may go on increasing her imports from the United Kingdom, she will certainly at no distant date swell her exports thither.

From Canada and British North America, imports increased by £3,040,000, and exports by only £100,000, Canada participating to the full in the active demand experienced for wheat, owing to the drought in Australia and the terrible visitation of famine in India, while she likewise increased her exports of dairy produce and timber. British India goes a long way towards making up the balance of enlarged exports, cotton yarns and piece goods alone being accountable for

£4,000,000 over 1895, though still £1,500,000 below 1894. Here again special circumstances were at work, and they were of a political nature. A British Government, in order to provide funds for the Indian exchequer, had, as we have seen, to impose a 5 per cent. duty, first on all commodities imported into India excluding cotton goods, and finally on cotton goods as well. But an important section of the Opposition stoutly resisted this, and when it was lifted into office, and the leader of this particular movement appointed Secretary of State for India, Lancashire confidently anticipated the repeal of the duties, and held back shipments. But she soon found, that having by her votes helped to place the party of her special choice in power, it meant in its security to do little or nothing for her, and the retarded shipments of 1895 helped to swell the figures of 1896.

And finally, despite the political unrest in South Africa, British possessions there absorbed goods to the value of £3,500,000 in excess of 1895, and paid for them in gold, the net import of the precious metal being £4,500,000 in excess of the previous year, owing to the demand for currency purposes having been satisfied.

Some knowledge of the actual state of affairs is necessary to enable us to appreciate the difficulties of the situation, and I have endeavoured thus briefly to supply it. These difficulties are enormously increased, the moment an attempt is made to mould so many discordant elements into a uniform system. The German Zollverein, or the Federated States of the United States Republic, have been frequently referred to as affording a basis for a similar union among the countries and territories constituting the British Empire, but these examples may be dismissed. The separate interests of the States may be no more identical than those of many of the British colonies, but they are at least geographically homogeneous, and there would be something inconsistent in adjoining territories, living under the same political institutions and governed by the same laws, levying discriminating duties one against the other. Something of the sort does exist, it is true, on the Australian continent, though for all practical purposes the different colonies are totally independent of one another, and only subject to a common sovereign rule. And there is even now a determined effort being put forth, which sooner or later is certain to lead to something practical, to draw more closely together, both in their political and economical relationships.

Still, schemes have been propounded with the object of stimulating Imperial at the expense of what may be termed foreign trade. A few years ago a London financial journal made the very tempting offer of a thousand guineas for the best plan of a workable customs union, and something like a hundred and fifty were submitted for competition. Two eminent economists and politicians were appointed adjudicators, and everything possible was done to attract the attention of the commercial community, as well as all others interested in the question. It is not doing the proprietors of the journal any injustice, to say that the offer was made from a business not a philanthropic point of view, and was looked upon as an excellent advertisement. It would have proved so had any really practical suggestions been forthcoming, but the value set upon the actual result by the proprietors themselves may be judged by the fact that no reference is ever made in the column of their paper to the selected essays or their writers, and the thousand guineas have no doubt long since been written off as an unrealisable asset.

Still, journal, essayists, and adjudicators combined, did render a public service in demonstrating the utter impracticability of the idea. The premium was divided, and the two successful competitors represented the opposing schools of thought —one being a colonial protectionist, the other an English free trader. The idea of the former was, of course, that Great Britain should impose duties on all foreign produce which could be raised in British possessions, and admit the colonial free; the other that every colony should adopt free trade, and model its Budget on precisely the same lines as the mother country. Both arrived at some very extraordinary results. One, for instance, proposed to levy a tax on foreign wool which on the statistics used showed an import of £2,750,000, out of a total of £23,000,000, and would have produced a revenue of £80,000, or about one-third of one per cent. *ad valorem*, for which all the costly machinery of custom houses and certificates of origin would have had to be introduced. Besides, London is the world's wool market, and fully half the import is re-exported to foreign countries after leaving substantial commissions to English merchants and brokers, and employing a considerable amount of labour. And this was to be imperilled, if not destroyed, for what?—£80,000, minus the cost of collection, plus a grain of sentiment.

The other would have compelled West Australia to raise its revenues from beer, spirits, tobacco, and a few comestibles, and make up any deficiency by a land and income tax. Now all the statesmanship of West Australian officials is at present being directed to encourage agriculture in the colony, as the population flocking in such numbers to the mining centres is constantly threatened with something approaching famine. Industry is not yet sufficiently developed to have created any desire for protection among the colonists themselves, even if eventually they lean in that direction, but responsible ministers do express a hope that the moderate duties levied on food, principally to obtain revenue, will stimulate home production as well, and under the circumstances even free traders may complacently wink the other eye. There is no question about the West Australian agriculturist being able to make a living without any protection at all, only at present fortune tempts in other directions. To impose a tax on agriculture would be economical if not physical suicide.

Any scheme of Customs Union in which Great Britain is expected to accord preferential treatment to the colonies, must necessarily include almost every food product now imported into the kingdom free. The total value of these in 1896 was £157,000,000, of which only some £23,000,000 came from British possessions, so that over 80 per cent. would have to be taxed, meaning a corresponding increase in price on all consumed, including what was produced at home. We might be inclined to lend a more willing ear to such a proposal, were the colonies able in case of need to supply the whole. Leaving out India, the production of which we know is not capable of any sudden expansion, while we have just had the most lamentable evidence of the possibilities of contraction, we find that the colonies contain a population of a little over twenty millions, of which between eleven and twelve are of European origin or descent. Is it conceivable that these twenty millions of people, allowing for natural increase and liberal immigration, will be able within any reasonable period to supply the 157 millions worth instead of the 23 as at present, without taking into account the probable increasing requirements of the kingdom? There is room for enormous expansion, but then Australia, where there is most, may, like India, fail us, as it has done for two successive years. And while the attempt was being made, we should give mortal offence to those countries which now supply us with the 134 millions, which in turn would forge every possible weapon of retaliation against our other industries. Possibly by the time our colonies were able to supply us with 157 millions worth of food products, they would find we did not require the half of them.

Besides, if anyone is to be protected, surely the British agriculturist has the first claim. He frequently pays a high rent, and has suffered grievously from the heavy fall in prices of recent years. True, the shilling duty on wheat asked for by the colonist would do him no good, but if granted he would hope later on to screw it up to five, ten, or even fifteen shillings, and what is more he would demand its imposition on Canadian as well as United States produce. If the day should ever unfortunately arrive when the fiscal policy so steadily pursued by Great Britain, and under which it has prospered so immensely, is reversed, it will be the landlords and the home producers who will fill their pockets first, though they may be knocking for admission at the workhouse door a few years later.

The kaleidoscope, true to its nature, has however recently presented us with an entirely changed aspect of the question. The Dominion of Canada, from demanding concessions, has suddenly and voluntarily granted them. A Government steeped to the lips in protectionist doctrine has been swept away by a mighty wave of public opinion, and replaced by one pledged to free trade. Its advent to office was accompanied by circumstances which made the pledges extremely difficult of fulfilment, inasmuch as Canada's great neighbour was on the eve of adding to the stringency of its tariff in general, and of that portion of it applicable to the Dominion in particular. Suggestions that the time had arrived for freer commercial intercourse were roughly received, and almost rudely repulsed at Washington, and made concessions in that direction an impossibility. The Canadian Government conceived a way out of the difficulty, and executed it with a brilliancy that startled the world, creating at the same time a fresh supply of economic problems.

Nothing leads to such prolonged and bitter wrangling as tariff reform, and heavily defeated though Canadian protectionists were, they might have been safely reckoned upon to give an excellent account of themselves on every separate proposal for reduction of duties. With the exception of iron and steel, nothing of any importance in that direction was attempted, and even then opposition was averted by an increase in the bounties on home production. But a far-reaching change was effected by a single resolution, which affirmed—

"That when the customs tariff of any country admits the products of Canada in terms which, on the whole, are as favourable to Canada as the terms of the reciprocal tariff herein referred to are to the countries to which it may apply, articles which are the growth, produce, or manufacture of such country, when imported direct therefrom, may then be imported direct into Canada or taken out of warehouse for consumption therein, at the reduced rate of duty provided in the reciprocal tariff set forth in Schedule D:

(a) "That any question that may arise as to the countries entitled to the benefits of the reciprocal tariff shall be decided by the Controller of Customs subject to the authority of the Governor in Council;

(b) "That the Controller of Customs may make such regulations as are necessary for carrying out the intention of the two preceding sections."

Schedule D referred to, provides that from the 23rd April 1897 to 30th June 1898 a rebate of one-eighth, or 12½ per centum *ad valorem*, shall be allowed off ordinary tariff rates, and on and after 1st July 1898 one-fourth, or 25 per centum *ad valorem*, on all goods except ales, beers, wines and liquors, sugar, tobacco, cigars, and cigarettes.

Thus a decided movement was made in the direction of free trade in the only way in which such a step should be taken, namely, moderate, gradual, and equal reduction in protective duties, which afford ample time to the protected industries to order their arrangements and avoid disaster.

Had this reduction been unconditional, every free trader would have had occasion to throw his cap in the air, and rejoice over a great and bloodless victory.

But conditions are attached which make it necessary to pause and consider. Canadian protectionists may, and do, detest the measure, but dare not declaim too strongly against it, lest by objecting to concessions to the mother country—for such this resolution really amounts to—their loyalty should be called in question. English protectionists welcome it, because, though no equivalent has been asked, or is at present expected, they foresee the day when hints will arrive that something of the kind will be appreciated, and if not promptly taken, unpleasantness if not estrangement may ensue. To avoid this some concessions may be made, and the principle of protection, disguised under a fair sounding title, established. There are consequently many pitfalls for free trade to avoid, all the more dangerous because dug by itself.

What then are the possible, not to say the likely consequences of this step? Great Britain has everything to gain and nothing to lose, inasmuch as the reduction of 12½ and eventually of 25 per cent. cannot operate against her trade and industries. But on the other hand, no British free trader desires concessions from Canada which will tend to her financial or material disadvantage. Nothing is more calculated to loosen the ties of kinship or of friendship than a business arrangement in which one side gets the kernel and lets the other take the husk, and it is of much more interest to know how the arrangement will affect Canada, than what it will do for the United Kingdom.

The geographical situation of the Dominion favours trade relationships with the United States. For the fiscal year ending 30th June 1896, the statistics were :—

|  | Total. | United Kingdom. | United States. |
|---|---|---|---|
| Imports for consumption, | $110,587,480 | $32,979,742 | $58,574,024 |
| Exports, | 121,013,852 | 66,690 288 | 44,448,410 |
|  | $231,601,332 | $99,670,030 | $103,022,434 |

The total trade with the two countries was thus apparently almost equal in volume, but statistics in this instance are more than usually unreliable. For several months of every year, St. Lawrence ports are closed to ocean traffic; all the year round some of the most thickly-populated districts are more accessible to New York than Montreal. As a consequence, much Canadian trade with Europe passes in transit through the United States, and it is more than probable that shipments entered for them find their ultimate destination in the United Kingdom, while goods entered from them are of British origin. No official care can well obviate mistakes of this sort, and as they all tell in the same direction we may fairly conclude that the total trade with Great Britain is already in excess of that with the United States.

But its distribution is most unequal. Canada imports much more than she exports across the border, and redresses the balance by reversing the operation with the United Kingdom. What Canada and Great Britain alike aim at, is to transfer as much as possible of these imports from the United States to the mother country.

The moment we begin to consider the question of competition, the figures must be cut down very materially, because of the $110,000,000 of imports—$43,000,000 were free goods, and would not be affected by any tariff arrangements, preferential or otherwise. It is upon the $67,000,000 of dutiable goods only that Great Britain can hope to make an impression, while even from this, considerable deductions must be made for sugar and other colonial produce, which she can never hope to supply. It is in fact only in the great realms of textiles and iron and steel, where a preferential tariff can exert any great influence.

Again, we examine the returns for 1896, and analyse the origin of the textile imports:—

| | Total. | From Great Britain. | From all other Countries. |
|---|---|---|---|
| Woollen Manufactures, | $8,670,691 | $6,930,350 | $1,740,341 |
| Cotton Manufactures, | 4,631,960 | 3,357,293 | 1,274,667 |
| Silk Manufactures, | 2,557,318 | 1,896,893 | 660,425 |
| Flax, Hemp, and Jute Manufactures, | 1,523,576 | 1,414,221 | 109,355 |
| | $17,383,545 | $13,598,757 | $3,784,788 |

This class therefore constitutes more than one-fourth of the entire dutiable import, and Great Britain already monopolises 80 per cent. of it. Only in cotton goods do the United States claim any important share, and under this heading about $1,000,000 fall to them. Of the foreign woollens, about $600,000 were of French manufacture. Canada is particularly anxious to encourage friendly commercial relations with France, and can hardly desire therefore to eliminate this particular item. It is not in textiles that any great advantage can accrue to British trade.

Iron and steel however have a totally different story to tell, and of imports valued at $8,463,747 Great Britain only supplied $2,352,581, most of the remaining $6,111,166 falling to the United States. Undoubtedly a preferential rate of 25, if not of 12½ per cent., will transfer much of this trade to the United Kingdom, to the loss of American manufacturers.

Of the more important of the minor articles, foreign countries, again principally the United States, supplied leather to the value of $1,150,000, out of a total of $1,250,000, but this is a trade England can hardly expect to win. Foreign drugs and chemicals were responsible for $1,000,000 out of $1,250,000; glass, $900,000 out of $1,100,000; paper, $750,000 out of $1,000,000; and gloves $380,000 out of $650,000. On the other hand, Great Britain supplied $800,000 out of a total of

$1,250,000 for hats, caps, and bonnets ; and nearly $400,000 out of $550,000 earthenware and pottery.

Iron and steel therefore remains the one important item which can be transferred to British trade returns, and another £1,000,000 might be added to the existing exports of nearly £50,000,000. Were we to increase this to the extent of another £1,500,000 for other goods, we should still have but £2,500,000 additional, as the direct result of the preferential tariff—a welcome, but of a total of £240,000,000 by no means an extravagant, contribution to the export business of the country.

Canada will in one respect benefit even more than Great Britain, inasmuch as she will obtain some twenty-five million dollars worth of goods first 12½ and then 25 per cent. cheaper than formerly, but then the benefit would have been still greater had the reduction been extended to all countries alike. The Dominion has now an opportunity such as has never before been offered it, and may never occur again. For four years at least the cost of production in the United States will be enormously increased, and one of the first, as well as the principal industry to suffer will be agriculture. If Canada will reduce the cost of living within its borders to a minimum, no preferential tariff will be needed to ensure its produce a profitable market in the United Kingdom, for that of its neighbour will be unable to compete against it.

We have only to glance for a moment at the

nature of the exports, to convince us as to what the Dominion is best fitted for. In 1895-96—

| | | | |
|---|---|---|---|
| Animals and Dairy Products constituted | 33 | per cent. of the exports. |
| Agricultural products | ,, | 16 | ,, ,, |
| Timber and other Forest products | ,, | 24 | ,, ,, |
| Fisheries | ,, | 10 | ,, ,, |
| Coal and other Minerals | ,, | 7 | ,, ,, |
| Manufactures and Miscellaneous | ,, | 10 | ,, ,, |
| | | 100 | |

It is the land and the water, of which Canada possesses a boundless supply, wherein lies her wealth, and it is to the industries connected with them that every energy should be devoted.

The possibilities of expansion can hardly be exaggerated. The provinces of Ontario and Quebec contain 450,000 square miles, and the population, according to the census of 1891, was under 3,300,000. Eight States bordering on these two provinces, enjoying very similar climatic and other natural conditions, contain 330,000 square miles. Their only city of first-class importance is New York; and eliminating its population entirely, they had in 1890 over 14,500,000 inhabitants. Pennsylvania with its 45,000 square miles and 5,250,000 inhabitants might be added, were we only certain that any part of the Dominion provinces contained its mineral wealth. What an attraction cheap markets would be to these twenty or twenty-five millions of people, many of whom would find it annually worth their while to cross the frontier, in order to avail themselves of the privilege of the free import of $100 worth of personal effects, were convenient stores provided for their sale. Nor would it stop there, for United States citizens, experiencing the advantages, and witnessing the prosperity of their neighbours, would migrate permanently, and within a decade the populations, now as four or five to one, might be fairly equalised.

Why therefore should Canada not avail herself of the cheapest instruments of production obtainable? If the United States can go on supplying agricultural implements and tools at lower prices than any other country, why refuse them? With a population advancing by leaps and bounds, Great Britain will increase her trade with the Dominion by thousands, where, under a merely preferential tariff, she will experience difficulty in adding hundreds. The prosperity of the colony is the first and should be the sole desire of the mother country, if from no higher motive than that she will herself participate in it.

We have seen that of the total foreign trade of Canada in 1895-96, amounting to a little over $230,000,000, less than the odd $30,000,000 was with countries other than the United Kingdom and the United States. Nevertheless, with two of these countries serious difficulties threatened to arise, owing to the existence of certain commercial treaties. Germany and Belgium were each accorded the same trading privileges with British colonies as were enjoyed by Great Britain herself, and their nature is best explained by the clause of the Belgian treaty.

"Articles, the produce or manufacture of Belgium, shall not be subject in the British colonies to other or higher duties than those which are or may be imposed upon similar articles of British origin."

The clause in the German treaty, though somewhat differently worded, has precisely the same meaning and effect.

When these treaties were concluded more than thirty years ago, it was not foreseen that British colonies would ever desire to discriminate in their tariffs; it was indeed rather hoped that they would adopt those free trade principles, which would render discrimination obsolete, if not ridiculous. That we know has not happened, and in so far as they are incompatible with the full freedom of colonial legislatures, they are utterly indefensible, and not to be longer tolerated when a serious demand was made for their abrogation. Whether British trade with these two countries is one half, or five times as great as with the colonies, is of no consequence; if the principle be wrong, they cannot be maintained.

But whether the method adopted of abrogating or "denouncing" them was the right one, is altogether another question. The conferences between the Colonial Office and the Colonial Premiers, at which this course was unanimously decided upon, only came to a conclusion early in July, and notice to terminate the treaties had to be given on the 30th of that month. It is obvious that there could be no time for serious negotiation with the governments concerned, unless another twelve months were allowed to lapse. To have secured the elimination of the objectionable clauses, while allowing the rest of the treaties to stand, would have been a real diplomatic triumph, which would possibly have been denied to Great Britain by Germany at least, though her own statesmen would be the last to tolerate them, if not the first to admit their inconsistency. But the British Government apparently preferred a display of fireworks to the exercise of a little statesmanship, and if any sparks fall into the powder magazine, the consequences may be serious.

On the other hand, a delay of twelve months would have been of small consequence. As far as Canada is concerned, the trade with Germany is but small, and with Belgium utterly insignificant. The imports from the former country in 1895-96 were a little under $6,000,000, and the exports but $750,000, a balance on the wrong side of the account, as far as Canada is concerned, of over $5,000,000. From Belgium the imports were $920,000, more than double those of the previous year however, and the exports $100,000, or less than half.

Canada consequently has nothing to lose by the denunciation, but with the entire British possessions it is different. German returns for 1895 show exports to them of £5,000,000, but imports from them of £16,000,000, so that while Canada stands to gain £1,000,000, her partners in the empire stand to lose £12,000,000. True, a great deal of the import is raw material—cotton and jute from India, wool and tallow from Australia, which Germany wishes to buy in the cheapest market. I have shown in a previous chapter that Germany does not hesitate to retaliate and strike hard, even though it be to her own injury, so that including the £34,000,000 of direct exports from the United Kingdom, £50,000,000 of British trade is imperilled. German manufacturers and German merchants may cry aloud against a tariff war, but they may also cry in vain, if German agrarians, who hate them quite as much as their British rivals, have any say in the matter.

Had every persuasive effort failed, had Germany turned a deaf ear to all argument, and insisted on the whole treaty or none at all, then the course would have been clear. But that all this should have taken place within a fortnight or three weeks is scarcely credible.

This is hardly the place to raise an important constitutional question, but as it so closely affects the commercial and industrial welfare of the kingdom, I cannot forbear.

Up to the very eve of the denunciation of these treaties, it was generally believed that no action would be taken for another twelve months, and the first intimation that anything had occurred came from Berlin. No doubt the denunciation of a treaty forms part of the royal prerogative, and may be exercised at the discretion of the responsible advisers of the Crown. But with Parliament in full session, and every facility for discussing proposals submitted to it, should a decision of such moment be arrived at without consulting it, especially on a point not of high politics, but affecting the bread and butter of every constituent of every elected representative? Party ties may be strong enough to confirm an unwise action when challenged by the Opposition, where they would have been proof against all cajolery to take a false step. We may well mourn the decadence of Parliamentary institutions, when the British House of Commons is not considered worthy of consultation on a matter of such supreme interest to its members.

The position of the Australian continent does not unduly favour trade with one country more than another, and the consequence is, that by far the largest part of its over-sea commerce is with Great Britain. But the continent is parcelled out into five separate divisions or colonies, and each includes the dealings with the others in the returns of foreign trade. Out of total imports in 1895 of £43,000,000 [1] this local movement was responsible for no less

---

[1] These figures include gold and silver bullion, which is as much a part of the industry of Australasia as of South Africa.

than £21,000,000, and of the total export of £54,000,000 for about the same figure, as it was naturally only an interchange, and any difference would be one of valuation merely. Of actual foreign commerce, the figures were—

|  | United Kingdom. | British Possessions. | Foreign Countries. |
|---|---|---|---|
| Imports, | £16,300,000 | £1,700,000 | £4,000,000 |
| Exports, | 23,500,000 | 2,000,000 | 7,000,000 |

The total trade of Tasmania, generally included in the Australian continent, though not an integral part of it, is some £2,500,000, but most of it is with Victoria and New South Wales, only about £500,000 being done direct with the United Kingdom. On the other hand, the distance of New Zealand from the mainland draws its relationships closer to the mother country. Of the total imports of £6,400,000,[1] £4,000,000 were from the United Kingdom, and only £1,280,000 from Australia, the remainder being divided between British possessions and the United States. Of the exports of £8,500,000, £7,000,000 were directed to the United Kingdom, and £1,000,000 to Australia.

We see at a glance therefore how comparatively little Great Britain stands to gain by preferential trading with the Australasian colonies, and how much Australasia stands to lose, inasmuch as while its imports from foreign countries amount to £4,000,000, exports thither are £7,000,000, much

[1] Most of the trade of the Fijian Islands is done with New Zealand.

of which would certainly be jeopardised, and most probably destroyed, under a tariff war, while in addition Australasian produce in Great Britain would suffer equally from the boycott of British. Especially is this the case with New South Wales, whose foreign imports were £1,650,000, against exports £4,600,000. Germany and Belgium shipped £425,000 and £150,000 of the imports, and took £1,150.000 and £780,000 of the exports. We are thus able to appreciate the magnanimity of the Premier of that colony in joining the others in their demand for the abrogation of the continental treaties.

Yet a great deal can be done to stimulate Australasian trade, both internal and external, and if the former assumes such large proportions under the existing restrictions, what possibilities there are were they removed. It is too much to expect that while the colonies remain separate they will adopt the liberal tariff of New South Wales; for one or two of them it would perhaps be false economy. But at least a step in the right direction would be to abolish all duties on agricultural products raised in any part of the continent, and leave its movement free from one end to the other. Victoria would be better, not worse off, were her farmers enabled to purchase their cattle and sheep in New South Wales or South Australia, if they so desired, without having to pay the obnoxious duty of 30s. and 2s. per head respectively, and her people would often be better and more cheaply fed were there no duty of 3s. per cental on breadstuffs. Let her, if she pleases, retain the tariff on manufactures for the present; increased prosperity for agriculture will eventually prove the best weapon with which to strike off the remaining shackles.

This can be accomplished without absolute federation, indeed one of the obstacles to this desirable end is the antagonism of fiscal policy. There are political difficulties, I am well aware, but with these I have nothing to do here, though I do not for a moment believe they would be allowed to stand in the way were the question ripe for settlement. Several unsuccessful attempts have already been made, and it does not at present appear as though the conference held in Adelaide in March and April 1897, and adjourned to meet in Sydney in September, will end in much better result. Possibly too much is being attempted at once, and were the journey made by slow and easy stages the goal would be reached much quicker.

I have suggested one stage of that journey, there is another for which the road is clear.

It has long been a sore point with colonial statesmen and economists, that the loans of their respective colonies should be excluded from the advantages conferred by the Trustee Acts of the United Kingdom. No British financier has hitherto seen his way to admit them within the sacred pale, and there have been good reasons for it. Not even the Australian colonies all stand on the same footing, yet it would be impossible to accord one the privilege, and ignore the others. One or two have been somewhat reckless in their borrowing, and though they surmounted the crisis of a few years ago, and are all the stronger for it, their financial position still excites some little amount of distrust. The present state of Australasian finances we will best gather from the following statistics [1]:—

|  | Public Debt, 31st December 1895. | Debt per head of Population. | Spent on productive Works. | Revenue from productive Works. | Charge for Debt. |
|---|---|---|---|---|---|
| New South Wales, | £62,263,473 | £48.5/6 | £48,525,410 | £1,522,063 | £2,318,392 |
| Victoria, | 46,939,328 | 39.15/6 | 43,860,479 | 1,229,620 | 1,884,812 |
| Queensland, | 31,873,934 | 69.4/2 | 19,982,863 | 506,673 | 1,222,509 |
| South Australia, | 21,770,456 | 62.18/5 | 17,303,184 | 484,354 | 883.981 |
| West Australia, | 4,736,572 | 38.17/1 | 3,860,537 | No particulars. | 194,623 |
|  | £167,583,763 |  | £133,532,473 | £3,742,710 | £6,504,317 |
| Tasmania, | 7,779,145 | 49.8/- | 3,807,413 | 18,127 | 332.197 |
| New Zealand, | 42,271,888 | 60.2/4 | No particulars. | No particulars. | 1,738,056 |
|  | £217,634,796 |  | £137,339,886 | £3,760,837 | £8,574.570 |

There is thus apparently a wide difference between the financial position of Victoria, and say Queensland or New Zealand, but the indebtedness per head is not always the exact measure of it. There are local as well as national loans, and local and national interests in the various colonies are not always upon identical lines. Queensland, for instance, has borrowed for the purpose of lending to municipalities, which have thus secured better terms, while making the finances of the colony appear more adverse than any of the others. New Zealand has admittedly played in the past the part of the prodigal son, but even she has stood the

[1] Extracted from Burdett's Official Intelligence for 1897.

strain. Much of her debt has likewise been spent on remunerative public works, so that the total revenue from this source may be set down as at least £4,500,000 per annum.

Whatever credit the separate loans may enjoy, there can be little doubt that were they consolidated and guaranteed, jointly and severally, by the seven colonies concerned, the £220,000,000 would rank with the highest securities in the British Empire, and therefore in the world. Their combined revenues, apart from the return on public works, are much more than equal to the £4,000,000 required, but then under present circumstances such joint guarantee would entail greater risks on one colony than another, which it is by no means called upon to incur.

No British Government, or Chancellor of the Exchequer, would need to hesitate for a moment about conferring the advantages of a trustee stock upon such a consolidated security. Again let us see what such advantages would amount to.

The market prices and interest yield of some of the principal colonial stocks are as follows :—

|  |  |  | Market Price. | Yield. |
|---|---|---|---|---|
| New South Wales, | 3½ per cent. | 111 | 3⅛ per cent. |
| Do. | 3 | „ | 102 | 3 | „ |
| Victoria, | 3½ | „ | 108 | 3¼ | „ |
| Queensland, | 3½ | „ | 108 | 3¼ | „ |
| South Australia, | 3½ | „ | 111 | 3⅛ | „ |
| West Australia, | 4 | „ | 111 | 3⅝ | „ |
| New Zealand, | 3½ | „ | 108½ | 3¼ | „ |
| Do. | 3 | „ | 100½ | 3 | „ |

The higher yield of the $3\frac{1}{2}$ per cent. stocks is due, it must be remembered, to the fact that they are redeemable at par at various times, ranging from ten to thirty years hence, and the market premium will consequently gradually disappear at the cost of the investor. An Australian 3 per cent. stock is valued in the market at about par, consequently the yield expected by the investor is just 3 per cent.

Let us turn now for a moment to the values and yields of securities recognised by the Trustee Act.

|  |  |  | Market Price. | Yield. |
|---|---|---|---|---|
| Consols | $2\frac{3}{4}$ | per cent. | 113 | $2\frac{1}{2}$ per cent· |
| Do. | $2\frac{1}{2}$ | ,, | $105\frac{1}{2}$ | $2\frac{3}{8}$ ,, |
| Lancashire and Yorkshire Railway Debentures . | 3 | ,, | 118 | $2\frac{1}{2}$ ,, |
| London and North-Western Railway Debentures . | 3 | ,, | 119 | $2\frac{1}{2}$ ,, |
| Midland Do. | 3 | ,, | 119 | $2\frac{1}{2}$ ,, |
| Do. Preference . | 4 | ,, | 150 | $2\frac{5}{8}$ ,, |
| Great Northern Do. | 4 | ,, | 150 | $2\frac{5}{8}$ ,, |
| North-Eastern Do. | 4 | ,, | 150 | $2\frac{5}{8}$ ,, |

There is no reason whatever why a colonial trust security should not rank at least as high as a British Railway preference stock, that is, a 3 per cent. loan should be worth 113 to 115, instead of as at present par.

To grant £220,000,000 of colonial loans this privilege, would mean presenting a bonus of some £30,000,000 to the present holders, which they have certainly done nothing to merit. The benefit, or at least the greater part of it, should accrue to the colonies themselves, and this is quite practicable.

The first step necessary is the inclusion of such a consolidated loan under the Trustee Act. The next is for the Commission appointed by the colonies for the purpose, to offer to inscribe all existing loans upon the consolidated fund, on payment of say 10 per cent., leaving 5 per cent. to the holder, of which he would naturally desire to avail himself.[1] A reserve fund of upwards of £20,000,000 would thus be formed, which might be invested in approved British securities—not colonial ones—and the interest applied towards that of the consolidated debt, while the principal of the fund would become available in the unlikely event of any of the colonies defaulting.

Nor would the advantages be limited only to the present, as all future issues of stock would be on so much better terms. No such issue could take place without the unanimous consent of the seven colonies, and no such consent would be likely, unless the proposed application of the money commended itself to them. On the other hand, there would be no captious refusals, because the weapon of retaliation would stare the objector in the face. Joint control of the finances would necessitate some joint control of the railways and other public works, from which so much of the revenue is

[1] Some allowances might be necessary on stocks approaching maturity. Though the scheme may not be quite so simple as I have made it appear for the sake of clearness, it is quite practicable.

derived, and all petty jealousies and attempts to favour one at the expense of another would naturally if not necessarily cease. Drawn together by such common interests, the advantages of still closer union would become more and more obvious, and the day hastened when Australasia will present as united a front to the world as the Dominion of Canada.

India loans enjoying the virtual, if not the actual guarantee of the British Government, are already under the Act. Canada with her indebtedness of little over £10 per head, but with of course smaller assets to show for it, would be entitled to full and free admission, and might likewise make terms with her creditors for the concession. South Africa would need to consolidate on similar lines to Australasia, while the case of the Crown colonies would demand separate consideration, and possibly more liberal treatment by the mother country.

But after all is said and done, and every plan for the future threshed out, are not the forces still at work which have made the colonies so prosperous, and drawn them so closely to the mother country? There are advantages in trade between them not enjoyed by foreign nations, and worth infinitely more than a shilling a quarter on wheat, or half-a-crown a hundredweight on butter and cheese. The fact that the greatest commercial houses engaged in the business are identical at both ends, is one the value of which cannot well be overestimated. Everybody knows that in these days when profits on large transactions are often cut to the barest commission, an order carelessly executed means loss. A foreign house of the very highest standing will often strain a point to put one through, and if the market should happen subsequently to go against the buyer, there are endless complaints and reclamations which the seller will not entertain, because they involve more than his entire profit on the transaction. Such disputes are almost impossible between great colonial or Anglo-Indian firms, though there must frequently be mistakes and severe criticism. But the interests of the traders are identical, or vary very slightly; what is loss to the one is loss to the other, doubtful engagements are avoided, and a more scrupulous care taken in those that are entered into. What does it matter if a profit is made in Bombay, or Montreal, or Melbourne, if it is to be dropped again in London or Liverpool, or Glasgow? But a profit in New York or Buenos Ayres is a profit, however the venture may turn out at its port of destination.

No more striking instance of this can be afforded than by the tea trade. The present generation has witnessed its transfer from China to India, and various are the conjectures put forward to account for this revolution. The quality is more suited to the English taste, the markets are nearer, and many others,—but is not the principal one, that Chinese traders are notoriously dishonest, and that no Englishman has ever yet fathomed all their tricks, while an importer of the Indian growth receives it from his own firm or agent abroad whom he can absolutely trust? What is the use of seeing 10 per cent. profit on paper, and finding 20 per cent. of rubbish at the bottom of each chest, when there is a certain 2½ per cent. to be made elsewhere? And while the average American or European trader is not to be mentioned in the same breath as a Chinese, there are plenty of rogues among them, while even the most honest have to study their own interests first. The instances could be multiplied indefinitely, but so long as the close relationship referred to continues, so long will colonial produce enjoy an important advantage over that shipped from foreign countries.

The best imperial federation that we can have for the present is an unwritten one. Common race, common speech, common religion, are the strongest ties ever created, provided they remain elastic. Once destroy that elasticity, and they are as useless as the common band of everyday use would be under similar circumstances. It will be an evil day for the colonies when Great Britain ceases to be the greatest and cheapest producer in the world, and that position can only be maintained by keeping the cost of living down to the lowest point experienced in any civilised country. The moment that advantage is lost, she parts with the whip handle, and gets the lash about her shoulders instead. The same free trade policy which suits Great Britain so admirably, would equally suit the genius of her colonial subjects, but she has no intention of forcing it down their throats. When they adopt it, it must be by persuasion, not by menace, and because they are convinced it will be for their own best interests. But so long as they attempt to exclude British manufactures, they must not be surprised at British manufacturers seeking markets elsewhere; and as trade is after all only barter, with money as counters, some sort of produce will be sent in payment which may compete with that of colonial growth. The real way to encourage trade is to remove existing obstacles, not to erect new ones, and in that respect the initiative lies with the colonies and not Great Britain.

Classical allusions are not always particularly appropriate to modern conditions. But it so happens that 2500 to 3000 years ago, two nations were busy colonising. Phœnicia sent forth merchants and ships to trade with the uttermost parts of the then known world, and true to the Semitic instincts of the people, established settlements only where profitable bargains were to be concluded. The colonies were mere outposts, until political revolution led to the foundation of Carthage, destined in time to utterly eclipse the mother country, for which it never showed any sympathy.

Trade and commerce, with their attendant moneymaking and luxury, were the sole objects of existence, and neither Phœnicia nor Carthage have earned any gratitude from posterity, nor erected any permanent landmarks of civilisation.

Greece at the same time was bursting the bounds of her confined area, and seeking breathing space across the sea. The greater Greece in Italy and Sicily grew up and prospered, free from all political dependence, until Sybaris and Croton, Syracuse and Agrigentum, completely overshadowed Athens and Sparta, Thebes and Chalcis. The western cities were Greek in origin, Greek in language, Greek in religion, and Greek in sentiment, and the very factions which rent the Ægean peninsula were faithfully reproduced in the Italian.

Two confederations stand out prominently in Greek history. The Amphictyonic Council pledged the several states to mutual defence and mutual assistance. Yet what did it ever accomplish? During its existence, the Persian army under Xerxes invaded Greece and laid Athens in ruins. Even the glorious day of Marathon was won while Sparta celebrated religious festivities, and would move neither hand nor foot to assist her neighbour. The final triumph of Salamis was achieved, mainly because the Spartan ships were so hemmed in by the enemy, that they could not escape without fighting beside their Athenian allies.

The confederation of Delos placed Athens at its

head. Under it that city rose to the supreme height of her grandeur, and but for it the Golden Age of Pericles might never have been experienced. But internal jealousies within, and active hostility without, eventually brought about its destruction, and with it, the final overthrow of the Athenian democracy, and the almost total disappearance of liberty for well nigh two thousand years.

The colonies were never drawn into either, and consequently took no part in the strife of the mother country. Then it was martial, to-day it is political and economical. Yet when Greece was hard pressed by the Persians, or Sicily by the Carthagenians, each was ready to fly to the other's aid, without written or verbal compact, and the bond of sympathy was never wholly broken until the all-pervading power of Rome absorbed both into its system. Which stood the strain the best, the Amphictyonic Council, the Confederation of Delos, or the invisible thread which bound Greece to her colonies?

# CHAPTER X.

## The Balance of Trade.

Mistaken Notions concerning it—The United Kingdom Balance of Trade—How it is made up—Influences affecting it—Its Fluctuations—The Meaning of them—Remedies when unfavourable—The United States Balance of Trade—Wild Fluctuations—Their Principal Cause—The French Balance of Trade—Its Dependence on the Wheat Crop—The German Balance of Trade—Influences affecting it same as in United Kingdom—Trade Fluctuations in the Argentine Republic—Trade Movements in Japan—Unreliability of some Trade Statistics—How Balances are Settled—Gold Movements—The Balance of Trade in South Africa—Why Great Britain imports so largely from France—The Importance of the Question.

There is no more favourite method in the popular mind of gauging the prosperity or otherwise of any particular country, than by striking a balance between its imports and exports, and there are few more fallacious ones. The contradictory results sometimes arrived at stagger thinking people, who are unable at the moment to assign any sufficient cause for what may look extraordinary, and possibly even appalling figures. There is a party in the United Kingdom always pointing to the enormous excess in the value of imports over exports, and claiming that the country is being ruined, because it is every year spending so much more than it receives.

On the other hand there is another party, equally emphatic about the immense advantage this affords, and the proof it gives of the great wealth of the nation, which has so large an annual tribute to draw from foreign sources. Again, we hear of much national rejoicing in the United States when exports greatly exceed imports, and because 1896 was in this respect a record year the utmost confidence was expressed that the economic crisis was past, and that trade and industry were on the eve, if indeed the morning had not already arrived, of a great revival. Some explanation is necessary why one country waxes enthusiastic over an enormous balance of trade in one direction, and another over a similar balance in quite the opposite one. The fact is, the figures themselves prove nothing, unless taken in conjunction with the circumstances which give rise to them.

The foreign trade of the United Kingdom is the greatest of any in the world, and the balance of it, adverse or favourable, from whichever point it is regarded, is likewise the largest, except possibly in some altogether exceptional year. We cannot do better therefore than enquire into the origin of this, and detail the items which go to make it up.

With those who favour a big rather than a little balance, it is a general argument that it shows the extent of foreign indebtedness for interest and freights, and that the larger the balance is, the greater must this indebtedness be.

But though the world does owe Great Britain a very important sum every year on these two accounts, it is certainly nothing like what the excess of imports over exports has been of late, and we must go further afield for an explanation.

Appealing once more to the income tax returns, we get an idea of the amount due for interest by foreign countries. Under various headings, this reaches about £55,000,000, and has not greatly varied for some years in amount, though it has in distribution. But as the balance of trade for 1896 was £145.500,000, this £55,000,000 goes a very little way towards accounting for it. We may concede that the sum is too small, and does not represent actual foreign indebtedness in this respect. There is a fair amount of domestic income which escapes the net of the Income Tax Commissioners, fine though its meshes are, and it must be much more easy to evade it when income is derived from foreign sources. True, most of it is received in coupons, or in the dividend warrants of corporations domiciled or banked in Great Britain, and the tax is secured at first hand, but a good deal comes into the country by remittance in drafts or commodities, and payment on these is not so readily assured. But if we make a very considerable allowance, and say that one-half the recent balances of trade are accounted for in this way, we have still a formidable sum left to deal with.

The amount due for freight is not of so much importance as is often supposed, and it is utterly impossible to ascertain what it really is. The largest freights earned by British shipowners are on homeward cargoes, and these must be considered as paid by the British consumer, except in the important item of foreign goods re-exported, the value of which in 1896 was £56,500,000, and the year previous had been £60,000,000. But then not all the imports are in British ships. Twenty-five per cent. of the trade is done by foreign vessels, and the net freights they earn must usually be remitted to their owners abroad. Not always though, because there are many vessels sailing under foreign flags which are British owned. Trade with Spain, for instance, can only be carried on, except under great disadvantages, by Spanish vessels, but much if not most of the capital sunk in them is owned in England, and the freights consequently remain in the country.

But if inward freights are paid by home consumers, outward ones are of course equally paid by foreigners, and three-fourths of them will have to be remitted to this country, the remaining fourth, or whatever it amounts to, remaining in foreign hands. Outward freights however are of very much less magnitude. We have seen in a previous chapter, that of some 52,000,000 tons cleared from the ports of the United Kingdom, 45,000,000 consisted of coal, and this will not bear a very high freight, indeed it is often carried for little more than ballast rates, and the 35,000,000 tons destined for foreign ports earn probably not more than five to ten shillings per ton on an average. The remaining seven or eight million tons cannot represent a very high figure, even when rates are satisfactory. A considerable proportion is fine case and bale goods, and does pay stiff freights on regular routes, where competition is guarded against by combinations of "liners," but when we have taken credit for everything, we are still a far cry from the £70,000,000 or £80,000,000 we want.

There is another source of freight-revenue, namely that from British vessels trading exclusively between foreign ports. That cannot be very great, because all expenses connected with loading and discharge are incurred and paid at foreign ports; the seamen's wages are often spent in them, and there is little more to remit home than the net profit of the voyage, not a very killing sum in these days. As freights are so constantly varying in all parts of the world, the difficulty of making even an intelligent guess at the result we are aiming at must be evident.

There is one important item of indebtedness to Great Britain which is invariably overlooked, probably because the aggregate is made up of small sums. The city of London is the banking house of the world, and few people realise what that means. We know bankers' profits are considerable, and joint stock institutions throughout the country earn and divide substantial dividends among their shareholders. But there are large concerns in London, both public and private, some of the latter among the wealthiest firms in the world, which confine their attention almost exclusively to foreign customers, who, needless to say, have to pay, and sometimes stiffly, for the accommodation afforded. Now and again a big profit is earned in this way, but as a rule they are made in comparatively trifling amounts. A foreign banking or mercantile firm may desire credit in London, or in some part of the world where London can easily grant it, for say £50,000. The security is unexceptionable, and the request is granted for a remuneration of perhaps no more than a quarter of one per cent. That is only £125, and counts for little. But the bills of exchange fall due, and require renewal. That means another £125, and this may be repeated several times before the transaction is finally liquidated. We can form some little idea of the magnitude of the financial business of London from the returns made by its clearing house. In 1896, the turnover reached the gigantic sum of £7,574,833,000. In the same year the Manchester clearing house dealt with £193,573,500, and Liverpool with £120,406,000, or about two and a half and one and a half per cent. respectively. As purely commercial cities, Manchester and Liverpool rank little if anything behind London, so that upwards of ninety-five per cent. of the London business must be financial. Of course there is much "clearing" done for the provinces, but that is every year becoming less, as provincial systems are inaugurated and perfected. Part of it again is Stock Exchange business, but some of that is for foreign account. A small fraction of one per cent. on this turnover represents many millions sterling, and some of them have to be paid by remittances from foreign countries, which usually come in the end in produce or commodities.

And lastly, there exists a strong tendency to undervalue British exports, due principally to protection abroad, particularly when it is on an *ad valorem* basis. Foreign customs authorities frequently require a consular invoice, certified by shippers, of the value of goods on which they may base the duties, and consignees, it may be sure, demand that they shall be made out at the lowest possible prices. The value of British exports to Great Britain is the sum charged for them up to the moment they are stowed in the ship's hold, but declarations often go no further than their value at the works, possibly without either profit or commission. In order that no questions may subsequently be raised, exporters make their declarations of value which go before the Board of Trade tally with those they have made in consular documents, whereas the cost may be increased by railway carriages and handling expenses, by five or ten per cent., before they have left port. The Board of Trade exercises an independent and intelligent judgment in dealing with exporters' declarations, but how are they to know whether a a case of goods is worth £15 or £20, when the value of such goods varies from a few pence to a few shillings per pound or per yard? Some, perhaps many millions sterling, must undoubtedly be added to the value of British exports on this ground alone.

We see therefore that in the natural order of events, foreign countries have each year to pay Great Britain for interest on money they have borrowed, for freights on goods they receive, and for commissions on financial accommodation they avail themselves of. There are other claims of a more or less indefinite and fluctuating character. For instance foreigners, especially United States citizens, spend large sums of money on holiday jaunts in Europe, and particularly in England, but against this must be set the amount spent by Englishmen abroad, though not largely in the United States. Adding these to the undervaluation of exports, we shall arrive at a figure, certainly exceeding £100,000,000, but how much there is no means of estimating. Even now we have not by any means exhausted the influences at work in building up the United Kingdom balance of trade.

A nation which has such an immense stake in foreign countries does not allow it to remain stationary. It is always adding here and diminishing there, either by lending, withdrawing, or transferring, and the movement at some period or other reflects itself in the trade returns of the kingdom. If money is being freely lent abroad, it is not usually sent out in gold or silver, but generally in some sort of manufactured or other commodities, of which the borrowing country stands in need. Similarly when loans are repaid or called in, they are not remitted in bullion, but in produce, and not necessarily in the produce of, or direct from the country principally concerned in the transaction. The balance of trade therefore is made up quite as much by movements of capital, as by receipt or expenditure of income.

At one time we find British investors placing their money in foreign loans and undertakings of all kinds, and exports are in consequence materially swollen. Then defaults are made, and there is a suspension of a portion or perhaps the whole of the interest. That would tend to reduce imports, but confidence has been lost, and determined efforts are made to get hold of whatever portion of the capital is left. Instead of drawing five per cent. of the amount invested in any one year as interest, 25 or even 50 per cent. of the capital may be withdrawn instead, and require remittance, and temporarily swell imports instead of reducing them.

There has been a conspicuous example of this during the last few years in the great realisation of United States securities in consequence of the gloomy financial and economical outlook in that country, and though much gold has had to be sent, by far the greater part of the liquidation has been effected in produce, stimulating the exports of one country, and increasing the imports of others.

While it is absurd on the one hand to contend that Great Britain is being ruined by her excessive imports, it is false logic on the other to regard with equanimity the continued growth of the balance between imports and exports. It does not represent increased income, but rather diminished interest in foreign enterprise, and consequently the limitation of industrial expansion. That may be wise or it may be foolish according to circumstances, but there is always a tendency to go to extremes in either direction. Because some foreign investments have turned out badly, is no reason to regard all of whatever nature with suspicion, and because others are doing particularly well, is equally no reason why capital should be blindly and recklessly invested in all directions. There is a tendency just now to ignore foreign outlets, and to favour what are called home industries. The consequence is that there is a want of expansion in the export trade of the country, but nevertheless great industrial activity in supplying the demands created by this advent of capital into domestic ventures. The result in the end will be the same as in foreign enterprise, the movement will be overdone, and a great deal of the money lost. But the adjustment will not affect the balance of trade. Those who dispose of their interest in doubtful or rotten concerns, will have what is left paid them within the country, and the transfer of capital will simply be from one internal bank to another, without the real exchange of anything more than a few slips of paper, whereas had the same adjustment been effected with a foreign country, it would have meant the handling of something of tangible value.

A glance at the figures of the last quarter of a century will show exactly how this operates. Prior to the Franco-German war, the balance of trade against the United Kingdom had not varied greatly for a good many years from £50,000.000, and this was on a total foreign trade of about £500,000,000. Then there was enormous activity, and the total advanced by leaps and bounds from £500,000,000 in 1867, to £682,000,000 in 1873. But still the balance scarcely varied, exports grew as rapidly as imports. It was a time of foreign loans, and though each year the amount of interest indebtedness was growing larger, and necessitated greater imports to discharge it, new loans carried off British manufactures in sufficient quantities to compensate for it. Then followed a sudden collapse, when it was found that parting with much of the money was like pouring water into a sieve. Exports fell away rapidly because it was no longer possible to borrow to pay for them. Investors, on the other hand, tried hard to get some of their money back, and all sorts of foreign produce was imported, so that the £371,000,000 of 1873, had steadily increased to £411,000,000 by 1880. Instead of a normal balance of trade of £50,000,000, plus perhaps twenty or thirty millions more for interest on the new loans, it rose to £118,000,000 in 1876, £142,000,000 in 1877, and £125,000,000 in 1878, and these figures undoubtedly meant considerable withdrawals of foreign capital. Then the panic subsided, and as investors have proverbially short memories, the decade of the eighties proved a time of outpouring of British capital all the world over, and particularly into South America. The adverse balance steadily fell, and that of 1880 was the largest during the entire period. In 1886 and 1887, it was down to £81,000,000, and it will be in the recollection of many that these years witnessed something like a climax in South American finance, and the immense schemes inaugurated in connection with it.

This culmination however was not for a little time apparent. Immense contracts had been entered into, requiring years to fulfil, and the value of exports went on steadily growing, until in 1890 they reached the unprecedented figure of

£328,000,000. But imports had grown still more rapidly, and the adverse balance had risen to £113,000,000 in 1889, only to fall again by £20,000.000 the year following. They were years of feverish excitement, the commercial atmosphere was laden with some strange force which nobody could quite measure. Then followed an event which will render the year 1890 ever memorable in commercial annals, the Baring collapse, and the fall of the gigantic structure which had been erected on the foundations of the credit of that great house. Once more the object was, not to lend further sums to foreign countries, but to recover all that was possible from the wreck, and the balance of £93,000,000 in 1890 sprang with one bound to £126,000,000 in 1891.

There perhaps it might have stopped, but the crisis was quickly transferred from South to North America. No sooner had British investors decided to await a return of prosperity in the Argentine Republic, than they became alarmed at the outlook in the United States. The M'Kinley Tariff, in conjunction with the Sherman Act thrown in to secure its passage, was leading to an inevitable crisis, and a scramble ensued to realise American securities, which intensified the crisis by the immense withdrawal of the gold bullion on which the stability of the currency depended. The result, as far as Great Britain was concerned, was not only the piling up of gold in the Bank of England until the vaults had to be enlarged to hold it, but a steady growth in the adverse balance of trade as well, which reached £131,000,000 in 1895, broke the record with £145,500,000 in 1896, and, so far as the returns of the year are published, threatens to go one better in 1897.[1]

These great balances are distinctly unsatisfactory, and there is hardly a redeeming feature in their favour. They mean that a small proportion of the population, probably less than 4 per cent., as we saw in a preceding chapter, have such immense interests abroad, that in order to receive the income from them, much less transfer them home intact, they have to import £100,000,000 to £150,000,000 worth of commodities every year, a little, if not a large portion, of which would otherwise be produced by the remaining 96 per cent. But the remedy does not lie in protection. The hundred or hundred and fifty millions would have to be imported all the same, and would only be rendered dearer to the consumer by the amount of the duty levied on it. Nor is it to be found in the withdrawal and concentration at home of capital invested in foreign countries. That would only make matters worse. Nor again do any of the socialist nostrums of the present day meet the case. The difficulty would be there just the same, if these

---

[1] At the end of July 1897 the adverse balance is £9,000,000 worse than for the same period of 1896, and circumstances point to its growing larger as the year advances.

imports were brought over by the 96 instead of the 4 per cent. The one and only antidote, is the continued investment of capital abroad. If the interest received be reinvested, either directly or indirectly, in the country which pays it, that obviates the remittance of produce, or if the produce is exported, as will likely be the case, something else will be taken in exchange for it. Failing such reinvestment, other outlets must be found, in order that it may not be dumped down without an equivalent in labour being exported elsewhere.

This is by no means as impracticable as it may appear. The world is not yet played out; it is in fact only just beginning to rub its tiny fists into its half-opened eyes. The United States have a population of seventy millions of people; there is room for seven hundred, and then there need be no crowding. Canada has an area as large as the United States, and five millions of souls distributed over it. The climatic conditions of a great portion of the territory are unfavourable for settlement, but fifty millions of people can lose themselves in one of the finest and most bracing climates in the world, every breath of which infuses energy. The capabilities of Australia, and Africa, and South America, nobody yet knows. British India has two hundred and seventy millions of people, and a shorter railway system than the United Kingdom with barely forty. Need we go farther, or draw the moral?

The United States, France, and Germany, may thrive upon a trade on which Great Britain would starve. The first has no foreign income to receive; it has to pay a very considerable sum instead. France and Germany have some, but not a great deal, and the competition of foreign products is not on so large a scale. The British industrial population may to a considerable extent be fed and clothed with imports from abroad, but they must have money to buy both the food and the clothing. That must be largely earned by supplying foreign countries with British productions, and money is wanted to pay for them. Four per cent. of the British population have it, and must lend it, not recklessly and under compulsion, but judiciously with the hope of gain. To encourage purely domestic industry at the expense of foreign exports is to commit industrial suicide. The one is good and should be promoted, the other is the nation's life blood. Protection may be good enough for the United States, for France, or for Germany. Cheap production is the first of all essentials for Great Britain, and Great Britain must not touch the unclean thing.

The day will come when a balance of £150,000,000 against the United Kingdom will be a normal and a satisfactory one. But it will have to be on a total trade some hundreds of millions greater than at present. Besides, it may mean in quantity considerably less than it does now, as commodities may again one day be on a much higher basis of value. The ability of Great Britain to purchase big and cheap lines from the foreigner is by no means an unmixed blessing. Suppose, for example, the balance of trade in favour of the country to be £100,000,000, and that it must be taken in wheat, of which we will say, likewise simply for argument, that the consumptive demand is 100,000,000 quarters. Were the price twenty shillings per quarter, the whole hundred million quarters would have to be imported, but if forty shillings, then only fifty million quarters, and the other fifty millions would either have to be produced at home, or purchased in exchange for home manufactures which would employ an equivalent amount of labour. A country like England therefore, which has annually to import so many products which enter into competition with her own, should do everything possible to encourage a moderately high level of prices, rather than a very low one.

The United States being a debtor, not a creditor country, we naturally look for the balance of trade on the opposite side of the ledger, nor do we look in vain. We might only be misled by going too far back into the figures of United States imports and exports, because until 1879 they were complicated by the greenback currency, which fluctuated in value until specie payments were resumed. Since that year however, we find the movements very much more erratic than any in the United Kingdom, nor is the explanation always quite so patent. It is considered a matter for congratulation when exports greatly exceed imports in value, and the balance of trade is supposed to be favourable. That by no means follows, and it may be no more satisfactory than a large balance the other way in the United Kingdom. It may simply mean draining the country to pay its debts.

Were the trade returns compiled for the calendar year, they would often be more erratic still, because seasons would overlap. United States exports are principally of agricultural produce, and there is little harvesting done before July 1st, and the product of what there is scarcely falls into the returns. By making the fiscal year to end on June 30th therefore, the comparisons are fairer, because they represent entire seasons.

In 1880-81 the balance in favour of the United States was $260,000,000, while the year following it sank to $26,000,000. The reason of the former was however eminently satisfactory. Europe had suffered from a partial failure of grain crops, the United States in that, as in the year previous, had reaped a bountiful harvest, and the value of the exports of breadstuffs during the two years touched the highest figures ever up to then recorded, $288,000,000 and $270,000,000 respectively. This has never been exceeded, except in 1892, when European crops again proved disastrous, and the figure rose to

$300,000,000. The United States in fact sold their breadstuffs for hard cash, and the net import of gold reached nearly $100,000,000, the country being fully that much to the good. In 1882, when matters had assumed a more normal aspect, very little gold was required to redress the balance one way or the other.

The climatic conditions of 1881 were repeated in 1892, and as far as the United States were concerned, resulted in a favourable balance of $203,000,000, while the year previous it had been under $40,000,000, and the year later was transferred to the other side of the account to the extent of $18,000,000. But there was no import of $100,000,000 in gold this time to redress it. The unsound economic legislation was even then beginning to tell, and though the very heavens had fought for the United States, they were throwing the result of the battle away. European investors were growing fidgety, and took the $203,000,000 in repayment of capital, thus staving off by a year the crisis which was preparing. 1894 saw this favourable balance run up to $237,000,000, yet despite it, the net movement of gold bullion resulted in an export of $5,000,000. The withdrawal of capital was going on apace, and when the following year the United States could only persuade their foreign creditors to take $75,000,000 excess in commodities, they had to supplement it with $30,000,000 in gold.

Here then we see the difference between confidence and distrust. A certain amount has to be paid every year to Europe for interest and other matters, only on ordinary occasions much of it is reinvested. But recent years have been extraordinary, and a tremendous strain has been placed on the United States, not only to pay up the interest, but to repay capital as well. Never was so large a favourable balance piled up in so short a time as during the last three months of 1896. It saved the country from the worst financial crash it has ever had to go through, and had not Great Britain been prepared to purchase and pay promptly for the great blocks of wheat and cotton literally flung at her, there would have been a catastrophe. Surely there can be no great cause for congratulation that an altogether abnormal balance of trade was the means of securing salvation by the skin of the teeth.

The magnitude of the British balance of trade, we have seen, is dependent more or less on foreign investment, and is not in any way influenced by legislation. In the United States however, economic conditions play by far the leading part in making it. Let us take in illustration of this three recent years, and compare imports with exports:—

|  | 1892-93. | 1893-94. | 1894-95. |
|---|---|---|---|
| Imports, | $866,000,000 | $655,000,000 | $732,000,000 |
| Exports, | 848,000,000 | 892,000,000 | 808,000,000 |
| Balance, | $18,000,000[1] | $237,000,000 | $76,000,000 |

[1] Adverse, under the M'Kinley Tariff.

Now, according to the American theory, 1893-94 must have been by far the most favourable of these three. If we examine the figures carefully, we will find that the great difference in those of that year is due principally to the large falling off in the value of the imports, and this is partly accounted for by the goods dealt with in the following table.

IMPORTS OF :—

|  | 1892-93. | 1893-94. | 1894-95. |
|---|---|---|---|
| Wool, | $21,000,000 | $ 6,100,000 | $25,500,000 |
| Woollen Goods, | 38,000,000 | 19,500,000 | 36,500,000 |
| Cotton Goods, | 33,500,000 | 22,300,000 | 33,200,000 |
| Flax & Hemp Goods, | 28,400,000 | 19,400,000 | 26,300,000 |
| Silk Goods, | 39,000,000 | 24,800,000 | 31,200,000 |
| Total of 5 Classes, | $159,900,000 | $92,100,000 | $152,700,000 |

The import of these goods in the middle year was little more than half the others, due entirely to the fact that the tariff was undergoing revision, and that great reductions in the duties were anticipated. But there is another important fact to be noticed, the trade was absolutely lost, and the recovery in 1894-95 was only to the figures of 1892-93. The American people knew that clothes would be cheaper in 1895 than in 1894, so instead of purchasing new supplies as they would have done under ordinary circumstances, they turned over their wardrobes, and made much of their contents last another twelve months. When they did eventually replace them, they did not lay in a double stock, because prices were so much lower, but just took their ordinary requirements. Will anyone say the United States were better off because they saved $60,000,000 in imported clothing, and perhaps three or four times the amount in that of domestic production? The individual wearers may have been, but what about those engaged in the trade, from the spinner to the seamstress?

An American protectionist would at once reply that this might have been obviated by leaving the tariff alone. But it was not due so much to the reduction of the duties, as to the fixing of them at so high a level, that the whole nation revolted. And this will occur again and lead to the same evil results, should another extravagant tariff be adopted. Meanwhile, the balance of trade will be affected in the opposite direction by a great rush of goods seeking entrance into the United States before the imposition of the higher rates.[1]

Violent fluctuations in trade are always to be deprecated. When deliberately brought about they are disastrous, and the see-saw legislation of the United States Government and Congress will, if continued, end in ruin. We experience wide fluctuations in British trade, and an increase in the balance from £81,000,000 in 1886 to £145,000,000 in 1896 is remarkable enough. But what would be thought, if some year the value of exports exceeded that of imports? The reverse in

[1] This has actually taken place since these remarks were written.

the United States seems quite as extraordinary, yet it actually occurred as lately as 1893. In 1889 imports also exceeded exports by $300,000, and the year before, the excess actually ran up to $28,000,000. What stability can there be in a commerce which shows a balance of £6,000,000 on one side of the account at one time, and only a few years later transfers it to nearly £50,000,000 on the other? It is certainly ruled by no fixed laws, and must depend largely on wild speculation.

A country which conducts its commerce on such conservative lines as France, might be expected to maintain a very steady balance of trade, and such is actually the case. If to be without a history really mean happiness, then is French trade in that enviable state. For many years there has been an excess of imports over exports, because France is a lending, not a borrowing country, though she confines her operations almost exclusively to Europe. From Spain, from Russia, and from Turkey, her investors have every year to receive considerable sums by way of interest, and this is reflected in the movements of commodities. The balance has never yet reached £50,000,000, and only once in recent years, until 1895, had fallen as low as £25,000,000, so that it is plainly seen how narrow these fluctuations are. A few figures which include the largest as well as the smallest difference, will both illustrate this, and show how uninteresting a discussion on French balance of trade usually is, compared with that of more enterprising rivals and neighbours.

|  | Imports. | Exports. | Balance. | |
|---|---|---|---|---|
| 1884, | fcs. 4,343,500,000 | fcs. 3,232,500,000 | fcs. 1,111,000,000 | £44,440,000 |
| 1889, | 4,316,700,000 | 3,704,000,000 | 612,700,000 | 24,508,000 |
| 1892, | 4,767,800,000 | 3,569,700,000 | 1,198,100,000 | 47,924,000 |
| 1894, | 3,850,400,000 | 3,078,100,000 | 772,300,000 | 30,892,000 |
| 1895, | 3,719,900,000 | 3,387,800,000 | 332,100,000 | 13,284,000 |
| 1896, | 3,837,100,000 | 3,404,700,000 | 432,400,000 | 17,296,000 |

1891 was the year of the crop failure, and the import of wheat and wheat flour the year following was the highest on record,—fcs. 2,035,000,000, or over £80,000,000. 1895, on the other hand, was a year of exceptionally small imports of this commodity fcs. 485,000,000, and for 1896 somewhat less still. This at least proves of what immense consequence a bountiful harvest is to France, and raises the question, whether from an economical point of view it is wise to artificially stimulate a particular branch of industry which is so erratic in its yield. If we concede that France was prosperous in 1895 and 1896 because its adverse balance of trade was so small, we must equally admit that 1891 was disastrous, and that 1897 promises to follow in its footsteps. France, in short, wagers too heavily on her wheat crop to be prudent.

The great industrial expansion of Germany has materially affected her balance of trade. For some years subsequent to the war, she was busily engaged putting her own house in order. She did not require to borrow money, neither had she much to lend, and the balance between imports and exports remained remarkably even. In 1884[1] there was an excess of the former of barely £3,000,000. In 1886 there was a balance on the other side of nearly £5,000,000, a year later there was nothing to choose between them, and in 1888 imports were again £4,000,000 in excess of exports. But German traders had been quietly making money, and looking about them for new investments, instead of putting all their foreign eggs in the Russian basket. United States and South American securities were freely bought, and Italy transferred her financial affections from France to Germany. The result of the outflow of capital is apparent, and may again be illustrated by figures :—

|  | Imports. | Exports. | Balance. |  |
|---|---|---|---|---|
| 1889, . | M 4,015,100,000 | M 3,166,700,000 | M 848,400,000 | £42,420,000 |
| 1890-93, |  | Exhibit no great variation. |  |  |
| 1894, . | 3,938,300,000 | 2,961,500,000 | 976,800,000 | 48,840,000 |
| 1895, . | 4,120,700,000 | 3,317,900,000 | 802,800,000 | 40,140,000 |
| 1896, . | 4,324,000,000 | 3,403,800,000 | 920,200,000 | 46,000,000 |

Yet people who claim that Great Britain is on the brink of ruin, because her adverse balance of trade has increased from £81,000,000 to £145,000,000, and point to Germany as the supplanter, entirely ignore the fact that the adverse balance of the latter has within the same period also grown, and now reaches nearly fifty millions

---

[1] German trade returns prior to 1889 are apt to be misleading, as it was only in that year that Hamburg and Bremen entered the Imperial Zollverein. The chances are that in the years mentioned the net balances were really against Germany as a whole.

sterling. Nor can there be any doubt that in strict proportion to the foreign financial interests of both countries, the German is relatively the greater of the two. It would be larger still were Germany to cease lending abroad, because some of her exports certainly represent capital.

The most violent reverses are naturally experienced in new and partially settled, or rapidly progressive countries, which every now and again receive a set back. We noticed in the preceding chapter how Australian trade in 1896 underwent quite a revolution—though of a temporary character — for amply sufficient reasons. There is a more striking instance still, and no bulky volume could record the modern financial history of the Argentine Republic in more eloquent terms than the following table of its trade statistics :—

|  | Imports. | Exports. | Balance Imports over Exports. |
|---|---|---|---|
| 1886, | [1]$95,409,000 | $69,835,000 | $25,574,000 |
| 1887, | 117,352,000 | 84,422,000 | 32,930,000 |
| 1888, | 128,412,000 | 100,112,000 | 28,300,000 |
| 1889, | 164,570,000 | 122,815,000 | 41,755,000 |
| 1890, | 142,241,000 | 100,819,000 | 41,422,000 |
|  |  |  | Balance Exports over Imports. |
| 1891, | 67,208,000 | 103,219,000 | 36,011,000 |
| 1892, | 91,481,000 | 113,370,000 | 21,889,000 |
| 1893, | 96,224,000 | 94,090,000 | 2,134,000 [2] |
| 1894, | 92,789,000 | 101,688,000 | 8,899,000 |
| 1895, | 95,096,000 | 120,068,000 | 24,972,000 |

[1] The Argentine gold dollar is about the same value as that of the United States.

[2] Imports over exports.

We see the gradually swelling imports as the loans increased, culminating in 1889, then we picture the anxiety of the early part of 1890, resulting in the first decrease for some years, and finally the utter collapse of credit, and the falling off by more than 50 per cent. in the imports of 1891. There were still some solvent individuals and corporations left in the country however who struggled to fulfil their engagements, and from a great import of borrowed capital, the country suddenly passed to an export of the interest on it, as well as a return of whatever capital could be liquidated. There is plenty of legitimate occupation for millions more in Argentina, and the day may come when imports will again considerably exceed exports without involving another financial crisis.

We get the reverse of this picture in another country which is just beginning to claim a large share of attention. The Japanese have long been the most progressive nation in the East, and their foreign trade has steadily grown. Prior to the conflict with China, their financial interests abroad were not great, though on balance they probably had a small amount to pay. Their victory ended in placing a large sum of money, received as indemnity, at their credit in Europe, and they have made use of it in adding to their naval power, and stimulating industry in various ways, meaning the import of a great deal of all sorts of material. The trade statistics best tell the story of this :—

|       | Imports. | Exports. | Balance Exports over Imports. |
|-------|----------|----------|-------------------------------|
| 1891, | [1]Yen 63,805,000 | Yen 78,806,000 | Yen 15,001,000 |
| 1892, | 75,903,000 | 90,481,000 | 14,578,000 |
| 1893, | 89,286,000 | 89,657,000 | 371,000 |
|       |            |            | Imports over Exports. |
| 1894, | 121,058,000 | 112,234,000 | 8,824,000 |
| 1895, | 138,498,000 | 135,065,000 | 3,433,000 |
| 1896, | 171,674,000 | 117,843,000 | 53,831,000 |

Scarcely less important than the way in which a balance of trade is created, is its method of settlement. The figures of exports and imports between any two countries may or may not afford a clue to their financial relationship. Spain, for example, is financed almost entirely by France, and French investors hold enormous blocks of government, railway, and other peninsular securities. The fact that in 1896 France imported from Spain £7,500,000 more than she exported thither, explains itself at once, though the real balance of indebtedness is probably more, and has to be settled in some other way.

Spain partially recouped herself from the United States through the medium of her colonies.

| | |
|---|---|
| U.S. Imports from Cuba and Philippines were | $45,000,000 |
| „ Exports to „ „ „ | 7,700,000 |
| Balance due Spain, | $37,300,000 |
| „ Imports from Spain, | 4,100,000 |
| | $41,400,000 |
| „ Exports to Spain, | 11,400,000 |
| Actual balance due Spain, | [2]$30,000,000 |

---

[1] The silver yen is worth about two shillings.

[2] A reference to page 283 will show to what extent the revolution has affected trade between Cuba and the United States.

A somewhat larger amount still, accrues to Spain from the balance of trade with the United Kingdom, but only a portion of this is available, as there is a good deal of British capital sunk in the country in industrial enterprise, upon which returns have to be made.

The trade between Russia and France resulted for many years in a balance of from one to three millions sterling in favour of the former country, but in 1895 and 1896 it rose to over six millions. Russia has been borrowing French money in large sums, and remits the interest in produce. This in its turn has resulted in the displacement of trade between France and the United States, for instead of taking wheat and petroleum from the latter, they are received from Russia, and American producers are compelled to seek other customers. The value of the French import of petroleum, for instance, is about £1,500,000, and of this the United States contributed in 1896 less than £100,000. France likewise imported large quantities of breadstuffs, of which the States shipped only about £350,000.

On the other hand, the British trade returns for 1896 exhibit an excess of no less than £29,450,000 in imports from France. Now France does not owe Great Britain such a sum, if indeed she owes anything at all. And strange to say, when we turn to the French returns of trade with Great Britain, the excess of exports over imports is only £20,000,000, which shows, not how unreliable trade statistics are, but how judiciously they must be handled. The British returns record imports from France of £50,105,000, but the French returned exports to Great Britain at only £40,336,000. The difference of nearly £10,000,000 was no doubt received in reality from other countries. Switzerland particularly, through French ports, which French trade statisticians record separately. Similarly the exports of Great Britain to France are given at £20,655,000, of which £6,500,000 was foreign and colonial merchandise, the principal item being wool, valued at £3,550,000; but France valued imports from Great Britain at £20,218,000 only. But even £20,000,000 was not owing by France, and must be accounted for in some other way. We will see what it is presently.

British imports from the United States are always greatly in excess of exports. This is natural, because there is so much owing by one country to the other. But the excess of £74,300,000 in 1896, or even that of £42,500,000 in 1895, requires more explanation. Capital withdrawals accounted for part of it, but the United States have every year to liquidate with Great Britain a much larger sum than they actually owe her.

The United States do not ship more than they receive to every country with which they trade.

We have already noticed that fact in their relations with Cuba. They want coffee from the Brazils, tea and other Eastern produce from India, China, and Japan, and like everything else, they must be paid for. These countries do not want American agricultural produce, but require enormous quantities of manufactured goods of the sort made in the United States, yet do not buy them because they are made so dear by protection, and can be obtained cheaper elsewhere. United States exports therefore are small, as we shall see from the following figures for the year 1895-96:—

|  | Imports. | Exports. | Adverse Balance. |
|---|---|---|---|
| Brazil, | $71,100,000 | $14,300,000 | $56,800,000 |
| India, | 20,400,000 | 3,200,000 | 17,200,000 |
| China and Hong Kong, | 23,500,000 | 11,600,000 | 11,900,000 |
| Japan, | 25,500,000 | 7,700,000 | 17,800,000 |
|  | $140,500,000 | $36,800,000 | $103,700,000 |

The greater portion of this balance, instead of being paid direct, is remitted to Great Britain in breadstuffs and meat and cotton, and helps to pay for British exports to those countries. The relationship between India and the United Kingdom puts it outside the ordinary current of foreign trade, but it is somewhat remarkable that the other three countries are among the few to which we send more than we receive. Brazil especially is considerably indebted to us, as Brazilian securities are largely held by British investors. This has to be paid by the United States, as well as the ordinary balances of trade, out of the $57,000.000 owing by them to Brazil.

|  | British Imports. | British Exports. | Favourable Balance. |
|---|---|---|---|
| India, | £25,300,000 | £30,850,000 | £5,550,000 |
| Brazil, | £4,050,000 | £7,000,000 | £2,950,000 |
| China and Hong Kong, | 3,775,000 | 8,825,000 | 5,050,000 |
| Japan | 1,250,000 | 6,150,000 | 4,900,000 |
|  | £9,075,000 | £21.975,000 | £12,900,000 |

There is another way in which the United States might have liquidated a large part of its indebtedness to the East, namely, by shipments of silver, the gross export of which for the year was $60,000,000. As a matter of fact $11,500.000 did go to China and Japan, but on the other hand, $43,000,000 was shipped to Great Britain, and most of it transmitted thence to India and other Eastern countries.

We see therefore how terribly complicated the settlement of trade balance may become, and how the intervention of half a dozen countries may be necessary before they are finally adjusted. Yet the huge machine works without friction, and the motive power is supplied by the exchange banks and bankers, located in every important trading city in the world. How it operates is beyond our province to discuss.

Balances are not always settled in commodities, gold and silver often play a most important part. Despite the heavy national indebtedness of

India to Great Britain, the normal trade balance exhibits in the former country an excess of imports over exports, and in addition, over a long series of years the import of specie has averaged £10,000,000 per annum. It has been principally in silver, which, though the money and treasure of India, is only now regarded in Europe as a commodity. This silver has been largely hoarded by the natives, who are able to accumulate small savings, but had it been spent in steel rails and locomotives, and other engines of industry, India would be much more prosperous than she is to-day. The habit of hoarding instead of investing is one of the strongest brakes that can be applied to the wheels of progress, and this is applicable to any country that endeavours to accumulate useless supplies of the precious metals.

London, as the banking centre of the world, is naturally often called upon both to receive and supply specie, and large movements of it frequently take place with little regard to any question of balance of trade. Now and again however a considerable real balance has to be settled by this means, as for instance in the last months of 1896, when the enormous purchases of United States produce had to be paid for partly in gold,—the object of the United States indeed in selling was principally to obtain gold, and few countries are more frequently compelled to liquidate their balances on both sides of the account in this metal. It is always an expensive process, and in most instances it would be more profitable to everybody except the bankers immediately concerned, were the debt discharged in commodities. It would be extremely interesting to know how many times certain American eagles have made voyages across the Atlantic and paid their passage-money, and yet not one has added a cent to its value in consequence.

The United States gold movement for six consecutive years will show how expensive and really wasteful this process may be :—

|  | Excess Exports over Imports. | Excess Imports over Exports. |
| --- | --- | --- |
| 1883-84, | $18,200,000 | |
| 1884-85, | | $18,200,000 |
| 1885-86, | 22,200,000 | |
| 1886-87, | | 33,200,000 |
| 1887-88, | | 25,500,000 |
| 1888-89, | 49,700,000 | |
| | $90,100,000 | $76,900,000 |

That is, $167,000,000 were moved to liquidate what proved to be a balance in the six years of no more than $13,000,000.

Silver is as much a United States commodity as wheat or cotton, and the annual export is steady and sometimes considerable, especially since the repeal of the Sherman Act.

The balance of trade between England and South Africa is at first sight heavily against the latter country. In 1896 British exports thither exceeded the imports by £9,600,000; in 1895 by

£6,000,000. This is really reduced however to the more moderate figures of £5,000,000 and £1,250,000 respectively, by the value of diamonds, which are not included in the British trade returns. No attempt in fact is made to ascertain the import of these valuable gems, and the figures are obtained from the Cape Government, which keeps a record of the export conducted through the post office.

There is another item complicating this account —namely, British trade with Portuguese possessions, that is, Delagoa Bay. Exports thither were nearly £1,000,000 and £600,000 respectively in excess of imports, which must be added to the balances, bringing them up to £6,000,000, and £1,850,000.

But in this particular instance movements of gold must be taken into account as well, because gold is as much a commodity in South Africa as wheat in the United States or Canada. When the figures are combined, they tell a very different tale. The net import of gold into Great Britain in 1896 was £7,180,000, so that the real balance of trade was upwards of £1,000,000 the other way. In 1895, while the import of gold reached £8,350,000, £5,620,000 was shipped back again in coin, and the real balance of trade was in favour of South Africa to the extent of £900,000.

When it is borne in mind what great amounts of capital were being sunk in that country in machinery and prospecting, a heavy net excess of imports over exports would have been by no means surprising, yet the profits realised by active and paying industries proved sufficient to enable a large sum to be remitted home as interest on capital.

There is one important point which must be borne in mind. Each country must regularly settle its balance of trade, whether adverse or otherwise, or go into bankruptcy. A nation that does not pay its debts finds its way there quickly; with a nation that does not collect them, it is only a matter of time. Whatever is due to Great Britain on a year's trading and investing must be remitted, and either received, or reinvested abroad. That Great Britain does not want so much of the various commodities sent her in payment is of no consequence. She may be surfeited with breadstuffs, and meat, and dairy produce, and still be compelled to go on buying them, and be much in the position of a child sent into a confectioner's shop with half-a-crown, and forbidden to leave until the money is spent, and what is purchased consumed. Had half the sum been spent in penny rolls instead, the child's digestion would have been none the worse, and half a dozen hungry urchins would have had full stomachs and light hearts. As it is the result is disagreeable, and Great Britain is sometimes at a loss to know what to spend her money on, without damaging her internal mechanism.

It is just here where France steps in, and obligingly relieves perfidious Albion of some of her shekels. We have already seen how French prosperity is largely dependent on the supply of luxuries to wealthy foreigners, and England in this respect is distinctly her best customer. Her exports in both the years 1895 and 1896, according to the French returns, which in this instance are more reliable for the purpose than the British, slightly exceeded £40,000,000, and the details for 1896 will reveal how it was largely made up.

| | |
|---|---:|
| Silk and Silk Goods | £5,040,000 |
| Wine | 3,130,000 |
| Spirits | 1,060,000 |
| Millinery and Flowers | 1,960,000 |
| Curios | 1,200,000 |
| Ornamental Feathers | 820,000 |
| Table Fruits | 610,000 |
| Oils, etc. | 520,000 |
| Ornaments and Fans | 520,000 |
| Pottery and Glass | 380,000 |
| Preserved Fish | 210,000 |
| Works of Art | 160,000 |
| Perfumery and Paris Articles | 210,000 |
| Preserves and Biscuits | 50,000 |
| | £15,870,000 |
| Woollen Manufactures | 5,430,000 |
| Leather Goods (including Gloves) | 1,450,000 |
| Prepared Skins and Peltries | 1,550,000 |
| Musical Instruments | 230,000 |
| Clocks and Watches | 180,000 |
| | £24,710,000 |

Many of these items differ materially from the British returns for the same period, which record for instance imports of silk goods from France worth £12,125,000, and watches and clocks £870,000, a large part in each case being of Swiss origin. In others, the classification varies and renders comparison difficult. Several important items like woollens, leather goods, wines and spirits, do not greatly differ, proving them to be almost entirely of French production.

There can be no doubt that a large part of this £25,000,000, as well as most of the remaining £15,000,000 of more commercial commodities, could have been produced at home, and afforded support to British industry. But what would have been taken instead? More wheat, or butter, or dead meat and cattle? Then would the farmer have been worse off than he actually was. Suppose that a duty on silk had thrown the manufacture into English hands, and that the £5,000,000, to say nothing of the £12,000,000, had been entirely eliminated. It would simply have meant so much greater value in other commodities to be imported instead, not necessarily from France, or even in the year 1896, but at some time, and in some way, it would have had to be made good. Yet it is a misfortune that it should be so. The wealthy must import their incomes earned abroad, and in doing it, they provide cheap food for those who can pay, but, at the same time, often take the bread out of the mouths of those who have to work for it. The remedy for this state of things has already been pointed out.

The great importance of this question of the balance of trade is sadly under-estimated by economists and practical business men alike. The object of the latter is to make profits and increase their capital, but they often fail to see that a temporary gain may result in permanent loss. They rejoice over a so-called favourable balance of trade, and think their country is growing wealthy because it exports so much more than it imports, while all the time it is being beggared by a steady drain on its resources, arising from too large a payment for the accommodation it has received, or the actual withdrawal of the capital with which it has been worked. Or, there may be jubilation at the contrary excess of imports over exports, set down as a sign of increasing prosperity, while all the time it is destroying it by reducing the demand for domestic labour, which is the source of it. The transactions of everyday life never have been, and never will be conducted on strict principles of political economy, but a knowledge and recognition of them may nevertheless reveal many a pitfall, and destroy many a false notion.

The Governments of nearly all civilised nations go to considerable expense and trouble in collecting and tabulating details and statistics regarding their commerce and industry. Could not a few of them go a little further, and append an intelligent account of the why and wherefore, which in future years would be of far greater value than the statistics? The English Board of Trade has not only the materials, but competent officials to deal with them. Each year it would be possible, not only to publish the bare figures of the balance of trade, and what countries contributed to each side of the account, but what particular forces were at work which compelled or permitted them to do so. Then there would no longer be the mistake made of supposing that adversity spelt prosperity, or that real prosperity meant the road to ruin. A country which either imported or exported too much, would have the reasons given it in black and white, and the opportunity, not now always afforded, of retracing its steps before it was too late.

# CHAPTER XI.

## Home and Foreign Trade.

Relative Importance—Effects of Protection—Arbitrary Divisions of Territory—Wasteful Labour—Incidence of Taxation on different Industries—The Agricultural Rating Act—Light Dues—Railway Preferential Rates—Reckless Foreign Trading—Education—Internal Competition—Independent Traders—Capitalist Influences—The Directions in which they are exerted—The True Aims of Home Traders—The West African Trade—General Possibilities of Foreign Development.

Though tariffs interfere directly with foreign commerce, they are ostensibly imposed, so far at least as they are protective, with the object of benefiting home trade. The latter is supposed to be, and undoubtedly is, of preponderating importance, and even in the United Kingdom, whose foreign commerce is the largest in the world, and the value of it per head of the population relatively greater still, the home trade must be many times more. Still, we must not lose sight of the fact that a reduction of 10 per cent. in the foreign turnover may, not necessarily must, mean a greater contraction internally. The foreign part of the machinery is a big cogwheel, with many smaller ones fitting into it. When the big one moves rapidly the little ones whirl; when it slows down to half-speed they do not make anything like half the number of revolutions. A large export order passes through few hands,—the merchant who executes it, the manufacturer who makes it, and the railway company and shipowner who eventually transport it. The merchant indeed may be eliminated, and the order passed direct to the maker. But when the proceeds are distributed, how many hands does it pass through? The banker upon whom the bills of exchange are drawn in payment, the sellers of the raw material, the workmen who have to receive their wages, the shopkeepers with whom they are spent, the dealers who supply the shopkeepers, and the merchants or manufacturers who stock the dealers. So that the value of the export has been turned over three or four times at least in internal trade, and each time ought to have secured a profit.

Thus we find that while nations jealously guard their own markets, they are always anxious to edge their way into other people's. The American protectionist is determined to capture the home trade, say in woollens or tinplates, but is equally keen about selling surplus products abroad, which he often succeeds in doing at about half cost price. He is fully aware of the value of foreign trade, and would like to double, treble, quadruple it. But then he has to meet competition and cut prices; at home a generous government guarantees him a hundred per cent. profit, so he prefers the smaller trade at the higher remuneration. From his individual standpoint he is quite right, and as long as the people of the United States are satisfied to legislate for the exclusive benefit of a few select individuals or classes, that is their business and nobody else's.

We saw in the last chapter how the United States are compelled to pay for the South American and East Indian produce they require, in agricultural products shipped to Europe. The four countries specially named are large buyers of cotton goods in Great Britain, part of which under favourable circumstances the United States might supply. They do supply a small quantity as it is, let us see how much.

|  | Total Import of United States from | United States Export of Cotton Goods to | British Export of Cotton Goods to ($5 to £1) |
|---|---|---|---|
| Brazil, | $71,100,000 | $1,000,000 | $11,300,000 |
| India, | 20,400,000 | 140,000 | 92,200,000 [1] |
| China, | 22,000,000 | 4,100,000 | 29,500,000 |
| Japan, | 25,500,000 | 100,000 | 12,000,000 [2] |
|  | $139,000,000 | $5,340,000 | $145,000,000 |

China is used principally as a dumping ground when the American home trade is depressed, as it was in 1896, and the chances are that most of the export to that country did not realise cost price. The previous year, when the trade was less depressed, its value was only $1,700,000.

[1] Yarn $10,200,000, goods $82,000,000.
[2] Yarn $5,500,000, goods $6,500,000.

The United States ought to be the great cotton manufacturing country of the world, and if there are any countries in which they should be able to compete against Europe, it is those of South America, as from every one without exception they import more than they export, and Brazil is the only one taking anything like a million dollars' worth of cotton goods. They should be able to supply that country with every yard it needs, except perhaps of specialities; and were they to pay India, China, and Japan directly in cotton goods, instead of indirectly in agricultural products, they would capture some British trade, but not on the whole affect it very seriously.

They prefer instead to make their own consumers pay high prices for the profit of the manufacturer, and in doing so deliberately throw away a foreign trade in a single speciality, which would be worth at least $50,000,000 instead of $5,000,000 in four countries alone, and probably another $50,000,000 in others that might be named. That is, the total value of the export of American cotton goods which now struggles hard to reach £2,000,000 or £3,000,000 per annum, might be made to touch £20,000,000. Nor would it mean much if any increased foreign competition in their own markets, for when they can manufacture cheap enough to do a trade like that, they will need no protection at home.

Nor would the farmer be any worse off through not being able to export his produce, for the additional hands required in the cotton mills would consume it. Either the dispossessed British cotton mills would have to find new customers elsewhere, from whom they would purchase food in exchange, or some of the hands would have to go back to the land, and produce more food at home.

Could anything afford stronger evidence of the false economy of protection than this? By building a high wall round home markets, people shut themselves in, as well as the foreigner out. They increase the cost of production and destroy home trade at the same time, for if instead of merely selling surplus products abroad to get rid of them, they cultivated a profitable foreign commerce, that would lead to a much larger domestic turnover. Besides, farmers as a rule get a better profit from a home industrial population than from a foreign one, and agriculture would be both stimulated and rendered prosperous.

It has hitherto been impossible to make nations see this, or to realise that the lines of demarcation they draw are altogether despotic. Why should they just be across the frontier of Mexico or Canada, and the United States, and not likewise between Wyoming or Nevada, and some point between them and Pennsylvania or Massachusetts? These four states it is true are all within a federal union, under one government, but in most respects their interests are so diverse that two might be at the poles, and the other two at the equator. Massachusetts can manufacture cotton goods if protected against Canada, and so could Wyoming if protected against Massachusetts. Wyoming is not allowed to do so because it is in the United States instead of Canada, and the inhabitants of the State are subjected to a real injustice. Its farmers may supply Massachusetts with food, but so they would Canada if they drew their cotton goods thence, and possibly obtain better prices. But Wyoming is not permitted to engage in foreign trade, because Massachusetts a couple of thousand miles away wants home trade. Where there are distinctions of race, or even language, which often produce national antipathies, one can understand barriers springing up, but between peoples identical in almost everything, they are wasteful and nonsensical.

Wasteful, because they prevent a fair exchange of labour, and often compel it to be employed on unprofitable work. In many a well-to-do household there is sufficient food thrown away every day to keep a needy family in comfort. It requires no effort of imagination to see that when it occurs. But when labour is thrown away, it is not so easily discernible. A mechanic in the United States is, let us say, engaged in making tin plates, and were he engaged in fruit-growing instead, his labour would be just twice as effective. The mechanic in England or Wales would have made two tin plates for the same price as one cost in the United States, and when cans had been made out of them, there would have been fruit to fill them. It is decreed however that tinned plates shall be a home industry, in order, so it is said, that two men may be employed instead of one. But the second need only work half time to keep up with the tinplate maker. Were both employed in growing the fruit instead, they would work full time, and keep two foreign tinplate makers fully occupied.

Now let us turn this into wages. The American tinplate maker receives, say, $10 for a week's work, and the fruit grower $4 for half a week, so that their joint production costs just $14 in wages. Had both men worked full time at fruit-growing at $8 a week, they would have produced four times the quantity of fruit for $16, but no tinplates to can them. The wages of the two foreign tinplate makers would have amounted to perhaps $15, so that for $31, four times the quantity of canned fruit would have been produced than actually was for $14.

But could it have been consumed? To begin with, four men were earning full wages where only one and a half were before, and they would eat some of the fruit. And were the same principle acted upon in other trades, the additional wage-earners would eat the rest. Over-production! There is no such thing while a man willing to work wants it, and while there are hungry people to be fed. Extravagant production there is, and that is why consumption lags behind. Had home and foreign trade divided the work between them, there would have been more food and more mouths to eat it; and the artificial monopoly by one branch was exactly as if a loaf of bread had been cut in two, and half thrown in the fire, while men, women and children were clamouring for it.

To remedy this, every obstacle to the free interchange both of labour and commodities must be removed. Of course a nation which has many saints' days, an occasional fast, and numerous feasts, does want protection against a more energetic neighbour, which rests only one day in seven, and takes but an occasional holiday in between. But in whatever latitude an active race is located, there is always plenty of work for it ready at hand without forcing any for which the natural conditions are not ripe. Men of the same race are fairly equal in aptitude and intelligence wherever they happen to be, and the Creator in His wisdom has given no country an advantage for which He has not provided another with some equivalent. A citizen of the United States would be indignant were it suggested to him that his country was less productive than England, or that his people were less intelligent or less energetic than the English. Why, then, is he so afraid of them? They offer to do certain things for him which he cannot do so well himself, and to take from him others that they cannot do as well as he. The fair exchange would save him hours of labour, and leave him dollars in pocket. But there is something wrong in his dictionary. When he turns up the meaning of foreign trade, it reads, " Selling your goods to the foreigner," and when he goes on further to home trade, it is, " Making what you want yourself." Half the real meaning has in each case been left out. In the first instance, it is, " And getting paid for them," and in the other, " When you can do it as well and cheaply as anyone else."

There is less wasteful labour in Great Britain than in any other country in the world, and that is why its foreign trade is so enormous, and at the same time its home trade *per capita* also the largest. No industry can long exist which is not on an economic basis. If cost of production is higher than elsewhere, it is soon discovered, and successful competition results. That rarely happens however, because men take care not to risk capital in such a business. Changes often occur from unforeseen causes, and what has been a profitable becomes a losing concern from no internal fault. That is a pity, but in the interests of the individual and the nation alike, the sooner the capital and energy are transferred to something more promising the better, unless the cloud is likely to prove but temporary. Occasionally the causes at work are grossly unfair, as in the case of sugar bounties, and then something may be done without placing any other industry at an unnatural disadvantage. And just so long as each trader, whether home or foreign, receives fair play, and none is favoured at the expense of another, will both share the same prosperity, or wade hand in hand through the deeper waters of adversity.

Protection as it exists in the United States and other countries is not however the only obstacle that may be thrown in the way of trade development, and while England gains much by free trade she parts with some of the advantage in other directions. We have considered taxation in its relation to tariffs, and found that as far as the United Kingdom is concerned the incidence is not unfair. But when practically half the taxation of the country is contributed by four per cent. of its population, the incidence on that half may be very unjust. The four per cent. represent almost every national interest, and certainly include all engaged in a large way in both home and foreign trade. The taxation therefore may be so divided, that it falls with undue severity on one, and rests lightly on another. A few hundred thousand pounds levied on one interest may almost destroy it, while upon another it would scarcely be felt.

There are two representative cases which illustrate this point. Agriculture is essentially a home industry, in fact the greatest of all home industries. A Royal Commission decided not very long ago that it was in a most depressed condition, and that the best practicable way of affording relief was by taking a large amount of taxation off land, which was done to the extent of over £1,500,000 per annum, and transferred to other shoulders. Probably one-fourth of this amount has afforded much wanted relief, and need not be grudged; the remaining three-fourths, if it has not already gone, will in a very brief period go into the pockets of landowners, who are the wealthiest class in the country—and do the least to promote its industrial prosperity. The same Commission subsequently found that agriculture was no longer so depressed, that it was really only the landowners with incomes ranging from a few hundreds up to tens of thousands per annum who were suffering, and that the agricultural labourer with wages of fifteen shillings a week ought to be the happiest and most contented of men, because food was so cheap. To put it in its most favourable aspect, a home industry has benefited by a million and a half per annum.

Shipping is as representative of the foreign trade as agriculture is of the home, and shipowners have a grievance. It is a very much smaller one than that of the landowners, and would cost much less to redress. Government undertakes, as it should, to light the coasts of the United Kingdom, at an expenditure of a few hundred thousand pounds per annum. It is no doubt theoretically just that shipowners whose vessels depend on the lights for safety should pay for them, and they not only do so, but contribute more than one hundred thousand pounds profit per annum into the bargain. Foreign vessels pay the same dues, but only when they enter a British port, and may make all the use they like of them, without charge, when on foreign voyages. But other Governments, with a far less important stake in shipping than the British, regard it as their duty to light their coasts at the national expense. They resent the charge made on their vessels in the ports of the United Kingdom, and show that resentment by imposing an equivalent tax on British ships entering their harbours, which their own escape. The consequence is, that while British and foreign ships alike pay dues in British ports, only British ships pay them in foreign ones, and the tax laid upon them by their own Government is doubled.

Here then is unfair discrimination between home and foreign trade. Wealthy landowners receive £1,500,000 per annum at the expense of general taxpayers, including shipowners, who in turn are refused remission of three or four hundred thousand pounds, which would be increased by a somewhat similar amount at the expense of foreign governments and foreign taxpayers. Though landowners and shipowners both belong to the rich, not the poor class, they are not by any means treated with equal justice.

There is a reverse side to this picture. Shipowners have so expedited the handling of their vessels, that the cargo of the largest steamer is now often discharged and sorted in less than forty-eight hours. This is true economy, and must be commended. The railway companies which have subsequently to handle a portion of these cargoes are also able to make such expedition, that they carry the goods at special rates. This is right and proper too, because the expense of handling a great bulk at one time is relatively much less than scattered quantities picked up here and there. But there is a limit to it, and it is often exceeded, so that produce brought many thousands of miles by land and sea, and then shipped over an English railway, sometimes pays less freight than British produce carried one or two hundred miles. Shipowners do not make railway rates it is true, but it is their business to encourage the companies to reduce their tariff to a minimum, in order that they may obtain full cargoes in foreign ports.

But all foreign trade is not favoured like this, and when it comes to conveying British manufactures to ports of shipment, much higher rates are exacted, though bulk and expedition may be the same. Imports are uncertain and must be attracted, exports are fairly secure and are bound to be moved, but in either case the home producer or the home manufacturer suffers by differential rates. It is a difficult matter to adjust, but the agricultural interest has a legitimate grievance against the railway companies, and indirectly against shipowners.

It may be claimed that one is a fair set off against the other, but no such happy-go-lucky method can be relied on to secure fair play to the multitudinous interests concerned in British trade, which cannot afford to depend on the chance result of a game at pitch and toss. These are questions which must be grappled with and settled equitably, not left to the arbitrament of the party which can make the first and most successful swoop on the spoils to be gathered in.

Similar problems are presented in Germany, and perhaps in most other countries likewise. Agrarian discontent throughout that Empire springs more from preferential railway charges than from any other cause, and hostility between the agrarian and industrial sections of the community often leads to open rupture. Though the latter is invariably favoured by the Government, the former occasionally gains a victory, as instanced by the legislation declaring time bargains illegal, which cannot but cripple legitimate as well as speculative commerce. An inordinate desire to increase the foreign trade of the country at almost any cost, has produced a conflict with those who believe that the home industry with which their interests are bound up is being ruined thereby.

It has done something more, apparent outside rather than inside the Empire. This was illustrated a short time ago by the political troubles in Crete, where the Greek insurgents, rightly or wrongly, believed Germany to be the instigator of the movement against them. They retaliated by boycotting German goods, and telegrams, it is said, were sent to German manufacturers countermanding orders. Most of the manufactures purchased in the island were of German origin, because that country gave every facility in the way of long credit and cheap articles, rendering it impossible for England and France to compete. If this went on in Crete, how much more is it likely to be in vogue elsewhere? A father in giving advice to a son who was about to start upon his career in the world, is said to have provided him with a motto, "Make money; honestly if you can, but make money." We can well imagine the German manufacturer's instructions to his foreign traveller or agent being "Book orders; at a profit if you can, but book orders."

And may not this explain why Germany sometimes captures British trade? The British manufacturer would indeed be foolish to compete against such instructions, and had much better let the business pass him than accept it at a loss. Much comment was at one time made on the progress made by Germany in the Eastern principalities of Europe, where Great Britain was rapidly ousted. But British Consuls were persistently warning their countrymen at home against extending their risks or giving protracted credits in these countries, and the warning was accepted, and no doubt many bad debts were avoided in consequence. It is worth noticing that while British exports to Egypt have been steadily growing in value, those to European Turkey have just as persistently fallen away. How much have German traders had to write off on this account? Every one interested in English Fire Insurance Companies knows that many of the principal ones, years ago, opened up numerous foreign branches. But a time has invariably arrived in the history of each of them when a balance-sheet has been published showing a more or less serious falling off in revenue, and the explanation has been, a wholesale relinquishment of bad foreign business, which agents, in their eagerness to increase premium income, had been induced to accept. British traders have every now and again to use the pruning-knife in the same way, and are able to regard with indifference, if not with amusement, the avidity with which their foreign rivals swoop down on the rejections.

There is a method of grossly unfair competition notoriously prevalent in Germany, and that is, the use made of foreign trade marks, either by direct forgery or colourable imitations. For her own credit, her Government should visit with severe penalties, when brought to its notice and convinced of the justice of the charge, such fraudulent attempts, not to capture trade, but generally to ruin the reputations of rivals who have spent large sums of money both to earn and to merit them.

There is no more important or far-reaching factor in trade economy than education, and unfortunately for England, most nations realised it before she did. The repugnance to a thorough and efficient mental training is often but ill-concealed where it is not openly expressed, and for what are called "the masses," the barest rudiments are regarded as amply sufficient. But a child is no more educated when it can read, write, and figure, than a steamer is equipped when the space has been made ready to receive the engines. It is only then that education begins, because these are only the rude implements with which it is forged. The increase of subjects is decried, and complaints made that the country is being over-educated. There has been no over-education yet, as far as elementary schools are concerned at anyrate, and the list of subjects wants increasing rather than diminishing in number. Three-fourths of them may never do the child any good, but who knows whether if the other fourth were omitted it might not contain the very matter which appeals to the mind of the dullest pupil, and excites an interest that develops an unexpected intelligence. Botany deals with trees and wood, but what practical use is it to a joiner? Similarly geology treats of earths and stones, yet it is not a necessary adjunct to efficient brick-setting. But the joiner who studies botany, or the bricksetter who interests himself in geology, is not likely to spend his leisure hours in the public house, or loafing at the street corners; he will employ them profitably, and very likely save his money, and will be a better joiner or brick-setter, and certainly a better citizen for it. Yet where is he to get a taste for such studies if not at school?

Much money is now being spent, and spent wisely, on technical education, but the foundation for it must be prepared beforehand. It is only when tastes have already been cultivated, and knowledge previously acquired, that such a course is likely to prove of practical value.

But the most extraordinary of all recent assertions is that the school curriculum of the country need not be so exhaustive as that of the town. It is exactly in the villages and sequestered hamlets of the land where it is most needed. The quick-witted town child may educate himself by observation even in the gutter, and without going to school at all may some day pick up a fortune, honestly or otherwise. Communion with nature may engender contentment, but it does not engraft the practical experience gained in the haunts of men, and, moreover, it is generally the town-bred population which most readily learns the lessons that nature has to teach. If there is to be a distinction between town and country, it is in the latter where school age should be the highest and the standard the most comprehensive. Yet the severest penalties of school managers are often visited on the village schoolmaster and schoolmistress who have ventured to teach more than they are paid for, which is often little enough.

England's trade competitors make no mistakes of this sort. In the United States there is no kicking against a school-board rate, and the statesman who ventured to suggest that threepence in the pound should be the maximum, would stand very little chance of having his term of office renewed. There, national elementary education costs nearly $3 per head of the population, against very little more than 6s. in England, while the redeeming feature of American millionaires is that they found and equip some of the finest educational institutions in the world. It is short-sighted policy no doubt, for some day they will be the means of rousing the nation to a sense of the rotten economical system which has allowed so many millions of the dollars to be accumulated. And what shall we say of Germany? There, if anywhere, the process is carried to an extreme, and in the construction of involved theories, practical considerations are sometimes lost sight of. But the Teutonic mind is eminently practical, and generally knows where to stop, and how best to adapt the knowledge it has absorbed.

Jealousies and rivalries are not always confined to international questions, and frequently do much to damage local interests. To all intents and purposes Great Britain is a commercial entity to the United States, and the United States to Great Britain. But when we come to examine these separate entities, we soon discover how heterogeneous is their composition, and how the different segments are warring against one another.

The desire of Manchester to become a seaport has stirred up bickerings and hatred between that city and Liverpool, such as would be discreditable between two rival nations. Fair competition is not only desirable but necessary, both to economy and efficiency, but when subterfuges have to be adopted, the result is demoralisation without either being attained. For Manchester to endeavour to fill her own docks at the expense of Liverpool is reasonable enough, but what is to be said of a system of attracting cargo to one port, the final destination of which is the other, and by taking advantage of a privilege specially conceded to a private undertaking, securing the dues legitimately accruing to one corporation for the benefit of the other? Or what is to be said of the English railway company, which, serving a port from which a foreign line of steamers regularly sails, advertises broadcast that the foreign government will grant special facilities for the clearance of cargo shipped by that route, as against a rival one served by a British fleet? Surely foreign governments might be allowed to do their own advertising.

These things and many others, too numerous and often too trivial to mention, rob Great Britain of a portion of the advantage she would otherwise derive from her system of commercial economy. Possibly it is well that it is so, otherwise the jealousy felt towards her by other nations might be strained to breaking point. But that is not what British traders have to take into account, and if they are to hold their own, they must consider what is to their own interests, and not what is likely or otherwise to provoke friction with the foreigner. Nor is there any reason why trade should be thrown deliberately in his way, as is only too frequently done, from pride, or stupidity, or both.

There is a manufacturing firm in the south of England, which is said never once to have altered its price list during the century. It keeps about a dozen customers on its books, and refuses to extend its connection, compelling all buyers of its goods to deal with those it supplies. Many attempts have been made to compete with it, but it holds its ground, and easily disposes of its entire production on its own terms. Nobody has ever yet been able to make anything quite equal to the goods it turns out. But if this firm looks rather sleepy, it apparently always keeps one eye open. It does not summarily dismiss the complaints of customers, even when received second or third hand, but diligently enquires into, and if it be in the wrong, promptly rectifies them. Besides, its special production contains probably more labour than material, so that the cost of making it may really be little if any less than it was a hundred years ago. Anomalous as such a position is, it is not this kind of trading that drives business out of the country.

But other firms and individuals have endeavoured to do the same thing without occupying so impregnable a position. There is another manufacturing house, located in another part of the kingdom, also of ancient lineage and high standing, but, unfortunately for itself, unable to retain the monopoly of its production. To my personal knowledge, a young and enterprising firm of traders, enjoying deservedly good credit, opened an account with it some years ago, and bought several small parcels of its goods. They turned out somewhat unsatisfactory, and a complaint was lodged, not vaguely and indefinitely, but specifically, of a certain defect which rendered them unsuitable for the express purpose for which they were required. The reply was that it was a piece of impertinence for a small firm a year or two old to criticise the business or manufactures of one that had been making the same goods for over a century. In due course the manufacturer's representative called on the traders, collected the account owing, referred briefly to the correspondence, and "supposed he need not call again." His supposition was correct, and now the offending but still unrepentant firm remit several hundred pounds per annum for goods made in Germany, which ought to be and could be supplied by British manufacturers.

Though such gross folly may be avoided, cross currents between home and foreign trade are bound to run swiftly and strongly at times, and it becomes extremely difficult for governments and legislatures to avoid taking sides. They would naturally incline to that of greatest importance to the country concerned. Though the internal trade of Great Britain is of greater volume than the external, still the industrial element inherent in the latter, is the prominent force in English life. Parliament and the nation are much more likely therefore to be engaged on industrial than on agricultural legislation, and the great principle of free trade was undoubtedly designed, and is steadily maintained in the interests of the former. But the friends of the agricultural or home interest are powerful, if they are fewer in number, and by almost entirely monopolising one Chamber of the Legislature are able to, and do, prevent legislation inimical to them, or likely to promote the welfare of the opposing elements at their expense. The landed interest, in consequence, still wields a power, and possesses an influence, such as it enjoys in few other countries, not even where it is by far and away the predominating factor in the national life; and though external commerce is of such vital importance, internal considerations sometimes block its way.

The agricultural element is as predominant in

the United States as the industrial in Great Britain, yet it is altogether over-ridden in the National Congress. Not by what may be regarded as foreign commerce, because that is of greater necessity in this instance to the agricultural than to the manufacturing element. But the secondary interest holds sway in America, as it often does in England, and for precisely the same reason, because immense wealth has given it immense power. Where land is so plentiful, the desire to possess it is less accentuated, particularly as it does not carry with it the social distinctions, so noticeable a feature elsewhere. Wealth always seeks to ally itself with patriotism, or to form a pseudo-patriotism of its own, and in one instance the watchword is, Home against foreign industry, while in the other it is Home against foreign agriculture.

But both in France and Germany we find the greater section exercising the greater influence. In the former country, nearly half the population is directly dependent on the land, only about one-third is connected with the ramifications of industry and commerce. The wealth of the country is divided on fairly equal lines, the enormous proportion of peasant proprietors having largely expatriated the old nobility from the soil. That is the reason, no doubt, why the scales of legislation are held so evenly, why industry is so ready to accord protection to agriculture, and agriculture to industry. At least it is impossible to contend that one is being ruined by the other, and if there is any undermining influence at work, it is not created by internecine warfare. If the agricultural interest slightly holds the predominance, it is only as it should be.

Quite the opposite conditions prevail in Germany, where it is the industrial and commercial section which forms nearly half the community, relegating the agricultural to the second place with one-third only. Bearing this fact in mind, the persistent endeavours of the Government to promote the former are more easily accounted for, while if the latter shout the loudest, they cannot bring up the brute force when it is wanted. Only, the position there is complicated by the intervention of a strong socialist element, drawn from both sections, which, by throwing its weight first into one scale and then into the other, tends to prolong and render the conflict doubtful.

Whether a country is stimulating more its home or its foreign trade, may generally be ascertained by gauging the respective influence of the sections of the community specially favouring them. The actual forces at work may not always be the most beneficial. If, for instance, they seek to destroy foreign commerce in Great Britain with her enormous income drawn from outside, they are crippling her resources. If, on the other hand, they endeavour unduly to restrict home industry, or to give it a wrong direction in the United States, which must develop their natural internal resources to enable them to meet their external liabilities, they are equally encouraging economic waste. Both countries, to ensure permanent prosperity, must lend their energies to the respective interests which provide the basis of the cheapest production compatible with a reasonable standard of comfort and workmanlike efficiency.

We have thus far dealt with positive forces, but there are others possessed of a negative tendency. Such for instance are the restrictions placed on the freedom of individuals, whether masters or workmen, in the pursuit of their respective callings. The British Parliament in particular has been long occupied with legislation of this nature, and though a great outcry is often raised against it, there is very little of it which has so far been unwise. In the interests of health, as well as life, it sometimes imposes onerous obligations, but they are rarely more stringent than a humane employer would voluntarily adopt were he unfettered. The competition of others less scrupulous than himself, forbids him to entertain conditions which are too costly, but when his rival is forced to adopt them whether he likes to or not, it is no hardship to institute them, though sometimes they go further than he would wish. The pressure of inspection or interference may be annoying, and men often ask what they have ever done to be called upon to suffer what they regard as an indignity. Nothing at all; but unfortunately there are others engaged in the same trade utterly reckless of life and limb of anyone about them so long as they make money, and we are taught that in this world the sheep and the goats cannot be divided. The falsest of all economy is waste of life or incapacitation of labour, and the country which does not afford every possible protection against both, is adding a heavy load to obligations which must be discharged, and the coin in which they are paid, while not always traceable, is never recoverable.

But the cost of such protection undertaken as a national duty, should likewise be at the national expense, and not imposed as a direct charge on industry, except possibly in such instances where interference proves to have been justified, and where the defect is due to preventible causes. Whether it be a mine, or a factory, or a ship, the maintenance of the machinery necessary to ensure their moral, apart from their industrial efficiency, is no just burden on those immediately concerned.

If trade prosperity is so dependent on the wisdom and discretion of employers, how much responsibility rests upon the employed? They can, and sometimes do, make or mar an industry. Their settled policy no less than their occasional acts would introduce us into a wide field, very germane to the subject in general, but hardly to that particular phase of it which it has been the object of this book to discuss. It is better to leave it entirely alone, than to deal with it in any fragmentary manner.

The principal lesson to be derived is, that each industry, whether attached more particularly to home or foreign trade, should conduct its affairs and arrange its economical organisation as though the prosperity of the entire nation depended on it. In a country like Great Britain, where the annual import must always be enormous, each home producer of a commodity which can be and is imported, should strive as far as he is concerned, to limit the necessity for the foreign product, and when he has done that he has fulfilled his duty. There are immense opportunities to be availed of at home as well as abroad, and as social evils are grappled with and eradicated, industrial activity will fill the vacuum, and make greater demands on home trade, without in any way curtailing the foreign.

We have witnessed during the last few years a striking illustration of how this same activity can be extended to foreign trade. There is a small group of West African merchants and shipowners who are very much on the alert, and never lose an opportunity of pushing their business and extending their influence. They have to deal with a broad area of country, capable no doubt of a good deal of development, but which, owing to the unhealthy nature of the climate, does not admit of the rapid progress which can be infused by the settlement of European or American peoples. Still, a glance at the trade returns proves that even during years disastrous on the whole to British commerce, this little group marched steadily onward. The figures are for the four districts usually included in British West Africa, namely, Gambia, Sierra Leone, The Gold Coast, and Lagos.

|       | British Imports. | British Exports. |
|-------|------------------|------------------|
| 1892, | £1,518,742       | £990,343         |
| 1893, | 1,866,578        | 1,213,263        |
| 1894, | 1,577,790        | 1,298,856        |
| 1895, | 1,685,541        | 1,197,221        |
| 1896, | 1,909,709        | 1,445,948        |

I have not included the figures of the Niger Chartered Territories, as they would altogether change the relative proportions. With the exception of Sierra Leone, these colonies have no debt, and consequently no interest to remit in produce or otherwise. The excess of imports over exports is therefore in some degree the measure of the profit of the merchants engaged in the trade, but as it may include movements of capital as well, too much reliance must not be placed on it. With the Niger Territories it is quite different, the exports being nearly double the imports, and represent to some extent at anyrate capital sunk in the country. There may be interchanges between them and the other British colonies, but the jealousies existing tend to reduce anything of the sort to a minimum.

Now these figures show that the imports and exports have increased in five years by 25 per cent.

and 45 per cent. respectively. Very satisfactory, though perhaps taken by themselves nothing very extraordinary. But there is more to follow.

The West Coast of Africa is peculiarly open to competition, inasmuch as both France and Germany are eagerly pushing their way there. These two countries protect their colonies as they protect themselves, and the protectionist, and especially the Imperial Federationist, would say that they thus secured their colonial trade and shut the foreigner out. But do they?

If France has expelled the foreigner, at least she has not gained much by it. Her returns of trade with her West African possessions are as follows:—

|  | Imports. | Exports. |
|---|---|---|
| 1892, | £990,000 | £800,000 |
| 1893, | 900,000 | 770,000 |
| 1894, | 910,000 | 1,000,000 |
| 1895, | 690,000 | 800,000 |

The figures for 1896 I am unable to give.

The progress here is crab-like, for while the exports have remained stationary, imports have fallen away 30 per cent.

But France has not expelled the foreigner, certainly not the Britisher. For while the latter has gone on exploiting his own preserves, he has been poaching most unmercifully on the French ones, as the following figures will show:—

BRITISH TRADE RETURNS WITH FRENCH
WEST AFRICA.

|       | Imports.  | Exports. |
|-------|-----------|----------|
| 1892, | £44,328   | £176,261 |
| 1893, | 68,437    | 174,580  |
| 1894, | 222,198   | 196,331  |
| 1895, | 221,704   | 308,017  |
| 1896, | 203,442   | 376,314  |

So that while we increased the import and export trade with our own possessions by 25 per cent. and 45 per cent., we actually added 340 per cent. to our imports from the French ones, and considerably more than doubled our export thither. And these imports, it must be remembered, do not compete with home products.

France might of course have returned the compliment, but her import of fcs. 9,250,000 from British West African possessions in 1892, had sunk to fcs. 7,250,000 in 1895, and her exports from fcs. 5,500,000 to fcs. 4,000,000.

The corresponding returns for Germany and German West African possessions are not so complete, either in length of time or detail, but what there are of them are quite creditable to Great Britain.

Had this enlarged British trade been due to the drink traffic, I would be the first to deprecate it. As a matter of fact, British traders do their utmost

[1] The actual export was £477,096, but included £300,000 for telegraph wire and apparatus, an altogether exceptional item.

to discountenance it, and many of them would leave it entirely alone were it not that the demand would otherwise be supplied by the vilest continental potato spirit. It is cotton goods that are chiefly responsible for the increase in exports, and though the volume of the trade may be smaller than that, say, with India or China, the West African shipper is proving himself to be Lancashire's best friend.

Now this is something like activity in foreign trade, and apparently no tariff wall can be built high enough to prevent the British trader clambering over, while the cheap production in his own country, due mainly to free trade, gives him practically a monopoly on his own side of it.

What can be done in West Africa is equally possible elsewhere, both in countries under British control and beyond it. All that is wanted is energy and intelligence—the one is useless without the other. Such an expedition as that sent recently to China by the Blackburn Chamber of Commerce, for instance, may be turned to enormous advantage, for crowded into that one country is a fifth of the world's population. Certain it is, that between home and foreign trade there should exist no jealousy, the latter cannot prosper without diverting the stream to the former.

# CHAPTER XII.

## Free Trade or Protection?

Slow Growth of Free Trade Principles—National and Individual Interests—General Growth of National Indebtedness—Decrease of the British Debt—Military and Naval Expenditure—The Commercial and Industrial Classes—Re-export Trade—Protection in its Relationship to Commercial Morality — The Causes of Over-production—The Working Classes—Spread of Protectionist Sentiment in Great Britain—Increasing Competition in Wholesale Trade—Great Prosperity of Retail Trade—Bullion Movements—What Free Trade and Protection do for the various Classes of the Community.

This is the question which naturally presents itself as we draw near to our conclusion. When rather more than half a century ago free trade was adopted as the economic basis of the commerce and industry of Great Britain, it was confidently predicted to be only a matter of a very brief period before every other civilised nation would be won over to support and adopt the principle. Yet so far from this being the case, protectionist doctrines are in many parts of the world becoming continually more rampant, and when facts and statistics are produced to show the favourable effects of free trade in England, others are promptly forthcoming which appear greatly to minimise them, or the contention is urged that protection has done more for the United States or some other country than the opposite policy has accomplished for England.

There is evidently then abundant room for difference of opinion, and personal opinion, as a rule, is little more than the reflection of personal interest. Opposing factions view things from totally different standpoints. A man to whom any particular system means prosperity, is often utterly at a loss to understand why other people can desire to subvert it, while a second to whom a change might bring fortune, regards the first as utterly selfish in his motives. In countries therefore where the voice of the majority is the final arbiter, the wishes of the majority will in the end prevail, unless indeed there be a powerful and wealthy minority constantly able to over-ride it. What for example are working men to do when, just before an important election, factories and workshops are closed on a large scale, and an intimation given that they will not be re-opened unless a certain candidate prove victorious? Or the majority may be misled, and the worse made to appear the better cause, but in that case it has only itself to blame if its interests suffer. Education is now sufficiently widespread to make it impossible for any mass of civilised people to be long kept under a delusion.

Still there are national as distinct from personal interests, which must be taken into account in judging the effects of economic policy. Individuals may make fortunes, but if in the process they involve their country in bankruptcy, the verdict will be that the system under which this has happened must be a very rotten one. There are only two methods of retaining wealth made in such a way, either by removing it as rapidly as it is made or by changing the system before irretrievable disaster overtakes it. As national indebtedness is one of the measures of the general well-being, we may first of all apply this test.

France, without any controversy, heads the list with a debt, which in 1896 amounted all told to over £1,200,000,000, and involved an annual outlay for interest on the consolidated portion of £28,000,000, and on the redeemable and floating of £10,000,000 more. The capital, though not the interest, has been steadily accumulating, for in France as elsewhere the value of money has undergone considerable depreciation, and refunding schemes have resulted in continual reductions in the charges; in 1890, for instance, on a smaller consolidated debt the outlay was £29,500,000. But it is very rarely a sound principle to continue borrowing because it can be done without further cost, and some day France will find this out. Her finance ministers do not blind themselves to the danger, and only go on piling up the debt because the resources of taxation are so severely strained, and nearly every year results in a budget deficiency, which has to be met by borrowing, at first on floating loan, and when this has so increased as to become unwieldy, by a conversion into funded debt.

How this accumulation has taken place is very simply related. In 1871 the funded debt was under £500,000,000, and the charge upon it about £15,500,000. By 1876 it had increased to £800,000,000, but of course there was good reason for it. France had to pay Germany a war indemnity of £200,000,000, as well as make good within her own territories the devastation which the war had wrought. Borrowing under such circumstances was not easy, and most of the new loans had to be raised at 5 per cent., which brought the charge up to nearly £30,000,000, or almost double on a debt which had not been increased by much over fifty per cent. By 1876 however it may be supposed that all urgent necessities had been provided for, and this supposition is confirmed by the very moderate increases which took place for several succeeding years. But with the beginning of the next decade it started a fresh advance, and went forward by leaps and bounds, until in 1885, by which time there was a large redeemable as well as irredeemable debt, it had reached £950,000,000. All the five per cents. had by then been converted, and no higher interest was paid than

4½, but the charge had risen to £33,000,000. Since then the increase has gone on at a quinquennial rate of about £50,000,000, and shows no sign of coming to an end, while the floating debt and other liabilities swell it up to the total named.

It would of course be ridiculous to directly associate the rapid accumulation of debt with a policy of protection. But at least the two must be considered together. France is supposed to have increased, and to go on increasing her wealth by means of it, yet either that or something else is having a most disastrous effect on the national finances. Were protection removed, the debt charge would have to be met just the same; but would the capital go on increasing ? The augmentation may be partly due to foreign expansion, and the so-called opening up of new markets to French industry. But it means a drain on revenue as well as an addition to capital, and the question may well be asked, whether the French people are proportionately enabled to meet this drain upon them as taxpayers, out of their increased profits as producers ?

This would become a very serious matter were France involved in another great war. On top of liabilities of £1,200,000,000, she could not expect to borrow much more on easy terms, and four, then four and a half, and finally five per cent. or more, would have to be paid for accommodation. That would not necessarily increase the charge on

# THE UNITED STATES NATIONAL DEBT 413

existing debt, but it would enormously depreciate its capital value, and French protectionists would not only find that the burden of taxation upon them was increased, but that the value of their investments had at the same time undergone a vast diminution.

At quite the bottom of the ladder in this respect stands Germany, with its Imperial debt of but £110,000,000. Still in 1875 it was nothing at all, the entire liabilities of the Treasury being represented by about £6,000,000 in Treasury Bills bearing no interest. There may to some extent be public works as an asset against the debt, and in any case it is trivial, and the taxation it involves hardly worth taking into consideration. But the tendency to increase is there nevertheless. Germany is an admittedly protectionist country, and at the end of twenty years is liable for £100.000,000 more than she was at the beginning.

When we come to the United States, we can weld debt and protection tightly together. In 1880, shortly after the resumption of specie payments, the total liabilities were about $1,950,000,000, of which only $1,725,000,000 was interest bearing, but even under the inconvertible currency previously in circulation, it had steadily diminished every year since 1867, that is, the civil war was scarcely over before the liabilities incurred by it began to be liquidated. The United States remained moderately protective down to 1890, yet in spite of it, or rather we might say in this particular instance, because of it, the debt continued steadily to decline. It had to be redeemed with the annual surplus of revenue over expenditure, and the only other way of disposing of the surplus being by reductions in taxation, that meant lower protective duties, and less protection. With the overflowing prosperity of the country, these duties were not high enough to keep imported goods out, the very fact of them being more or less luxuries adding only to their popularity among the wealthy classes. But few people would contend that the prosperity of the United States up to 1890 was due to a policy of protection. Indeed the cry of the protectionists in the election of that year was, that a much larger measure of prosperity would be the outcome, if only real instead of what they regarded as sham protection were adopted.

Its adoption and the cessation of debt redemption were almost simultaneous. The capital amount of the interest paying debt on the 30th June 1891, after protection had been in force barely a year, was about $600,000,000, and it never after fell much below this figure. The lowest point ever touched was in September of that year, and the exact amount was $585,024,720. The protection of commodities in general, and of silver in particular, created deficit after deficit in the national revenue, and led to drain upon drain on the national treasury, which it was only possible to meet by a succession of loans, beginning in February 1894, and continuing steadily until February 1896, until they amounted in the aggregate to upwards of $260,000,000. Circumstances compelled the issue of bonds bearing a much higher rate of interest than the credit of the country necessitated, and the sales actually realised close upon $300,000,000, the premium having practically to be refunded before maturity by an annual payment of excessive interest. During a period of nearly a quarter of a century therefore, under a policy of what may be termed non-effective protection, the finances of the country flourished, the debt was reduced to a very low level, and would in time have been extinguished; while the moment protection became effective, the reverse tendency asserted itself, and in two or three years debt was increased by some £50,000,000 to £60,000,000. There is no contention that the burden of debt in the United States is even now oppressive, but it soon would be, if added to at the rate of £25,000,000, or even £10,000,000 per annum.

And now, what has happened in the United Kingdom, the only country of the four where free trade has remained pure and undiluted? Going back to the earliest period with which we have dealt, namely 1875, we find that the national debt in that year, funded, unfunded, and approximate value of terminable annuities all included, was £769,000,000. For several years it exhibited a tendency to increase; it was the period of the Russo-Turkish war, when

England was much involved in Eastern complications, and a great deal of money was spent on warlike preparations. Yet the maximum reached was only £773,000,000 in 1879, and since then it has undergone rapid diminution, scarcely a year with the movement in the opposite direction, until in 1896 it had sunk to £648,000,000. But this is not all, the redemption is automatic and increases in velocity as it proceeds, because a fixed sum is set apart every year for the debt, and as capital, and consequently interest, decrease, there is a larger amount available for sinking fund purposes. An addition to the debt of any other country would involve an immediate call on the pockets of the taxpayers, but Great Britain could increase hers by £200,000,000 without adding a penny to its annual cost, until such time as was again considered ripe to re-establish the sinking fund.

While France and Germany therefore have been steadily increasing their national indebtedness, and the United States have been playing hide-and-seek with theirs, free trade England has reduced hers by £120,000,000. From a purely national point of view which is the better policy?

Nor is the contention admissible that the continental increase is any way due to their military systems. If Great Britain maintains a small army, she keeps afloat a huge navy, and the respective charges under this heading, inclusive of pensions, speak for themselves.

GREAT BRITAIN, BUDGET ESTIMATE 1897-98.
Army        £18,140,000 [1]
Navy    .    21,890,000 [1]
            _____
             £40,030,000

FRANCE, BUDGET ESTIMATE 1897.
Army    .    £28,800,000 [2]
Navy    .    11,750,000
            _____
             £40,550,000

GERMANY, BUDGET ESTIMATE 1897-98.
Army    .    .    £29,700,000 [2]
Navy    .    .    4,500,000 [2]
                 _____
                  £34,200,000

The expenditure of the United States on these services has hitherto been comparatively trivial, which would in itself account for the substantial decrease in debt over so long a period. It amounted for the year ending 30th June 1896 to $56,000,000 for the army, and $31,000,000 for the navy, about one-half the smallest item of the three European Powers, though what it may amount to if the country plunges into a spirited foreign policy, is utterly impossible to predict. The tendency in

[1] There is considerable extraordinary expenditure in addition under Special Defence Acts, but as the credits are not exhausted during the year, the amount is uncertain.
[2] Inclusive of extraordinary expenditure.

Europe has been steadily to increase, and in Great Britain perhaps more than elsewhere, but the figures prove conclusively that it must have been years since she enjoyed any financial advantage in this respect over her neighbours.

Next to the nation as a whole, the commercial and trading classes of it loom largest on the horizon, as though they may not constitute the majority of the population they keep the whole machinery of industry moving. It will not be a difficult matter to prove that free trade rather than protection affords the incentive to their energy, and leads directly to increased operations.

A country which seeks to retain its trade and industry in its own hands, does not need many distributors. Between the manufacturer and the consumer there are at most but two middlemen, the dealer and the retailer; often the first is knocked out altogether, sometimes both. But the moment a foreign commodity is dealt with, a small army is employed. There is the shipowner with his office staff, or his agent, the harbour officials and labourers, the draymen and warehouse keepers, importers and brokers, and then dealers and shopkeepers, and all expect to make something out of it. A commodity that can afford to bear all these charges must be more cheaply produced elsewhere to be imported and disposed of on economical principles. Similarly the goods purchased in exchange will go through much the same routine, and while they have employed the same number of hands in producing, they engage more in handling, and yet arrive eventually at the consumer cheaper than if made on the spot. A fair exchange of manufacturing labour therefore means the employment of a more or less important quantity of intermediate labour as well.

We can again illustrate this from what are known as foreign exports, that is re-exports of imported goods. The figures for France and Germany are quite unreliable, because they include so much merely in transit from elsewhere. Switzerland, for instance, must conduct the whole of her very extensive foreign trade through one or other of the countries named. Austria-Hungary sends and receives much through Germany. Some parts of Germany make free use of Dutch ports, and Northern France avails itself of Belgian inlets and outlets. But it is certain that neither France nor Germany have any important markets for foreign produce destined for distant lands, other than their own colonies.

Neither have the United States. The value of this trade is more distinctly traceable, and in 1895-96 fell short of $20,000,000, which is decidedly above the average. Yet the United States are situated most favourably for commerce of this sort. There are important consuming centres in Central and South America, which cannot afford to keep large stocks of foreign commodities, and are therefore in constant need of replenishment. A port like New Orleans should be a busy centre of such commerce, yet it is almost entirely absent. The total value of foreign merchandise shipped from Gulf ports was only $825,000, while the total shipments from all United States ports to South America was under $800,000. Two-thirds of the total went to Great Britain or British possessions. The prevalence of protection enhances the cost of dutiable articles, even where the full drawback is allowed, and so handicaps if it does not entirely destroy the business.

Great Britain on the other hand, as a free trade country, has a large annual turnover in this respect. In 1895 the value touched very nearly £60,000,000, in 1896 it was £56,250,000. What does this mean? In the first place, shipping was employed to convey over £100,000,000 worth of commodities. Dock and harbour dues were charged on them, and so helped to lighten the burden on those retained for home consumption. Employment was given in various directions, brokerages, commissions, and profits, aggregating in all a considerable sum, were earned, and helped to swell British incomes. And all this occurred because there was absolutely no restriction on the trade. Anything that is wanted hastily, from a drug at a guinea an ounce, to scrap iron at twenty or thirty shillings a ton, is to be had for the asking, and shipped at twenty-four hours' notice. And because British ships are always ready to go anywhere, and carry anything, the British merchant navy, without subsidy or bounty, maintains its pre-eminence on the ocean.

Protection not only restricts, if it does not entirely prevent this trade, but throws all sorts of obstacles in the way of that done for home consumption. There are constant disputes as to the meaning of clauses, and what they do or do not include; in the United States litigation has been known over the placing or misplacing of a comma. New and sometimes forced interpretations are given to meet special cases, and the French tariff in particular is deluged in explanatory notes and amplifications, constantly being added to.[1] Only those subject to such interference can realise the worries, resulting generally in more or less serious loss, which are the direct outcome of continual friction. I mentioned in a previous chapter that there were 43,420 undecided disputes pending in the United States at the date of the last return.

Passing for a moment to an entirely different aspect of the question, there is little doubt that protection has a direct tendency to lower the moral tone of the commercial classes. A determined attempt is being made in the United States to substitute wherever possible specific for *ad valorem* duties, on the direct ground that imported goods

[1] The French Customs Authorities in 1896 alone, issued 126 special circulars supplementary to various clauses of the tariff.

are systematically undervalued in the sworn declarations of their owners, and that the protection afforded to home manufacturers is in consequence often more apparent than real. Laws which are not only evaded, but broken without any compunction of conscience, savour more of the relationship of conqueror and conquered than of a free and self-governing people. Commercial morality is not assisted by a Government which puts such stringent regulations in force, that men otherwise honest in their dealings are for ever seeking to circumvent them.

Next we pass to the industrial community, and the most noticeable feature is the wave of prosperity or depression which is always passing over it. At one time these waves were of fairly equal force and duration, but of late years the depression has been severer and more prolonged than the prosperity, and this may be directly ascribed to protection.

Under protection each country desires to supply all its home requirements, and to be independent of foreign producers. It seeks therefore to keep the plant of its own production equal to the maximum demands of consumers. In the United States, for instance, the output of Bessemer steel rails in 1887 was nearly 2,050,000 tons. But in 1894 it fell to 900,000 tons. Presumably there was in the latter year a plant equal to the production of double what it was used for, indeed in the following year the output rose again to 1,250,000 tons.

There was loss of interest and depreciation going on on the idle plant, helping to add to the cost of what was actually made. But that is not the worst feature of it. Plant would not be thrown idle until there was distinct over-production, and the chances are that the 2,050,000 tons were far more than were required in 1887, and that the surplus had to be worked off gradually afterwards.

Extend this principle to France and Germany and other protected countries, and we see the same forces at work. Everywhere there is a maximum plant capable of producing the maximum demands of home consumption. That demand actually springs up in two or three countries, and it is filled at once. But under a free trade system manufacturers would probably have been content, even where they were able to compete successfully against foreign rivals, to maintain a medium plant, and any unusual demand would have been distributed in all directions. It would have taken time to fill, there would have been less disposition to anticipate a continuance of briskness in a foreign market than in a home one, and over-production would have been more promptly checked. The period of prosperity would have been prolonged, there would have been a smaller surplus to work off during the subsequent depression, the period of which would consequently have been shortened.

We have only to extend this to all the industries stimulated by protection, and we soon arrive at universal over-production. Labour is as much a portion of the plant as the engine which drives the machinery, and it too for a time is attracted in unduly large quantities. Then it is suddenly thrown idle, but instead of being content with an occasional turn and oiling, it starves, and those dependent on its earnings with it. The farmer goes on growing his corn and vegetables and feeding his cattle, but there is not the money to purchase them. They remain in his granary, or rot in the fields, or eat their heads off, and their owner complains of bad times and over-production, whereas were everyone properly fed there would be something approaching a famine in the land. Free trade therefore not only opens many markets to surplus products, but in three years out of four stimulates the consumption of them at home.

And what of the great mass of wage-earners and those dependent on small or moderate incomes however received? Where wages are proportionate to prices, free trade or protection is of little consequence. If bread and all the necessaries of life are 50 per cent. dearer in one country than another, and wages are likewise 50 per cent. higher, the labourer might rest content. But how often is this the case? The skilled mechanic in the United States may be quite as well off financially as his brother in England. In any case he is not so physically. The same precautions are not always taken to ensure his health and comfort while at work, he has not the same redress if permanently injured, or even temporarily disabled, and if he is discontented and strikes, there may be judges who will construe the laws against him, and send him to jail, though he may not have been guilty of any violence. He really wants a higher proportionate wage to compensate him for the disabilities he is under.

But the moment he is idle, or his wages are reduced, he begins to feel the pinch. The commodities he requires are not necessarily cheaper, he has less money to buy them with, and must either save less or reduce consumption. And it must be remembered that in every country a very large number of wage-earners are not skilled mechanics receiving high pay. They are the flotsam and jetsam of humanity, cast hither and thither, and earning a precarious livelihood. An average of two, three, or if they are lucky, four days' work per week is all they have to look forward to. If food and clothing are plentiful and cheap, they may be able to eke out a fairly tolerable subsistence, but increase the cost of these and life becomes one continual fight against starvation. How essential therefore that the barest necessaries should be maintained at the lowest possible level of value. If the well paid mechanic in England and the United States are on fairly equal terms, there is no comparison between the lot of the casual labourers in the two countries, for while in the one a few coppers will always secure food and shelter, it is only a silver piece will provide the equivalent in the other.

Very low prices are of less consequence than that they should be at the lowest practicable level. To those who rarely if ever have any money at all, it matters little whether the quartern loaf is at fourpence or eightpence; to those who are able to earn something, however little, it may make all the difference in the world. But when natural causes keep the price at the higher level, they will also to some extent raise the remuneration of even casual labour. When these causes are, like protection, purely artificial, they may, and very likely will, operate in one direction without exerting any corresponding influence in the other. What each nation must aim at, is not to reduce prices to the lowest point in order that the most needy of the community may benefit, but to take care that they are kept as low as anywhere else. And only free trade can accomplish this.

It is always difficult as well as dangerous to attribute far-reaching consequences to narrow causes. The contention that free trade has been the sole, or even the principal reason of the past industrial supremacy of Great Britain, is almost impossible of proof. We do not know what would have happened under protection; other nations have advanced under it, and one at least appears now to be making more rapid industrial progress than Great Britain, though, as we have seen, it is the least protective. But there are landmarks which should at anyrate be noted.

Were the demands for protection in England confined exclusively to agriculturists and landowners, it might be dismissed as a purely class agitation. But it now finds considerable support among manufacturers, who were at one time almost to a man fervent adherents of free trade. They feel the pressure of competition, particularly of what we may term the "balance of trade" competition, and though that must continue in one form or another, each individual wishes to transfer it to some other industry. Under it profits have been grievously reduced, while they have been further cut at the other end by a steady rise in wages. Invested capital generally, being worth so much less than it formerly was, it is but natural that capital invested in industry should likewise yield a smaller return, though this may be made good to some extent by increased personal energy. But the fact remains, that only in exceptional years and under very favourable circumstances are industrial magnates able to earn the profits to which they had grown accustomed by long usage, and because they are growing poorer, or not increasing in wealth as they think they ought, they imagine the country is losing ground.

The favourite figures used to disprove this are not always very convincing; the value of property assessed to the income tax does not show any great increase in recent years, while the larger deposits in the Post Office savings banks are known to be very largely on behalf of well-to-do people, who use them as a safe investment while the rate of interest is everywhere else so low. And truly, a system which has only succeeded in placing a bare four per cent. of the population within reach of an income of £400 per annum and upwards, has nothing very great to boast of.

Nevertheless the country has been and is making steady progress, and increasing in wealth, in ways which are not perceptible to the statistician. My own memory carries me little further back than twenty or twenty-five years, yet in the city with which I am best acquainted I have in that time witnessed a transformation. In every direction it has extended itself, and rows of goodly-sized houses, semi-detached villas, and spacious mansions have sprung up everywhere. I have sometimes wondered where the people came from who inhabit them, for the actual population has not increased in anything like proportion to the accommodation provided for it. The answer is probably to be found in the wholesale migration of shopkeepers moving their private residences from their places of business to suburban districts. The cheapness of nearly everything, undoubtedly due in some measure to free trade, has not only stimu-

lated the demand, but has increased retail profits ;
and while the great merchant or manufacturer
finds it difficult to make a fair percentage on an
annual turnover of hundreds of thousands of pounds,
the retailer makes his twenty, thirty, and even
fifty per cent. on his hundreds or few thousands.
The dwellings which at one time would have been
regarded as at least the homes of large wholesale
dealers, are now inhabited by people who sell
sugar by the pound and calico by the yard. This
means not only enormous activity in the building
trades, and all in any way associated with them,
but growing receipts for the railway companies,
and new demands for omnibus and tramway routes,
with all the employment they necessarily afford.

In the same city there is a district notorious
as the centre of everything that is vicious and
criminal. Until recently I had not passed through
it for some years, and I was surprised to find
that the narrow streets, and still narrower and
more confined courts, had been cleared of the
high and tumble-down tenements with which they
had so abounded, and that rows of neat-looking
workmen's cottages had largely taken their place.
How much wretchedness, vice and crime there still
is in that district, God only knows, but at least an
attempt has been made to provide the people with
decent surroundings. Not much can be expected
while there is a public-house at every street corner,
and very often one or two in between; but there is

an evident tendency to improvement even among the most debased, assisted and expedited by the very cheapness of all the necessaries of life.

And between these extremes there is an enormous population dependent on one to three pounds per week, living in comparative comfort, where half a century ago they would have been unable to make ends meet. Free trade may not have lifted them into the class of the rich, but it has at least handed down to them many of the comforts, and some few even of the luxuries of that class.

While these classes have been prospering, perhaps to some extent at the expense of those above them, the nation in the aggregate has certainly not been growing poorer. We have noticed that already in connection with the reduction of the national debt, but there are other means of gauging it as well. All the new buildings, whether for residential or business occupation, are a permanent addition to the wealth of the country, and though some of the old property may have greatly depreciated in value, much of it on the other hand has steadily risen, as it has become the centre of growing business activity. And even when we come to that very popular test, the accumulation of the precious metals, we find the same story told. However else the excess of imports over exports has been paid for, it certainly has not been in gold. Every year from 1887 to 1895 inclusive, more gold was received into the country than was sent out of it. The aggregate excess of the years 1874 to 1896 inclusive amounted to upwards of £60,000,000, and whatever else is wanted in the land, there is plenty of the precious metal for all needful requirements.

Silver renders a somewhat different account, as during the same period the exports exceeded the imports by upwards of £8,000,000. This is strange, considering that nowhere in the United Kingdom are there any silver mines; but the explanation is that some lead containing silver is produced, and that a great deal of rich silver lead ore is imported from Spain and other countries for treatment by English smelters, and that the quantity so extracted has been sufficient to provide all that was necessary for coinage purposes, and for use in the various arts, leaving a considerable surplus for export. In British trade returns, silver should really appear as a commodity, and that would slightly rectify the adverse balance. In 1896, if so included, it would have operated in this way to the extent of £720,000, a figure rather below the usual average.

The United States have on the other hand lost much gold in recent years, again directly attributable to fiscal and currency legislation. The countries of continental Europe have gained largely, but that has been of set and deliberate purpose, while in England it has taken place in the natural course of events. The banks of France, of Germany, of Austria, and of Russia, accumulate great supplies of gold as a precaution against military eventualities, and nothing would induce them to part with it. London is a free market, and the gold is as much at liberty to go as it is to come.

What free trade does for the many, protection would undoubtedly accomplish in an accentuated degree for the few. The increase in the price of any commodity rarely passes intact into the hands of the producer, but as one producer supplies many consumers, a small portion of it soon enriches him. Were protection afforded to agriculture in the United Kingdom, the net result would be a rise in the rent of land, which would come out of the pockets of food consumers and pass into those of the landowners. Were it extended to certain manufactures, such as clothing, the woollen or cotton spinner and weaver would profit; the wearer would pay. How it would operate in Great Britain, is exactly how it does operate in countries where it exists. Protection is the paradise of the rich, Free Trade the salvation of the poor.

# APPENDIX.

## THE NEW AMERICAN TARIFF.

The "Sound Money" victory of November 1896 has already borne its fruit in the United States, but it is distinctly of the Dead Sea variety. Not the slightest attempt has been made to reform the currency, the basis of which remains as rotten as ever, while the assets held against it have been further depreciated by at least $50,000,000 through the continued heavy fall in the price of silver. The hundreds of thousands, if not the millions of United States electors who were deluded, cajoled, and forced into voting for President M'Kinley on the specious grounds of his transparent "honesty"—save the mark—now discover to their cost that they are delivered over, bound hand and foot, to be mercilessly plundered by his friends. For the loud boast of these latter is, that the new or Dingley tariff imposes an average duty of 56 per cent. against the 40 per cent. of its immediate predecessor, and the 50 per cent. which was all Mr. M'Kinley as a plain Congressman could screw it up to.

The first object of the M'Kinley Act was to reduce the revenue; the purpose of the Dingley tariff however is to "provide revenue for the Government, and to encourage the industries of the United States," a curious combination it must be admitted, for in the way in which it is here meant, the one is altogether antagonistic to the other. The framer of the measure claimed for it indeed that it would shut out foreign imports, and enable home manufacturers to supply the goods instead, and then in the same breath, and with an audacity of which only an American protectionist could be capable, proceeded to show that taking the previous year's imports as a basis, the Treasury would gain to the extent of $110,000,000. In the form in which the Bill has finally become law, the duties payable on the goods imported during the last year of the Wilson Act would be $276,000,000, against the amount of $156,000,000 actually collected under that Act, that is, the additional levy would amount to $120,000,000, or £24,000,000. As the quantities of these imported goods constitute under many of the schedules but a very moderate percentage of the total consumption, it is quite safe to estimate that the cost of the new tariff to the consumers of the United States will be somewhere between £50,000,000 and £100,000,000 per annum. Just a little instalment to be going on with of the price for "Sound Money."

The Dingley Bill as it emerged from the Ways and Means Committee of the House of Representatives was almost a recast of the former M'Kinley Act, with one important exception. That exception was sugar, which had formerly enjoyed a bounty costing the Treasury some $12,500,000 annually, but now followed the lines of the Wilson Act, and imposed instead a duty on the basis of $1\frac{7}{8}$ cent per pound for pure sugar, which was calculated to yield $50,000,000, that is, on this one schedule alone the gain to the Treasury was estimated at upwards of $60,000,000 per annum upon the M'Kinley Act.

The Bill was forced through the House of Representatives without amendment, and practically without debate, the closure having been applied in an unusually drastic manner. The measure however so greatly exceeded in stringency what had generally been anticipated, that a strong movement set in to import as much as possible of every article affected, prior to its becoming law, and the protectionists made a counter move to prevent this. They tacked on to the Bill a retroactive clause, that is, although it might not become law for some time, the duties under it were to become payable on the 1st May, and ample security taken on goods which should be imported subsequently, and cleared from bond before the final enactment of the new tariff. Unfortunately for these enthusiasts, they had been engaged some years previous in defeating a clause of a very similar character.

The Wilson Bill had been framed to come into operation on the 1st August 1894, which would have allowed ample time for its discussion, but owing to the obstructive tactics of the Senate, its passage was delayed until the 28th of that month. Protectionists, grasping at any straw, moved for and obtained a decision from the Supreme Court that all imports cleared from bond prior to that date fell under the old tariff, and consequently had to pay the old duties, though they no doubt hoped that the judges of that court would now reverse the decision for their special benefit.

But there was no need to appeal to the Supreme Court in this instance. The retroactive clause did not suit the Senate, and was promptly banished to the limbo of obscurity whence it sprang. Many of the members of that body were busy in one way or another importing all they could themselves, and otherwise making money out of the new tariff, and they wanted delay, not speed, any loss to the National Treasury being to them of utter insignificance when compared with their personal interests. It was consequently not until the closing days of July that the Bill actually became law.

Meanwhile it had passed through many vicissitudes. Despite the pharasaical utterances of its official sponsors there was less concealment than usual about the real objects of the Bill, and the fight for the spoils was open and flagrant. It was no longer a case of asking for a duty to keep an industry on its legs, but rather of demanding a licence to pilfer the American public, and the man who could steal the most became the hero of the hour. An ardent supporter of the measure when asked if he was aware that one of the clauses assured an annual profit of $3,500,000 to one of the smaller trusts, blandly responded that he "Didn't know and didn't care."

The House of Representatives having looked carefully after its own interests, it was but natural to expect that the Senate would follow so excellent a precedent, one indeed which in times gone by it had itself created. It became therefore no longer a question of how much Congressman Brown or Congressman Jones was going to make out of it, but whether it suited the pockets of Senator Smith and Senator Robinson.

The result was very tersely put by a leading New York journal on the day the Bill emerged from the Senate Tariff Committee, an event which was announced as "Dingley Bill went in, Jones Bill comes out," Mr. Dingley being the representative of the Eastern manufacturers as well as the author of the measure, and Senator Jones of Nevada, the champion of the interests strong in the Senate.

In one respect at least the Senate was honest. It brushed aside the nonsense about the Bill providing ample revenue for the Government, and sought to ensure that in a practicable manner. Tea, previously on the free list, was charged with a duty of 10 cents per pound, and the excise tax on beer was raised from $1 to $1.44 per barrel. On the basis of existing consumption these new taxes were estimated to yield $30,000,000 per annum, and so help to adjust the national balance-sheet. They were subsequently eliminated, as to the out-and-out protectionist an annual addition to the national debt is far preferable to an admission that protective duties do not provide sufficient revenue.

But for all that, a very considerable number of changes were made in the original measure, and as some of them were in the direction of reduced rates, credit is claimed for the Senate for having somewhat modified the measure. Little is due to it however, for the changes are more apparent than real, and are principally conspicuous in the schedule devoted to iron and steel, where the Wilson rates are as a rule retained, and in one or two instances further reduced. Here it has been lately demonstrated that the interests principally concerned are unable to avail themselves of the protection already afforded, and that the ordinary laws of supply and demand hold sway. To reduce the duties $1 or $2 a ton, is consequently but to make a virtue of necessity, for nobody is either the gainer or the loser.

Had the Senate really desired to demonstrate its ability, as well as its desire to modify the metal tariff, there was ample scope for it in the section devoted to cutlery. On cheap penknives and pocket-knives for instance, the Wilson rate was 25 per cent. *ad valorem*, the Dingley is 40 per cent. on top of a graduated specific rate. A knife, the wholesale price of which is 5 cents, pays another 5 cents duty, and then the 40 per cent., making the duty 140 per cent. against a former 25 per cent. Razors and razor blades are very similarly treated, and instead of 40 per cent., pay, if valued at say $3 per dozen, another $1.75, and 20 per cent. additional, or about 80 per cent. Similarly all sorts of nails, paying mostly under the Wilson Act 25 per cent., are now charged at specific rates varying from $\frac{1}{4}$ cent to $2\frac{1}{4}$ cents per pound, in some instances a very material increase.

Again, in the schedule devoted to cotton goods, many of the Wilson rates are left. But they are solely in the cheaper fabrics in which foreign competition is altogether out of the question, and in which over-production at home occasionally brings prices down to a lower level than the tariff would warrant. Had American cotton manufacturers been able to demonstrate that an extra 10 or 20 per cent. would have enabled them to exact that much more from the consumer, the Dingley Bill would undoubtedly have granted it to them.

But the moment we pass to the more expensive goods, in which there is foreign competition, there is a different tale to tell. Here duties have been raised all round, and sometimes raised heavily. Fine cotton cloths of over 200 threads to the square inch have been increased $\frac{1}{2}$ cent a yard, and on the very finest 1 cent a yard, equivalent to about 20 per cent. Stockings and hosiery have suffered just as severely, and whereas the former rate was an even 50 per cent. *ad valorem*, it is now under mixed, specific and *ad valorem* duties raised to from 60 to 75 per cent.

In one or two directions the Senate sought to introduce decided improvements. Owing to the basis of the constitution of that Assembly, it is much more representative of the South and the West than the lower chamber. The Wilson Act, it will be remembered, made important concessions to agricultural industry by placing cotton bagging and ties, and grain bags, on the free list. The Dingley tariff sought to reintroduce these duties in nearly all their former unblushing extravagance, and the Senate once more abolished them. A compromise was eventually arrived at, under which cotton ties now pay \$11.20 per ton instead of the \$30 under the M'Kinley Act, and the bagging $\frac{6}{10}$ cent per square yard, instead of $1\frac{6}{10}$ to $1\frac{7}{10}$ cents. Grain bags fare less favourably, and have to pay 15 per cent. on top of specific duties of ⅜ to ⅞ cent per pound.

But the Senate made ample atonement for this in other directions, and particularly by the transfer of raw cotton from the free to the dutiable list at 20 per cent. *ad valorem*, aimed of course at the Egyptian staple, and by the imposition of 1½ cents per pound on raw hides. These duties were particularly obnoxious to Eastern manufacturers, and the angriest protesters against them were the bitterest protectionists. They were meant to afford an advantage to western and southern producers, and hitherto American protection has always meant that the western and southern citizen was to pay, not receive. Logically the duties are absurd, but not more so than the wool duty, and there is no more reason why a flockmaster should be protected than a cotton planter or a cattle breeder. The former duty was got rid of, but that on hides the Senate insisted on retaining, though it was compromised by a reduction to 20 per cent. *ad valorem*.

This is a severe blow to the leather-tanning industry, one of the very few in the United States which has prospered in late years, and likewise one of the very few which has hitherto been conducted free from artificial restriction. The value of the leather export has steadily mounted from under $12,000,000 in 1893 to upwards of $20,000,000 in 1896, and despite the drawback to be allowed on exported leather tanned from imported hides, the industry is certain to receive a severe check. Moreover, it affects trade relationships with South America, whence fully half the raw hides are imported, and Uruguay and the Argentine Republic, who are constantly being invited to increase their takings of United States manufactures, are already threatening serious reprisals. One would feel some sympathy for those engaged in the American leather trade, did one not feel certain that had protection suited them they would have demanded it for themselves long since.

Mexico is another country with which the United States are anxious to extend their connections, at anyrate as far as selling them manufactured goods is concerned, and there is perhaps no country at the present moment whose friendship is better worth cultivating. Mexico is likewise a considerable exporter of hides as well as cattle, the duty on which is also largely increased. But the great industry of that republic is silver and lead mining, and once more the Western Senator has intervened to destroy trade. The natural source of supply for the deficiency in the United States lead production is Mexico, so the duties on pig lead and lead ore have been doubled, the former now standing at \$47.50, the latter at \$33.50 per ton. Again however, the Western Senator and those he represents are amply justified from their own point of view.

The last serious difference between the two houses which I shall notice for the moment, arose on the Wool Schedule. The M'Kinley Act, it will be remembered, divided the fleeces into three classes. The commonest is used principally by Eastern carpet manufacturers, and when not imported is grown principally on the backs of sheep in the Rocky Mountain districts. As they thus belonged to Western owners, the measure of protection extended to them was much less than to those of the Middle and Eastern States. Against this Western Senators rebelled, and while reducing the duties on first and second class unwashed wools from 11 and 12 cents per pound to 8 and 9 cents respectively, they materially increased those on third-class wools. Once more was heard the wail of pharasaic hypocrisy as the sponsors of the Bill declaimed against greed and selfishness, but nevertheless, to keep what they had already secured for themselves, they agreed to give what the West demanded with some slight modification, with the result that the old M'Kinley Woollen Schedule is re-enacted in more than its old iniquity.

The new regulations regarding tourists' wearing apparel and personal effects, naturally fall to be reviewed under this schedule. I referred to a probable attempt to put an end to this abuse, and it too has resulted in compromise. Instead of everything of foreign production being made dutiable, an import is permitted of $100 for each person; a slender margin for some, but a fairly wide one for those who are not inclined to extravagance. Already endless disputes have arisen regarding the interpretation of the clause, and among other things a wrangle has occurred over the value of the clothing on the corpse of an unfortunate passenger who died while at sea. The customs landing depots attached to the various ports promise to become veritable houses of detention, and there will be no need shortly for penitentiaries like the "Tombs."

On the other schedules, with one important exception, there appears to have been something like agreement. That devoted to chemicals afforded perhaps the widest field for fresh pilfering, and it was fully availed of. Since the days of the M'Kinley Act, a Drug Trust has come into existence, which has sought to impose its terms on every retail chemist in the Union, and failing, has deliberately set to work to ruin him. The ten per cent. duty hitherto imposed on raw drugs was insufficient for its purpose, and as it no doubt contributed handsomely to the Republican campaign fund, its orders despatched to Washington to impose an additional specific duty were promptly and implicitly obeyed. Bleaching powder, which even under the M'Kinley Act had been left free, was transferred to the dutiable list, and rated at ¼ cent per pound, equal to $4.50 per ton. Argols or crude tartar was treated in the same manner, and instead of being free, is now charged at 1 cent to 1½ cents per pound, equivalent to 10 to 15 per cent. of its value. The Wilson rates on the remainder, with scarcely an exception, were raised to, and sometimes beyond, the M'Kinley ones, and American industry utters a deeper groan than ever.

Schedule B devoted to earthenware and glassware shared a similar fate, though as absolutely nothing had previously been left out, nothing could well be added. As far as possible this was atoned for by raising some of the items to an unprecedented altitude, where the keen air may be expected to nip any little foreign trade that was left.

The warfare against Canadian lumber was renewed in all its intensity in Schedule D, and though the Senate uttered a mild protest, it complacently voted the duties. The genius who discovered toothpicks as the apex of the Wilson Act, has however again been exercising his nimble wittedness, and this time lighted on firewood, which must in future pay $\frac{3}{10}$ cent per quarter cubic foot. We can pity the kitchen maid, who, living in the vicinity of the Canadian frontier, has every morning to repair to the local custom house to measure a cubic foot of chips, and pass entries for them before she can kindle her fire and prepare her master's breakfast. At the same time the opportunity has been discovered for building up another great American industry, and as a consequence foreign manufactured butchers' skewers will henceforth have to pay 40 cents per 1000.

Agricultural products are generally restored to M'Kinley rates, and once more fresh milk and cabbages have their nakedness covered. Green fruits have been generally advanced, but against this remains the fact that sage has been permitted to halt at 1 cent per pound against 3 cents formerly.

What the M'Kinley Act endeavoured unsuccessfully to accomplish for tinplates, the Dingley tariff is bent on doing for flax and silk manufactures. Over and over again the people most interested in the establishment of a flax and hemp industry have maintained that climatic conditions are unsuitable for the cultivation of the fibres, or for their subsequent treatment. But the Dingley Bill decrees that the American people shall be forced to use any rubbish that can be produced in the United States, in preference to the beautifully finished and bleached fabrics of the North of Ireland and Yorkshire. A duty of $20 per ton (2000 pounds) has been imposed on the raw materials, which under the Wilson Act were free, and even under the M'Kinley just half this rate. The tissues which were dutiable at 35 per cent. and 50 per cent. respectively, are now reduced to 30 per cent. *ad valorem*, but on top of a specific rate ranging from 1¾ cents to 9 cents per square yard, with the added proviso that in no case shall the combined duty amount to less than 50 per cent. One of two things is likely to happen, either Americans will pay utterly extravagant prices for linen goods, or they will discard them in disgust, and fall back on the cheaper and less serviceable cotton fabrics.

With silk it is somewhat different. The raw material has never yet been produced in the United States, while there has long been a more or less important manufacture of it. The former consequently remains on the free list, while the duties on the fabrics are heavily enhanced. Spun silk is raised from 30 per cent., to equal to 35 to 40 per cent., while the tissues themselves are based upon most elaborate calculations of a very technical character, but also with the proviso that in no instance shall they be less than 50 per cent. Probably they will more often than not be in the neighbourhood of 100 per cent.

A United States Tariff Bill without the Sugar Schedule, would be like a performance of Hamlet without the Prince of Denmark. The Sugar Trust probably spent more millions of dollars in securing the return of President M'Kinley than any other corporation or individual spent thousands, and for every million it advanced, it has been permitted to put its hands into the pockets of the American people and take out at least ten.

The House Bill started well, and established a differential rate between raw and refined sugar, which, though enigmatical to the uninitiated, afforded at least double the protection attainable under the Wilson Act. This was not good enough for the managers of the Trust however, who despatched their agents to Washington—men, who in case of anything some day going wrong, may have to do penal servitude in place of their principals—not to negotiate with the Government, but to dictate what the schedule should be. As a consequence, when it appeared in the Senate it had undergone a total transformation, and though more complicated than ever, its framers frankly avowed that it gave them $\frac{1}{4}$ cent per pound certain protection, and did not deny that the real figure was probably $\frac{1}{2}$ cent. As the annual consumption of sugar exceeds 4,000,000,000 pounds, this meant over $20,000,000 per annum, fully three-fourths of which would have been secured by the Trust.

The Senate forced the schedule through as it stood, and individual Senators are known to have made moderate fortunes by speculations in the stock. The Republican leaders in the House of Representatives professed much righteous indignation, and vowed the Trust should not have so much. The Trust knew better, and when the House finally settled the matter, it juggled the text, and left the result very much what it was. All this time sugar stock had been steadily rising from about par, until it stood at over 130. On the day the House practically conceded all that had ever been demanded, the market value of the stock appreciated a further $5,500,000.

The final basis of the duty is $\frac{95}{100}$ cent per pound on sugar testing 75 degrees by the polariscope—an unusually low grade — increasing $3\frac{1}{2}/100$ cent for every degree. Absolutely pure sugar testing 100 degrees would consequently work out at 1.825 cents, but there can be no such thing as pure raw sugar, and to be in this state it must be refined. $\frac{1}{8}$ cent, that is, .125 is added as a gratuity to the Trust, bringing all refined sugars up to $1\frac{95}{100}$ cent per pound.

The enormous advantage accruing to the Trust may be seen at a glance, though without the possibility of calculating it with exactitude. Nobody in fact can do that without access to the books of the company. On the basis of 1.825 cents for 100° sugar, each degree should pay .01825 cent, but as a matter of fact an allowance is made of .035 cent. That is, in addition to the $\frac{1}{8}$ cent out and out which the Trust fought for and obtained under the Wilson Act, it now gets .01675 cent per degree per pound. The lower the sugar the Trust can buy for refining purposes therefore, the greater will be its profit, consequently all the low-grade sugars produced throughout the world, together with any filth containing sugar, will henceforth be purchased for the consumption of United States citizens.

The Trust has at least several years before it in which to plunder, if it does not previously poison the public; its time for robbing the Treasury was limited. It was made the most of however, and the Bill delayed until every available nook and cranny was filled with raw sugar imported at the old duty. For many months to come the United States Treasury will draw no revenue from sugar — it has gone into the coffers of the Trust instead. The American consumer will get none of it, it is certain, as the moment the question was settled, and before the Bill became law, the retail price was raised to the extreme limit of the new duties, and the

Trust's profits on the imported sugar alone are estimated to exceed $10,000,000.

These plums all fall to the Trust, and the shareholders participate in them like the managers, though as the latter were always aware of what was taking place at Washington, their opportunities for manipulation were very great. But they wanted something for their own exclusive benefit, and President M'Kinley almost stumbled over his own shadow in his haste to procure it for them and place it at their disposal.

The group of islands in the Pacific, known as the Sandwich Islands, has Hawaii as its centre. The principal industry is sugar growing, and ever since there has been a duty on raw sugar in the United States, an American syndicate has run the islands and secured the free import of the produce of the cane into the States. The intimate connection of the Sugar Trust with this syndicate may be gathered from the fact that the chief sugar estates in Hawaii are known as Spreckelsville, and the Spreckels of California are the western managers of the Trust.

Under the stimulus of unlimited capital and gigantic profits, the production of sugar in Hawaii has enormously increased, and the 130,000 tons of 1895 rose to close upon 200,000 in 1896, and will no doubt be again exceeded in 1897. Now 90 per cent. raw sugar pays about $1\frac{1}{2}$ cent per pound import duty, say $30 per ton of 2000 lbs. On the latest production of Hawaii, this would mean $6,000,000 per annum, which instead of going into the Treasury is henceforth to be divided among some half-dozen managers of the American Sugar Trust as their perquisites.

That is the meaning of the annexation of Hawaii. A mere treaty of commerce admitting the produce of the islands free is not secure enough, so they must be incorporated as part of the federal union. And what matters it if the annexation does bring the Republic into deadly conflict with the rest of the civilised world, so long as sugar kings fill their pockets ?

The M'Kinley administration acts on the assumption that the annexation is an accomplished fact, though it has yet to be ratified by the Senate. Will the Senate again succumb and cover itself with infamy, or will it for once refuse to be dragged at the tail of the Sugar Trust, decline to ratify the annexation, abrogate the treaty, and make Hawaiian pay the duty like any other foreign sugars ?

The unblushing effrontery and unalloyed success of this Trust is already stirring up powerful imitators, ready at any moment to raid the small amount of liberty the American people still enjoy. A group of bankers and financiers is even now planning its arrangements to secure entire control of the national currency, first by compelling the public to accept its promises to pay, or bank notes as they will be called, and then forcing the Government to guarantee them and keep some sort of metallic reserve against them, though it may only be a cent in the dollar. The profits of such a combine would put those of the Sugar Trust to shame, and at the same time fetter the industries of the country to an extent that would render the future of the Republic almost hopeless.

What the eventual outcome of all this will be, one would have to venture too far into the realm of prophecy to say. A bountiful harvest, once more accompanied by high prices, may stave off the evil day, but no foreigner should permit himself to be deluded into the idea that legitimate prosperity is possible, while the present state of things is permitted to continue, and those who are lured by a gleam of sunshine will only have to return sooner or later drenched to the skin. The rush to pay duties went far to equalise revenue and expenditure in the fiscal year just ended. The payments in April exceeded anything previously recorded, and reached nearly $30,000,000, those in March having already been $17,500,000, or for the two months combined, double, if not treble the average. The delay in passing the Bill brought a renewed flood of imports, and for the last month of the fiscal year the duty payments rose once more to $21,500,000. This must have a most detrimental influence on the revenue of the current year. The first month of it was again affected by uncertainty, the second enjoyed the advantage of being entirely under the new tariff. It resulted in an excess of $15,000,000 of expenditure over income, and any schoolboy who has advanced to the stage of multiplication by 12, will be able to calculate that continued for a year this means a deficit of $180,000,000. It will not be quite as bad as this, but the Treasury will have a lucky escape if the promised surplus of $50,000,000 does not end in a shortage of a like amount.

That the Dingley Tariff will sooner or later be interred in a dishonoured grave is more than certain. The M'Kinley administration has only to continue as it has begun, to expire amid the execrations of the populace, and to pass down to posterity as the most iniquitous Government that ever presided over the destinies of the great American people.

Here is protection, pure and unadulterated. Is there any Englishman who would like to see it introduced into his own country?

# INDEX.

Abbreviations :—U.K., *United Kingdom;* U.S., *United States;* Fce., *France;* Gmy., *Germany.*

## A

Adverse trade balances, 345, 349.
Africa, U.K., 304, 403 ; Fce., 286, 405 ; Gmy., 285, 406.
Agrarian agitation, Gmy., 275.
Agricultural implements, U.S., 149.
 ,, Rating Act, U.K., 385.
Agriculture—Basis of industry, 30.
 ,, Protection, U.K., 39, 76, 309.
 ,, Tariffs, U.S., 127, 442 ; Fce., 169 ; Gmy., 184.
Algerian trade, 289.
America, discovery of, 280.
American Line subvention, 215.
Argentine trade, 361.
Australasian finances, 325.
 ,, trade, 302, 323.
Australian federation, 325.
Austrian shipping subsidies, 212.

## B

Balance of trade, U.K., 337 ; U.S., 352 ; Fce., 358 ; Gmy., 359 ; Argentine, 361 ; Japan, 362 ; S. Africa, 369 ; Settlements of, 363.
Bankers' profits, 340.
Beer duties, U.K., 69 ; U.S., 252, 436.
Belgian treaty of commerce with U.K., 319.
Blackburn Chamber of Commerce mission, 407.
Board of Trade returns, 374.
Bounties, Canadian iron, 233.
 ,, origin of, 193.
 ,, from over-production, 233.
 ,, miscellaneous, Fce., 232.
 ,, sugar, U.S., 124 ; Fce., 197 ; Gmy., 196.
 ,, sugar, cost to consumers, 198.
Brazilian trade, 366, 378.
Breakfast table duties, U.K., 75.
Brewing, sugar used in, 81.
British national debt, 115.
British railway system, 222.
 ,, shipping subsidies, 205.
 ,, trade with U.S., 365 ; Fce., 364, 372.
Building materials, U.S., 111.
Bullion movements, 367, 430.

## C

Canadian expansion, 316.
 ,, fiscal policy, 293.
 ,, iron bounties, 233.
 ,, preferential tariff, 310.
 ,, shipping subvention, 219.
 ,, trade, 295, 303, 313, 320.
Cement, U.S., 111.
Checks on consumption, 13.
Chemicals, U.S., 105, 441 ; Fce., 168 ; Gmy., 178.
China, trade of, 366, 378, 107.
China and earthenware, U.K., 95 ; U.S., 112, 442 ; Gmy., 183.
Chips, U.S., 442.
Cigar industry, U.K., 71 ; U.S., 252 ; Gmy., 177.
Coal, U.K., 49, 339 ; U.S., 117 ; Fce., 167 ; Gmy., 50.
Cocoa, U.K., 75 ; Fce., 154 ; Gmy., 176.
Coffee, U.K., 75 ; Fce., 154 ; Gmy., 176.
Colonial policy and trade, U.K., 292, 301 ; Fce., 269, 286 ; Gmy., 285 ; Spain, 281 ; Portugal, 283 ; Greece and Phœnicia, 333.
Commercial morality, 421.
 ,, treaties, 191, 318.
Competition in trade, 394, 398, 427.
Conservatism ,, 395.
Construction bounties, Fce., 209.
Contraband trade, 15.
Conventional tariffs, Fce., 174 ; Gmy., 187.
Copper, U.S., 122.
Corn Law League, 10.
Cotton, raw, U.S., 47, 139.

Cotton, manufactured, U.K., 88 ;
    U.S., 131, 378, 438 ; Fce.,
    166 ; Gmy., 180.
    ,, ties and bagging, U.S., 117,
    118, 438.
Cost of collecting revenue, U.S., 255 ;
    Fce., 269.
Cost of living, U.S., 255.
Cuba, 201, 282, 363.
Currants, reduction of duty, U.K.,
    63.
Customs Union Schemes, 305.
Cutlery, U.S., 121, 437 ; Gmy., 179.

## D

Dangers of tariff legislation, 9.
Danish subsidies, 212.
Denunciation of commercial treaties,
    319.
Diamond trade, U.K., 95 ; U.S., 148;
    S. Africa, 370.
Disorganisation of mail service with
    U.S., 218.
Disputes, tariff, 421.
Distribution of taxation, U.K., 244 ;
    U.S., 252 ; Fce., 271 ; Gmy., 278.
Drawbacks, customs, 194.
Drink traffic and public opinion, 16,
    18 ; West Coast Africa, 406.
Drugs, U.S., 106, 441.
Dutch subsidies, 212.

## E

Earthenware and China, U.K., 95 ;
    U.S., 112, 442 ; Gmy., 183.
Economic conditions, Fce., 153, 162.
Education, 270, 392.
Egyptian trade, 291.
Excise duties, 10, 65.
Export duties, 44.
Exports of foreign goods, 419.
    ,, under-valuation of, 342, 421.

## F

Failure of sugar bounties, 201.
False economic conditions, 41.
Feathers. Ornamental, 96, 158, 372.
Federation of Australia, 325.
Fiscal year, U.S., 353.
Fishery bounties, Fce., 232.
Flax ,, ,, 232.
    ,, industry, U.K., 95 ; U.S., 133,
        145, 443 ; Gmy., 181.
Fluctuations in trade, U.S., 357.
Food imports, U.K., 308.
Foreign exports, 419.

Foreign investments, 344.
    ,, trade, nature of, 376, 384.
Forgery of trade marks, 391.
Freights, 339.
Free trade and Trusts, 60.
    ,, ,, the masses, 429.
French bounties, sugar, 197. Other,
    232.
French colonies, 162, 174, 269, 286.
    ,, conventional tariff, 174.
    ,, economic conditions, 153, 162.
    ,, exports, nature of, 156.
    ,, industrial limitations, 161.
    ,, national debt, 270, 410.
    ,, population, 162.
    ,, railway subventions, 227.
    ,, shipping subsidies, 209.
    ,, surtaxes, 172, 201.
    ,, trade with U.K., 364, 372.
Fruits, U.K., 75 ; Fce., 171 ; Gmy.,
    177 ; Canada, 295.
Furs and skins, U.K., 97.

## G

German colonies, 285.
    ,, conventional tariff, 187.
    ,, industrial expansion, 192.
    ,, national debt, 271, 413.
    ,, shipping subsidies, 205.
    ,, State railways, 222.
    ,, sugar bounties, 196.
    ,, tariff, moderation of, 175,
        186, 274.
    ,, ,, Wars, 187.
    ,, trade with British colonies,
        321.
    ,, treaty of commerce with
        U.K., 191, 319.
    ,, Zollverein, 305, 360.
Glass, U.K., 90 ; U.S., 113 ; Gmy.,
    183.
Gloves, U.K., 93 ; U.S., 147 ; Gmy.,
    183.
Gold production, S. Africa, 370.
Grain bags, U.S., 145, 438.
Greek colonies, 333.
Growth of industry, 27.
Gunpowder, U.S., 148.

## H

Hawaii and U.S., 446.
Hides, U.S., 439 ; Fce., 173.
Home trade, 384.

## I and J

Imperial federation, 330.
Import duties, 53.

Incidence of protection, 53, 61, 253.
" revenue taxes, 62.
" sugar bounties, 198.
" wheat taxes, U.K., 56; Fce., 55.
Income tax, U.K., 240, 245, 248; U.S., 251.
Indian trade, 303, 366, 378.
Indo-China, 288.
Industrial Expansion, U.S., 35; Gmy., 37.
Industry, natural growth of, 27.
Insecurity of protection, 20.
Intercourse between nations, 383.
Internal competition, 394.
Iron and steel, U.K., 91; U.S., 115, 437; Fce., 167; Gmy., 179.
Italian shipping subsidies, 212.
Japanese trade, 362, 366, 378.

## L

Labour, waste of, 381.
Lace, U.K., 96; U.S., 136; Gmy., 182.
Lead, U.S., 122, 440.
Leather, U.K., 89; U.S., 146, 439; Gmy., 183.
Legislation and trade, 401.
Licensing systems, 17.
Light dues, 386.
Linens, U.K., 95; U.S., 145, 443; Gmy., 181.
Local taxation, 53.
Luxuries and necessaries, 8.

## M

Madagascar, 290.
Mail contracts, 208, 211, 213, 218.
Mexican dollars, 45.
Mexico and U.S., 110.
Military expenditure, 417.
Morocco, trade of, 46.
Musical instruments, U.K., 95; Fce., 161.

## N

National Debt, U.K., 415; U.S., 413; Fce., 270, 110; Gmy., 271, 113; Australasia, 325.
National finances, U.S., 258, 417.
" " and protection, 20.
Naval expenditure, 417.
Navigation bounties, 210, 212.
Necessaries and Luxuries, 8.
New South Wales tariff, 297.
" " trade with Gmy., 324.
New Zealand tariff, 299.
Nitrate of soda duty, 11.

## O

Over-production, 234, 382, 422.
" bounties arising from, 233.

## P

Paper, U.K., 91; U.S., 145.
Pension list, U.S., 258; Fce., 267.
Phœnician Colonies, 333.
Political uses of protection, 25.
Poor, taxation of the, 12.
Portuguese Colonies, 283.
Postal revenues, 239.
Post office and rubber trade, 78.
Preferential railway rates, U.K., 388, Gmy., 275.
" tariff, Canada, 310.
Prohibition, dangers of, 15.
Protection in U.K., 38.
" France, nature of, 171.
" Gmy., moderation of, 175, 274.
" U.S., results of, 151.
" incidence of, 53, 61, 253.
" and revenue, 25.
" insecurity of, 21.
" when legitimate, 10.
" who responsible for it, 30.
Prussian budget, 277.
Public opinion and drink traffic, 16, 18.

## Q

Queensland tariff, 298.

## R

Railway systems and subventions, U.K., 222; U.S., 231; Fce., 227; Gmy., 222.
Railway preferential rates, U.K., 388; Gmy., 275.
Raw materials, U.K., 77; U.S., 132; Fce., 169; Gmy., 275.
Reckless trading, 389.
Re-exports, 119.
Restrictive legislation, 101.
Retail profits, 428.
Retroactive tariff, 135.
Revenue, cost of collection, U.S., 255; Fce., 269.
Revenue from commodities, 238.
" incidence of taxation, 62.
" and protection, 21.
Royal Commission on Agriculture, 385.
Russia and France, 364.
Russia, tariff war with Germany, 188.

## S

Salt, 41, 49.
Settlement of trade balances, 363.
Shipping competition, 213.
  ,,     light dues, 386.
  ,,     subsidies, 205-221.
Silks, U.K., 93 ; U.S., 144, 143 ; Fce., 158 ; Gmy., 182.
Silk bounties, Fce., 232.
Skins and furs, U.K., 97.
South African trade, 304, 369.
  ,,   American finances, 347.
Spain, tariff war with Gmy., 190.
Spanish colonies, 281.
  ,,     trade, 363.
Specie movements, 367, 430.
Specific and *ad valorem* duties, 421.
Spirit duties, U.K., 67 ; U.S., 127, 252 ; Gmy., 177.
State railways, Gmy., 222.
Steel rails, U.S., 58, 117 ; Fce., 167 ; Gmy., 179.
Straits Settlements, 297.
Subsidies to shipping, 205-221.
Subventions to railways, 222-232.
Sugar consumed by brewers, 81.
  ,,   consumption, 202.
  ,,   bounties, 195-204.
  ,,   duties, U.K., 63, 79 ; U.S., 124, 134, 443 ; Fce., 154 ; Gmy., 176 ; various, 203.
Sugar tax in West Indies, 45.
  ,,   Trust, U.S., 124, 443.
Surplus products, 6, 234.
Surtaxes, Fce., 172, 201.

## T

Tariff for morality, 13.
  ,,     protection, 19.
  ,,     revenue, 4.
Tariff reforms, U.K., 98.
  ,,   revisions of, 13.
  ,,   wars in Gmy., 187.
Taxation, U.K., 240 ; U.S., 250 ; Fce., 261 ; Gmy., 273.
Taxation of necessaries, 6.
  ,,     indirect, 5.
  ,,     of the poor, 12
  ,,     unequal, 385.
Tea, U.K., 76, 80 ; U.S., 436, Fce., 154 ; Gmy., 176.
Tea, sources of supply, 87.
Textile machinery, 51.
Timber, U.S., 123, 442 ; Fce., 171 ; Gmy., 184.
Tin, U.S., 115.

Tinplates, U.S., 119, 382 ; Fce., 167 Gmy., 179
Tobacco. U.K., 71 ; U.S., 126, 252 ; Fce., 155 ; Gmy., 177.
Tobacco monopoly, Fce., 265.
Trade fluctuations, U.S., 357.
  ,,   legislation, 401.
  ,,   mark forgery, 391.
Trusts, U.S., 60.
Tunis, 289.
Turkey, fiscal policy, 203.

## U

Under-valuation of exports, 342, 421.
Unequal taxation, 385.
United States balance of trade, 352, 365.
  ,,     coastwise service, 216.
  ,,     expansion, 35.
  ,,     finances, 258, 447.
  ,,     mail service, 218.
  ,,     national debt, 413.
  ,,     natural advantages of, 31.
  ,,     railroads, 231.
  ,,     shipping subventions, 214.
  ,,     trade crises, 348.
  ,,     ,, fluctuations, 357.

## V

Viticulture bounties, Fce., 232.
Victoria, tariff of, 298.

## W

Wages, U.S., 32.
Wasteful labour, 381.
Watches and clocks, U.K., 92.
Wearing apparel, U.S., 149, 441 ; Gmy., 182.
West Africa, U.K., 403 ; Fce., 405 ; Gmy., 285, 406.
West Australia, tariff of, 296, 307.
West Indies, sugar tax, 45.
Wheat, U.K., 56, 309 ; U.S., 47. 127 ; Fce., 53, 170 ; Gmy., 184.
Wholesale profits, 427.
Wine, U.K., 71 ; U.S., 126 ; Fce., 154, 171 ; Gmy., 177.
Wool, raw, U.K., 2, 307 ; U.S., 133; Fce., 169.
Woollen manufactures, U.K., 88 ; U.S., 137, 440 ; Fce., 165 ; Gmy., 181.
Working classes, 402, 424.

www.ingramcontent.com/pod-product-compliance
Lightning Source LLC
Chambersburg PA
CBHW022115300426
44117CB00007B/721